THE BEST OF BURNLEY VOLUME 2

Another Burnley FC Anthology

Compiled by Dave Thomas

This book is dedicated to the memory of the great Jimmy Mcilroy.
1931 to 2018

THE BEST OF BURNLEY VOLUME 2

Another Burnley FC Anthology

Compiled by Dave Thomas

Vertical Editions
www.verticaleditions.com

First published in the United Kingdom in 2018 by Vertical Editions, Unit 4a, Snaygill Industrial Estate, Skipton, North Yorkshire BD23 2QR

www.verticaleditions.com

ISBN 978-1-908847-12-6

A CIP catalogue record for this book is available from the British Library

Cover design by HBA, York

Printed and bound by Jellyfish Solutions, Swanmore, Hants

Contents

Source Material

Publications

The London Clarets magazine: *Something to Write Home About*

David Saffer: *Revie's Unsung Heroes*, Vertical Editions, 2017

Tim Quelch: *Underdog! Fifty Years of Trials and Triumphs with Football's Also-Rans*, Pitch Publishing, 2011

Leon Barton: *Brian Flynn: Little Wonder*, St David's Press, 2017

Peter Swann: *Swanny: Confessions of a Lower-League Legend*, John Blake Publishing, 2008

Dave Thomas: *Jimmy Mac: Prince of Inside Forwards*, Hudson and Pearson, 2009

Paul Fletcher: *Magical: A Life in Football*, Vertical Editions, 2012

Simon Hughes: *On The Brink: A Journey Through English Football's North West*, De Coubertin Books, 2017

Photographs

My thanks to Gary 'Rocket' Jenkins for the front cover. To Burnley Football Club for permission to use photographs of various players from their archives and programme front covers. And also to Vertical Editions, Sandria Burkinshaw, David Eaves, the Jimmy McIlroy family, Simon Hughes, Brian Speak, David Saffer and Mick Warn.

Introduction

This is the fourth Burnley Anthology, the first two being *No Nay Never Volumes 1 and 2*. They all follow the same pattern, however, being collections of articles and chapters taken from football books and magazines.

One excellent magazine is *Something to Write Home About*, the magazine of the London Clarets. You certainly don't have to be in London to be a member. There are members all over the UK and around the globe. One of the membership benefits is the six-times a year magazine, a production that is scholarly and erudite. There are a number of contributors but one thing they have in common is that they are all Clarets and all skilled writers.

The pen pictures of Ade Akinbiyi, Clarke Carlisle and Robbie Blake have all previously appeared in that magazine. All three made great contributions to Burnley, particularly Robbie Blake and Clarke Carlisle in Coyle's promotion season. Which of us will ever forget the catalogue of Blake's stunning 30-yard goals? None of us will ever fail to remember Akinbiyi's equaliser at Chelsea in the memorable League Cup tie when Burnley went on to win on penalties.

I remain fascinated by the 1950s. Perhaps that is because I was brought up back then and well remember just what life was like. But season 1952/53 was a fascinating time at Burnley Football Club with Jimmy McIlroy and Jimmy Adamson already well established in the side. Managed by Frank Hill they came close to winning the title but faded in the final weeks. It is this season that forms the basis of Chapter One.

Several books provide more chapters and I am grateful to the authors for their permission to use their work.

Vertical Editions allowed me to use the chapter about Burnley starlet

Ian Lawson, from David Saffer's 2017 book *Revie's Unsung Heroes*. Lawson burst onto the scenes as a 17-year old at Turf Moor but then could never really break into a side that featured Ray Pointer and Jimmy Robson.

One of the great heroes of Burnley FC is Brian Flynn. Credited also with the re-awakening of the Welsh national team, his biography written by Leon Barton and published by St David's Press should be on the bookshelf of every Burnley fan. I offer grateful thanks to Leon Barton for his ready permission to use the opening chapters of *Brian Flynn: Little Wonder*.

Many thanks too, to Tim Quelch for permission to use chapters from his book *Underdog! 50 Years of Trials and Triumph with Football's Also-rans*. Much of the book is about teams well below the radar as well as small clubs that have been giant-killers, such as Wimbledon at Burnley way back in the 70s. Tim would like credit to go also to Niall Cooper author of *Spirit of Wimbledon*.

SWANNY: Confessions of a Lower League Legend, is one of those rollicking, rumbustious football biographies that are so readable and entertaining and that you are sorry to finish. It goes back to 2008, published by John Blake, but is still available and certainly recommended.

Thank you to Simon Hughes for his permission to use the Burnley chapter (essentially a Sean Dyche chapter) from his splendid book *ON THE BRINK: A Journey through English Football's North West*, published by De Coubertin Books. The chapter on Accrington Stanley is a joy to read.

There is one lengthy chapter on Jimmy McIlroy. It is from the McIlroy biography *Prince of Inside Forwards* and pays homage to the genius of the man. In that same chapter is included a piece about Jimmy by Paul Fletcher that was taken out of the book *Magical* simply because we had exceeded our word limit. It is therefore good to be able to see it in print in this anthology. In his pomp he was virtually unplayable.

Jimmy passed away just before this book was due to go to print. It was an absolute joy to work with him for over a year on the two books we did together. He was a friend to so many people in Burnley. I doubt we will see his like again in claret and blue. Is it really ten years since Jimmy and I did the biography and the scrapbook? It seems like yesterday. Maybe that is because there are so many memories of that year that are still imprinted in my head. On only my second visit to his home he sat and read the newspaper for a little while and then suddenly smiled.

'Sorry Dave I was just reading the obituary page – to see if I was in it,' he said. Sadly he now is.

There was an occasion at Turf Moor when we launched the Harry Potts book with a grand dinner and a packed room. Jimmy was there and agreed to say a few words. We all know what it is like trying to get a room to be silent on such occasions so that the speaker can begin, but when Jimmy stood there was an almost instant silence as people turned to listen. You could have heard a pin drop. He smiled that gentle smile. He spoke in his quiet Irish lilt. And said ...

'If only Bob Lord could see me now,' with a twinkle in his eye and the room roared with laughter.

He spent a couple of weekends over in Leeds and on the Sunday morning of the first weekend he stood in the kitchen in his pyjamas with a mug of tea. I had to pinch myself. This was THE Jimmy McIlroy, in my home, in my kitchen, the player I had revered as a boy. In the playground playing football it was always, 'baggsie being Jimmy Mac.'

I used to say a little prayer the night before each Burnley game. 'And please dear Lord, let Jimmy Mac win us the game.'

On one occasion we sat in the design studio at Dunnockshaw, as was our custom every week, looking at the onscreen pictures. For each one he had a story and a memory. Slowly, one by one, staff quietly began to gather behind us, until there were maybe seven or eight people standing there hanging on his every word.

Most if not all obituaries and the articles about him say he was from Lambeg. Jimmy always chuckled about that. 'That's because they probably couldn't spell Ballyskeagh.' Here he was brought up in his grandmother's house having been born in Greenhill a mile or so away, and close to Lambeg.

As ever there is the recommendation that you seek out the books that are featured in this anthology and buy them. The vast majority of authors make precious little money out of writing unless it is supplemented by journalism, or they strike lucky and pen a 20,000-copy best seller.

No Nay Never Volume Two and *Jimmy Mac: Prince of Inside Forwards* are both still available direct from the author Dave Thomas. www.burnleyfcbooks.co.uk

Many thanks to Gary 'Rocket' Jenkins who provided the front cover picture.

Many thanks too to John Gibaut over there in Seattle who proofed the pages and to Mrs T who puts up with my curses when the computer is on the blink and then she fixes things.

1

Frank Hill and Nearly the Title

The Team of 1952/53. From *Something to Write Home About,* the magazine of the London Clarets. Article by Dave Thomas

I was brought up in the fifties, so for me they are not just history, they are real and I can still draw on the memories. I started the decade as a five-year-old and ended it as a fifth former at the local Grammar School. Today, for many, those who were born after the fifties and did not experience them, they are indeed just distant history and history is a much neglected school subject. How many people have any knowledge of the times? The social background, the political events, the slow progress that was made in living standards, the great divide between those who 'had' and those who had nothing, not to mention the death of King George in 1952 and the first British atom bomb test, the coronation of 1953, Ian Fleming's first James Bond novel, the first ascent of Everest, the death of Stalin, the Korean war, Winston Churchill, the Rillington Place murders, the Lynmouth flood disaster. Hundreds of orphans and destitute children were being sent to Australia; and we still hanged people.

They were the years of austerity, polio, rickets, tuberculosis, malnutrition, of drabness, real poverty for many, the lingering remnants of rationing, cold winters, and for many the absence of anything resembling luxury. And yet, as with all things to do with the past, we who were brought up in the fifties, despite the authoritarianism, restraint and uniformity, look back on them as an era of trust and law-abiding neighbourliness. We view them through rose-tinted spectacles and think of them as 'better times' even though few people had washing machines, fridges, televisions, or dishwashers, and telephones were strictly limited. There were 'town-centres' for shopping and 'corner shops' but no supermarkets. Shopping malls and shopping centres were non-existent. The Co-op was all important and getting your 'divi' once a year. I can remember our number. It was 6014 and we queued to claim our 'discount' on what we had bought at the Co-op. I never wore long trousers until I was 14 and my education was formal, strict and disciplined. By the age of seven I could already chant most times tables. The 11+ ruled our life and determined our secondary education. At home there were coal fires not central heating. In winter my bedroom had ice inside the window. There were no ready-made meals, freezers, ranges of designer clothing or instant entertainment. For thousands of people there was an outside toilet, gas lamps not electricity and still no running water or baths. Money was in short supply; the nation in the early fifties was still recovering from the draining war years. Few people had cars, there were no motorways, we travelled by steam train, holidays abroad were unheard of.

Yet now, today, there is this nostalgic picture of a 'simpler, happier' life; of neighbourliness, children behaving themselves, make do and mend, getting on with things, improvising, and being content with one's lot. What we remember above all is that there was no hooliganism, violence, stabbings or drunkenness every Friday and Saturday night in any town centre. But, at the same time, what is absolutely true for the vast majority was that life took place in black, white and shades of grey. Colour was in very short supply except at the cinema as more films were produced in Technicolor.

How we soon forget ... or never knew in the first place. 1952 and 1953 saw the birth of rock and roll, Charles Chaplin driven out of the USA, the Comet jet airliner began first commercial flights, the Goon Show began on radio, children watched *Bill and Ben the Flowerpot Men* if they had a TV, adults *The Quatermass Experiment*. The big films were *High Noon* with Gary Cooper and *The Greatest Show on Earth* with Charlton Heston or *Shane* with Alan Ladd. Rocky Marciano won the World Heavyweight title. Russian tanks rolled into the streets of Berlin and quelled a workers' uprising. On a more humorous note the Piltdown Man was revealed as a hoax.

Personal memories range from the good to the bad: "We could walk to school and play out at night in the streets or fields. We played outdoors in all weathers; there were no computers or TV's in bedrooms. We climbed trees, got a clip round the ear if we were naughty, we had teaspoons of cod liver oil, played cards and board games. It was an innocent time now gone forever. We played Cowboys and Indians, and English and Germans. There was no such thing as political correctness. People were courteous and polite."

On the other hand, meat, cheese, sugar and sweets were still rationed; cities blitzed in the war were still half derelict. Respectability was all-important, being deferential to your 'betters' (the doctor, the bank manager, the teacher, the headmaster) was the norm. What many people remember, too, are the endless fogs closing in, at their worst making life intolerable and a walk down the street hazardous and risky as a huge bus would loom out of the mist. Smog was even worse and the result of factory chimneys and of hundreds of streets of homes burning coal fires and churning out smoke mixing with the fog. Sometimes visibility was so bad it was unsafe to walk along a pavement. It got into your eyes and down your throat; you could smell and almost taste it. On truly dreadful days we wore primitive masks.

The official 1950 Burnley Corporation handbook made fine reading despite Burnley being a place of noisy mills and towering chimneys, smoky back to back terraced rows, and hardship. It was a place of small shops, street traders and delivery men selling bread, meat, fish and groceries, of rag and bone men with their horses and carts, the market and neighbourhood pubs, of men in overcoats and caps, and by and large where a woman's place was to be seen and not heard. In 1950 it was a thriving place with an official population of 84,590, although within a couple of years workers would be laid off in the textile mills. Cotton was still king but only just with the industry facing recession. In June 1951 town unemployment stood at just 197. A year later it was 15,205 because of 12,000 'temporary' stoppages in the cotton industry. In addition to the cotton mills there were attendant engineering firms, loom makers, bleachers, dyers and sizers. There were acres and acres of factories, mills, and rows and rows of terraced workers' housing with their chalked stone steps. It was not all cotton. There were coal pits, leather tanners, a rope works, clothing firms, bottle makers, paper works, sheet metal works, tin and copper works. There were manufacturers of steel springs, washing machines, weighing scales, raincoats, kettles and kitchen tools, uniforms, toys, and furniture. There was electrical engineering, breweries and brickworks. There were two theatres and cinemas in several parts of the town. The Empress Hall catered for roller skating and dancing. Thompson Park and boating lake covered 480 acres. The town was proud of the building of the first new and modern housing estates although masses of housing still remained cramped and lacking in many basic facilities. Though the handbook presents all the positives to be found in the town, it fails to mention exploitation and low wages, the palls of coal-fire smoke and for those who were unemployed the helplessness of poverty and despair. Once a year the whole town seemed to decamp and vanish to Blackpool for 'Wakes Week'. On a Saturday they wanted their football team to do well and to provide a brief respite from the drudgery of daily life. Mostly menfolk streamed in from all over the town and the surrounding areas, clambering aboard the special buses, then to alight and surge like a human tide underneath the canal bridge and up Yorkshire Street to Turf Moor. Final decay, the disappearance of old industries, demolition and ultimate regeneration were still years away.

Football in the 1950s was lacking in glamour and gloss. Glamour comes in short supply when the mud is two inches deep. In a very early edition of *Charles Buchan's Football Monthly*, in May 1952, the spotlight on Burnley had them down in a full page article as the most improved side in the First Division. At the beginning of the previous season they had begun badly, but new players and better performances established them as a comfortable mid-table side. At the end of 1951/52 Manchester United were the champions. Some top footballers in those days regularly advertised cigarettes. Eminent author Norman Giller wrote that the fifties were "when the beautiful game was in black and white … they were the best of times and the worst of times." It is a description that might be applied to the fifties as a whole by those who still have memories of that time.

The big names of the early fifties were Wilf Mannion, Raich Carter, Tommy Lawton, Joe Mercer, Joe Harvey, Stan Milburn, Bobby Mitchell, Gil Merrick, Stanley Matthews, Tom Finney, Jimmy Hagan, Billy Liddell, Nat Lofthouse, Stan Mortensen, Billy Wright, Jimmy Dickinson,

Jimmy Scoular, Ivor Allchurch, Sam Bartram, Ted Ditchburn and Len Shackleton. The football match on a Saturday afternoon was a release for men who were cooped up and worked in the mills for long, long hours, and was the topic of conversation for much of the week. It was an exciting time on the football pitches of dribbling wingers beating their full-backs, powerful centre forwards who could head a ball with venom and power, and shuddering physical confrontations the like of which we cannot imagine in today's sanitised game. Referees rarely took names even though it was a game of intense and bone-jarring tackles. Opposing fans mixed happily on the terraces. At Easter there were three games in the space of four days. Nor did Christmas Day see any respite as games took place on that special day until 1957.

Jimmy McIlroy had arrived at Burnley in 1950 signed by manager Frank Hill. By season 1952/53 he was an established player and rising star, already a Northern Ireland international. "The first game I ever went to see at Burnley was in 1955," I told him during a visit when we talked about his time with Frank Hill. He and I talked about how different things were then; hardly a foreign player to be seen, mudbath pitches, the heavy ball, laced and made of stitched panels. Head the stitches and it left a clear, deep and painful imprint. Players lived next door to the supporters in many cases; walked to the ground on matchdays or got on the bus. They were still seen as working class, still on a maximum wage no matter how big their name, still at the beck and call of the club, the manager, the chairman and the directors. They were still very much the bloke next door and on the way to or from the game talked about it with the fans. The players walked from their homes down Brunshaw Hill. Brian Pilkington well remembers getting the bus back home after training and talking football with other passengers. If he was tired after a gruelling session, he would go on the top deck to hide and bury his head behind a newspaper.

It could be argued that manager Frank Hill is only ever remembered at Burnley for one thing – because he signed Jimmy McIlroy. And even then there is the caveat that it was another player who was being watched and McIlroy was 'discovered' by accident. In fact, Hill is more important than that, having given the club a firm footing and making a number of astute signings whilst he was manager from 1948 to 1954. Sandwiched in between the success of Cliff Britton in 1947 and the huge influence of Alan Brown for the three years following 1954, Frank Hill merits more than just a passing mention. As a player he won three title medals with Arsenal, a stunning achievement and at his later clubs he was a natural captain. As soon as he himself went to Ireland to see McIlroy he snapped him up and gave him his chance, recognising that when Harry Potts left McIlroy was good enough to replace him without the need to look elsewhere. He signed other excellent players: Billy Gray, Bill Holden and Billy Elliot. The sale of Billy Elliot after just two seasons did not go down well, however.

Born in Forfar in May 1906, Hill started his career as a wing-half with his home-town club in 1924. He moved to Aberdeen in 1928 and played over 100 Scottish First Division matches. At right-half, he earned the nickname "Tiger" for his tigerish tackling and in his time at Aberdeen earned three caps for Scotland. He left Aberdeen under something of a cloud, being one of five players dropped by manager Paddy Travers in November 1931. The reasons were unclear but the club's official history claims that several players had been involved in a betting scandal. No players were ever charged with an offence, but none of them played for Aberdeen again. By the time he left he had played 106 games and scored 10 goals.

In 1932 he was signed by Herbert Chapman for Arsenal who had just finished runners-up in both the First Division and the FA Cup. He made his debut against Blackburn Rovers in October 1932. Although Arsenal were spoilt for choice for wing-halves – the legendary Wilf Copping was one of them – Hill still featured in all three of Arsenal's hat-trick of League title wins, 1932 – 1935, earning winners' medals for each, as well as the 1934 Charity Shield. He usually played right-half, but could also play on the left and even on the wing. Copping and Crayston eventually squeezed him out of the side and he only featured in ten games in '35/36 and was not a member of the Cup winning team that season. He requested a transfer and was sold to Second Division Blackpool in the summer of 1936. In all, he played 81 games for Arsenal, scoring four goals.

Hill captained Blackpool in '36/37 helping them to the runners-up spot and promotion to the First Division. He did not stay there long before moving to Southampton in September 1937. He was recruited by manager Tom Parker in a bid to strengthen the promotion bid from the Second Division. Southampton paid £2,000 for him and acquired a "half-back with strong personality and ball-winning abilities." His resolve and leadership helped the club away from relegation during '37/38 but a series of injuries then side-lined him for long periods. He eventually fell out with the Board of Directors when it was revealed he had been secretly applying for managerial posts and he left the club in 1939 to join Preston North End as assistant trainer. But Southampton, where he played 53 times and scored three goals, refused to release his player registration until 1943.

During the war, whilst football was suspended, Hill served in the RAF in India. Returning to Britain in 1944 he became player-manager of Crewe Alexander and his career as a player continued until he was 42. From Crewe he moved to Burnley as manager in 1948 where he remained until 1954. From Burnley he moved to Preston until 1956.

From Preston he moved abroad and in January 1957 he coached the Iraq military team and then came back to manage Notts County. He helped them to promotion to the Third Division in 1960 and watched with satisfaction as two of his former protégés, McIlroy and Adamson, helped Burnley to the Division One title. From Notts County it was then to Charlton Athletic who were bottom of the Second Division, in 1961. He saved them from relegation and eventually took them to fourth in 1964. The good form did not last and he was sacked in the summer of 1965.

Before retiring he worked as a scout for Manchester City and then moved to Lafayette in California where, with his wife and son, he ran the *Piccadilly Circus Fish and Chips*. He never lost touch with football though and refereed college games into his 70s. He died in California in June 1993, aged 87.

Peter Fyles in *Burnley's Greatest Ever Goal* described him: 'Ex-players have described Hill in different ways but usually with hesitant overtones. Most descriptions have been succinct: "a real Arsenal type" or "a pleasant enough manager". A heavy smoker and always immaculately dressed, Hill would confiscate players' cigarettes when he had none himself. Yet an incident regarding the sale of FA Cup tickets seems to characterise Hill's main weakness. In those days before an FA Cup tie every player would be allocated two complimentary tickets. Selling them on was common practice. After one particular Cup match, several team members were rebuked by the club for selling tickets for private profit. At the same time, Hill entered the dressing room wearing a new pair of fashionable ankle-length boots, boasting that they had only cost him one Cup ticket. It was Hill who had the perception to buy Jimmy McIlroy from Glentoran, Northern Ireland, in March 1950. (A signing that was illegal as it took place in the early hours of Sunday morning, a day when it was prohibited to buy players). Whatever Hill lacked in close relations with his players, he compensated for in football astuteness and determination. He was described by one former player as "a hard little devil of a character". He loved playing five-a-side soccer and often matches would last several hours until his side eventually edged into the lead. Only then would the game end; Hill was a bad loser.'

Jimmy McIlroy tells the story that when he first signed his father was worried that Jimmy would suffer from rough treatment. Hill rolled up his trouser legs and displayed his legs saying 'don't worry, look at these there isn't a mark on them.' It was either Ray Bennion or Billy Dougal who jokingly quipped 'that's because he never made a good tackle in his life.' Bearing in mind in his playing career his nickname had been 'Tiger' on account of his tigerish tackling, it was a good-natured jibe.

Billy Dougall was Hill's right-hand man, a terrific influence and, like Hill, was another Scot. Along with Ray Bennion he had been there many years and Bennion was someone whom Tommy Lawton praised highly for the influence he had had on his training and development. Dougall by 1952 had been there over 20 years and had a huge authority over the players with his common sense and wisdom. He spoke and they listened. He aimed for perfection and always told his players to make the perfect pass or strive for the perfect ball. Even if a pass resulted in a goal, he could still be constructively critical and suggest how it could have been better if it was less than perfect and this is something that Jimmy McIlroy remembers well. In training Dougall would insist on repetition until flawlessness was achieved. 'Do what the opposition don't expect or want you to do,' was the maxim he drilled into players. Wingers would practise crossing the ball at speed and if the inside forward or centre-forward had to break his stride to head or strike the ball it was deemed not good enough and it was repeated.

Peter Fyles continues: 'With such meticulous preparation, the Clarets never finished the season out of the top ten from 1952 to 1964. Training sessions took place from Tuesday to Friday mornings and, for those engaged in other trades, Tuesday and Thursday evenings. Laps around the cricket field, sprints, ball control, running in and out between the girders under the Brunshaw Stand, and five-a-side matches would make up a session. Pre-season training was particularly unpopular after a summer of non-activity. Many players including Harold Mather and Les Shannon were physically sick during these sessions. As for tactics, Burnley were regarded as a good defensive side and possibly because of this and also being a small-town club, had already acquired the tag 'unfashionable'. Burnley played to their strengths. In 1951 football operated in a much more restricted fashion and players played with a specific zonal mentality. Centre-halves were there to prevent centre-forwards scoring and would rarely stray into the opposition's half. Full-backs were there to stop wingers. Everyone knew what area of the pitch they were going to operate in. As one player put it, 'Mac was the general, Elliot was the strong man, Attwell was the genius, and Mather kept his man under control.'

Hill aged 46 had inherited several good players and also gathered a group of younger ones he could call his own. It was a settled team, more often than not made up by Jimmy Strong or Des Thompson in goal; Harold Mather and Jock Aird at full back, Reg Attwell and Jimmy Adamson the half-backs, Tommy Cummings centre-half. And a forward line of Jackie Chew on the right, Jimmy McIlroy inside right; Bill Holden at centre forward, Les Shannon at Inside left and Billy Elliot at outside left. It was a good mix of craft, guile and toughness where it was needed. How they lined up in the early fifties was far different than today.

Thompson or Strong

Jock Aird **Harold Mather**

Jimmy Adamson **Tommy Cummings** **Reg Attwell**

Jackie Chew **Jimmy McIlroy** **Bill Holden** **Les Shannon** **Billy Elliot**

It was an old-style formation still in use in 1959/60 when Burnley won the Championship. It lingered well into the sixties until the middle of the decade when a 4 – 2 – 4 formation emerged. It was Strong who began the season playing 20 League games in goal and kept his place until Thompson took over in December '52, the latter completing 22 games in the League. Jimmy Strong was one of the legends who played at Wembley in the '47 Cup Final and then went on to win promotion to Division One at the end of that memorable season. Until he was clattered by the burly Bobby Smith at Chelsea he hardly missed a game. He was never really the same after that injury and Thompson eventually took over. After retirement he ran a poultry farm near Burnley, his ability to catch a football finding good use for twenty years catching chickens. Des Thompson too was a class act and was on the fringe of selection for England. Only the emergence of the outstanding Colin McDonald cost him his place and but for that he was good enough to have held on for a good while longer. Thompson might well have achieved far more in football had he not been up against first Colin McDonald at Burnley, and then Alan Hodgkinson at Sheffield United after he moved there.

Jock Aird was Burnley's first Scottish international right-back winning four full caps in 1954. He had pace and stamina and replaced the great Arthur Woodruff. For Scotland, however, he played at left-back. He was described as feisty and aggressive (even though he was only 5' 8"), which meant in those days that wingers were given short shrift and unless they were nimble enough to avoid it, they ended up several feet over the touchline following a suitably full-blooded tackle. Defenders were rarely ornamental wallflowers in the fifties. In 1955 he left for New Zealand and eventually settled in Australia. In his eighties, he visited Burnley Football Club in September 2009 and was given a warm reception as he made the half-time draw.

At left-back Harold Mather harked back to the iron-curtain team of 1946/47, Wembley and promotion. The full-back's commandment was simple. 'Thou shalt not pass.' He was a no-nonsense, no-frills, tough defender who on winning the ball usually decided that the best place for it was somewhere way up the field. Butch Mather was described at the time as 'a particularly sound positional player who seldom found his defensive powers seriously undermined by any winger.' Prior to a

Stanley Matthews encounter Mather would intensify his sprint training and follow Ray Bennion's instructions to 'show him the touchline.' The outcome was usually a subdued and intimidated Matthews. Jimmy McIlroy tells the story that he once ran back towards him and shouted for him to play him a short pass. Mather looked askance and replied, 'Get back up that bloody field where thee belongs.' And then he booted it high over his head for him to chase. He was quite slow but with great timing rarely let a winger get the better of him. After Burnley he continued in football for many, many years in different capacities.

Reg Attwell, who was another one of the team of '46/47, was one of Jimmy McIlroy's favourite players and would feature in any of Jimmy Mac's best Burnley Elevens. He was stylish, cultured, wonderfully accurate with short and long passes, cool and unhurried. The word 'class' would not go amiss. Some players are just naturally elegant and he was one of them. In another age he would have received England call-ups but this was a time when there were so many great players. The decline of his Burnley career is sometimes thought to date to an incident when he was caring for his mother after his father's funeral and failed to inform manager Hill, missing a key game against Arsenal. He was a great favourite with the Burnley crowd. What happened to Attwell after football though provided a perfect example of how many players were unprepared for life after the game. Today even an average player receives a wage enough to set him up for life. But in the fifties players had no such money to fall back on. When Jimmy McIlroy finally finished with football he went back to bricklaying. Reg Attwell, sadly however, eventually appeared in court for handling stolen goods. It was stated that he had received no training for life after football and was unemployed. The judge was lenient, fining rather than imprisoning him.

Tommy Cummings, from the North-east, was an unusual centre-half. He was never just a big, muscular, bruising 'stopper', although ironically he replaced one – iron-man Alan Brown. He was outstandingly quick and relied on speed, interceptions and intelligence rather than just kicking the centre-forward from pillar to post. In an age when he was up against players of the calibre of Len Shackleton, Jackie Milburn, Nat Lofthouse, Stan Mortensen and Trevor Ford he rarely put a foot wrong. He refused attempts to persuade him to sign for a South American club when there were huge financial temptations to lure British players. His goal against Newcastle United in the early fifties has long been thought of as Burnley's greatest ever goal. In those days centre-halves rarely ventured beyond the halfway line but on this occasion he took the ball on the edge of his own penalty box, took it forward, went on … and on … and on … passing several players … and then crashed home an unstoppable, thunderbolt shot. Such a goal was unheard of. Cummings remained to win a 1959/60 medal and play in the 1962 Cup Final. His was a long and distinguished career.

Jimmy Adamson missed just one League game in '52/53. He had been a professional at the club since January 1947; he made his debut in season '50/51 when he was already 22. Not until he was moved back to the half-back line did his career begin to blossom. He was tall, thin, gawky; all arms and bony legs, hardly the perfect physical specimen. Yet his thin legs won countless midfield tackles and he distributed the ball to all parts of the field. As he went forward with the ball his long legs ate up the ground with slow, elongated strides and his timing was immaculate. He was a thinker, a schemer, a tactician and his contribution as a player to Burnley Football Club is simply immense. Like Cummings and McIlroy he played in the title winning and Cup Final team.

Jackie Chew, a member of the 1947 Cup and promotion team, provided shooting power and accurate crosses from the right wing. On account of his bandy legs he was affectionately known as 'Cowboy'. By the summer of '53 he was 33 years old and approaching the final days of his career and in 1954 moved to Bradford City. As a winger in the '50s there was nowhere to hide. His job was to beat the full-back and get the ball over. Being in a position that was so close to the crowd, if you had a poor game, they let you know in no uncertain terms. On some days he left the field black and blue after the treatment he received from snarling full-backs out to do just one thing – stop him by any means foul or fair. He was also a fine cricketer for Rishton in the Lancashire League which in those days had many outstanding players.

A young Jimmy McIlroy was the rising star and Irish international. He caught the eye and made the headlines with his performances. In his very early days he was lightening quick, and in '52/53 scored 11 goals. The name later bestowed on him by journalist and author Dr. Malcolm

Brodie, *'The Prince of Inside Forwards'*, summed up this exquisite player perfectly. Certainly Burnley's best post-war player, only the legendary Bob Kelly rivals him for the title best-ever player; although Jimmy himself tells the story that someone he knew who saw Kelly play always told him that Kelly was just that little bit better. His complete story is in his biography published in 2009. 'Magical McIlroy' was a description of him and a headline that was written over and over again. In today's game he would be worth millions. He remained at Burnley until 1963 when Bob Lord deemed him expendable; the club was desperate for money after weeks without matches and income following a dreadful winter and manager Harry Potts told a mystified McIlroy he was not satisfied with his playing efforts.

Centre-Forward Bill Holden played all 42 League games during the season and scored 22 goals. Bearing in mind what a rough, tough position this was, and the treatment centre-forwards got, to complete every game was a tremendous achievement. Against Sunderland he scored four of Burnley's five goals. In his younger days he had been overlooked by Bolton but spotted by Everton. When he was unsuccessful there he was snapped up by Hill who took him to the fringes of the England team in the early fifties. He was big enough to be physical when necessary but he was also two-footed and mobile using the full width of the pitch instead of simply being the traditional battering ram down the middle. 1952/53 was his best season even though he had broken his leg in March '52 at Aston Villa. Top scorer again two seasons later, he then moved to Sunderland.

Les Shannon was one of Jimmy McIlroy's favourite players. From Merseyside, he made his first appearances in the '49/50 season. When he was eventually converted to playing a deep-lying, inside-forward role he at last found a place that suited him. Yet still he scored 15 goals in '52/53 including two hat-tricks. He had a terrific football brain and this, allied to his stylish play, brought him several representative honours. He continued to have a distinguished career in football after he finished playing.

Completing the line-up was the incomparable Billy Elliot at outside left. It is the much later Mike Summerbee of Manchester City – and briefly Burnley – who is often seen as the winger who first decided that roles should be reversed and wingers should stop being delicate little orchids there to be kicked black and blue by ugly full-backs. It was Elliot who decided that it would be he who ferociously tackled them and gave them a taste of their own medicine. It was Billy Elliot, one of the hardest men in football, who turned the role upside down long before Summerbee. He was signed by Hill from Bradford Park Avenue for a then record fee of £25,000, and whilst at Burnley won five England caps. Hill could most certainly spot a player. Even by the standards of the 1950s Elliot was a hard man, and his meetings with Willie Cunningham of Preston North End had spectators open-mouthed at the ferocity of their confrontations. Such was the aggressiveness of it that during one game the Preston captain moved Cunningham to the other full back position before there was a serious injury, something quite unheard of in that era. Elliot then became the first Burnley player to be sent off after the war for threatening behaviour. Nor did he spare his own team-mates. His crosses came over low and very hard with regular and frequent precision. In one game no-one was getting a head to them which may have been something to do with the velocity at which he was sending them over. He was furious after one cross and well known for his bad language demanded to know: "Which of you fuckers ducked?" with Jimmy McIlroy convinced he would have thumped anyone who owned up. Before one game, McIlroy remembers him sitting in the changing room holding his face, clearly in pain. He asked Billy Dougall if he had a file and Dougall asked what for. Elliot explained that his false teeth were killing him. He took out the dentures and blood trickled down his chin. With the file he smoothed some of the edges on the bits that were rubbing his gums. He looked at them, slipped them back into his mouth, nodded, and then went out to play. He moved to Sunderland after just two seasons, eventually becoming a coach and manager, working in football until 1983.

Twenty players were used in all during the season but just twelve of them played the bulk of the games, resulting in a very settled team so that the players knew each other's game instinctively. Just a small number of reserves played a handful of games between them. All in all it was very fine team, a mixture of youth and experience and of power and skill. The balance was exactly right and for almost a month in March 1953 it was top of the division and on course for the title. Just prior to this the Sheffield Wednesday programme of February 7th referred to them as possible candidates for the double.

With McIlroy and Les Shannon leading scorers with three goals each, five of the first six games were won and everyone became aware of what this team was capable. With Billy Elliot then away playing for the Football League, a future star was drafted in, Brian Pilkington. The game against Tottenham was lost but Pilkington served notice with a fine display against top full-back Alf Ramsey. Another player who came in for just a handful of games was Joe Brown who would later progress through the ranks of the backroom staff to become manager, albeit briefly. It was significant that the Tottenham game was lost to an 89th minute goal.

The success that came Burnley's way up until March 14th came in short runs of games where there were consecutive victories; a run of five at the beginning of the season after the opening game was lost; a run of four in October/November and then a run of three in February. There was a run of eleven unbeaten games spanning late November to the end of February but six of them were only draws. After the victory over Manchester United on March 14th there were only two more wins and only six points from a possible twenty. March began with a visit from Blackpool who proceeded to win and do the double over Burnley, the only side to do so that season. Wins against Chelsea and Manchester United saw a return to form, top place and press predictions that here were the champions. But then anti-climax set in. A last minute goal at Fratton Park gave Portsmouth revenge for their FA Cup defeat and a run of five games garnering just one point saw the Clarets disappear from contention. Manager Hill shuffled his pack and brought in fresh players: Stephenson, Brown and Winton. Hope came with a 5 – 1 demolition of Sunderland with Holden scoring four of them. But inconsistency reared its ugly head again and Burnley were hammered 5 – 1 away at Wolves. The season faded rapidly. The title opportunity vanished and it was Arsenal who went on to win, claiming it in the very last game of the season. They had also ended Burnley's Cup run in February. In their three Cup games Burnley were watched by a staggering 143,000 people. In the League a golden opportunity was missed by a side that had only conceded 52 goals all season, the second best defensive record. But they scored a mere 67; by today's standards a high total, but in the goal-filled fifties not enough. Six points separated Burnley and Arsenal. Two games were lost to goals in the 89th minute, another to an 88th minute goal. Another two games were lost to goals in the final ten minutes. Had these defeats been avoided and Burnley managed a win against eventual champions Arsenal, it would have been Burnley crowned champions and not Arsenal.

Disappointment was the key feeling but Hill had achieved success, limited though it may have been. Sixth place was no mean achievement. Entertainment had replaced the dour, 'iron-curtain' defence of previous seasons. Crowds were good with an average attendance of over 28,000. Bill Holden was the first player since the war to score over 20 goals. In McIlroy, Adamson, Cummings and the emerging Pilkington a third of the team that would win the title in 1959/60 were in place.

At the end of the season the players dispersed. This was a time when there was a proper 'close season' that lasted all summer for three months. The pay they received was less in this period and several found extra work to help make ends meet. The ground was still very basic with the Longside and the Bee Hole End uncovered. Advertising was in its infancy; football was untainted by greed; a footballer then was classed as a tradesman; Bob Lord was accumulating shares with the intention of joining the board. There were no designer shirts (in fact training gear was threadbare and heaped on the floor with a first come first served rule) or club shop and it was a time when the mud-laden 'casey' took some shifting according to Jimmy McIlroy. Commentators today make the point that the stars of yesteryear would have struggled in today's super-fast, athletic game. The other side of the argument is that the stars of today would equally have struggled back then in the fifties playing under such crude conditions. Someone like Jimmy McIlroy, however, looks with envy at the light ball of today that dips and swerves; the bowling-green pitches, grassy all year and referees giving so much more protection.

Frank Osborne in *Soccer Star* complimented Burnley who had become an attractive side to watch. Quite what he meant by 'big-money' football in the 50s is anyone's guess: 'One secret of manager Frank Hill's success at Turf Moor is the unity and comradeship both on and off the field. The lads who don the claret and blue may not be the boys with the glamour of big-money football, but they can be credited with switching the spotlight to the drab and colourless streets of the

Lancashire mill town.'

Jon Spurling described the final dramatic game of the 1952/53 season in *Highbury: the Story of Arsenal in NE5* (published by Orion). Arsenal had to beat Burnley to pip Preston North End for the title. A Burnley win would have given them a total of 50 points, leaving Arsenal on 52 but Preston on 54. A crowd of over 51,000 watched the game on an atrocious day.

'As (Arsenal winger) Don Roper recalled, this would be no easy task: "By the end of the season we were very tired. The pitches became really heavy. I remember Wolves' and Preston's pitches were total quagmires and your legs felt they weighed a ton. For the Burnley match, I'd say that the Highbury pitch was the worst of the lot by a long way. I don't think there was a blade of grass on it and when we went out for the pitch inspection that morning, it was obvious that the edges were completely unplayable. Either the ball would get stuck, or you'd fall over. It was terrible. We felt the pressure. We had the chance to win the League in front of our own fans at Highbury, which would be a huge honour. Even Joe Mercer, who was normally the life and soul of the group, was noticeably quiet when we ate our eggs on toast at King's Cross Station. It was always our meeting place, and for many, it was the biggest day of their lives. What was funny was that lots of Blackpool and Bolton fans were milling around because the FA Cup Final was being played the next day. And all of them were coming up to us and wishing us well because Preston were the local enemy. And they weren't overly keen on Burnley either."

'The match kicked off at the early time of 6.30 p.m. on Friday, 1st May. This was due to the absence of floodlighting at Highbury. Arsenal fan Harry Wright ensured that he got to the ground early: "People were milling around the ground from midday onwards. You sensed that this would be a great occasion. Weather-wise it was a very odd day. There were constant showers, and in my mind's eye, every man-jack seemed to be wearing a raincoat. But they were happy to be standing out in the rain as well. I think that many people believed that the game would be a sell-out, so they were ready to rush in and have a beer when the gates opened. When it got to about 6 o' clock, the atmosphere got really intense. For the first time in what seemed an age, the Arsenal crowd seemed as one that night. There was a big crowd, around 50,000, but it wasn't full to capacity which amazed me and my pals.

'"Lots of fans wore rosettes and colours, which was quite rare for those days. The crowd actually worked together to produce the atmosphere. All of us clapped 'Arsenal, Arsenal' in unison, that's the North and South terraces. Even the stands joined in. It was a marvellous atmosphere." Doug Lishman concurred: "The crowd was at their best that night. The noise they made was unbelievable, it really was ear piercing, enough to make the hairs on the back of your neck stand on end. However much the players and fans were in conflict that season, I can't deny they were superb on the night."

'The action was frenetic. After six minutes, Burnley's Des Thompson put Burnley ahead against the run of play. *(Spurling has that wrong it was Roy Stephenson who put them ahead. Dave Thomas.)* Midway through the first half Arsenal found their attacking rhythm. Alex Forbes, courtesy of a huge deflection, equalised, and two minutes afterwards Jimmy Logie ducked out of the way to allow Doug Lishman to put Arsenal 2 – 1 up. ("I just smacked the loose ball as hard as I could. It was the greatest moment of my life when it went in.") Just before half-time Jimmy Logie pounced from five yards out to snaffle a poacher's goal. At half-time, Harry Wright recalls: "There was this horrendous downpour. It absolutely teemed it down. The buoyancy of the crowd suddenly disappeared. From talking about how many goals we might score, the talk was, would the game be abandoned? You could see the puddles developing. After the restart, Burnley proved they weren't dead and buried. If they won, they would finish fourth, no mean achievement for a team which had laboured around mid-table until March. Five minutes into the second half, the Clarets' Billy Elliot pulled the score back to 3 – 2.

'At that point, the Arsenal players attempted to shut up shop; a risky strategy with 40 minutes left. Don Roper recalled: "I noticed that Joe Mercer's legs had gone. And the thing was that Joe later admitted that they went for good that night. He reckoned it was the last time he operated as a top-class player. Half the team were struggling now as the ball weighed twice as much as it did at the start of the game due to the wet pitch. Every time you kicked the ball, your whole body ached. I had a knee injury, and at one point I thought I'd collapse with pain when the ball caught me on the side. It later turned out I'd torn a ligament, but these were the days before substitutes, so you had to carry on. Jimmy Logie and Peter Goring were virtual passengers by now. They could barely walk and so we just stuffed them behind the ball. We had no option but to stand firm in the final half-hour.

'"Manager Tom Whitaker couldn't stand the tension. He walked out and poured himself a double brandy. Arsenal fans told me it was just unbearable to watch. A single Burnley goal would have finished us because there was no way we could have summoned the energy to come back at them. By now we were all defenders, and we knew that one careless tackle could be curtains for us. With about a minute to go I caught Billy Elliot in the box. These days he'd have gone straight to ground and won a penalty. To his credit he stumbled and carried on. He said: 'There are better ways of denying you the title than that Don.' I still smile at the sportsmanship of that moment today. Then he hit the bar with a minute left, and I think all of us filled our pants. 'Bugger,' he grinned. 'I should have dived when I had the chance.'"

'Finally, at 8.01 p.m. the referee blew his whistle. Arsenal had won the title on goal average by 0.099 of a goal. Harry Wright recalls: "The rain had eased off and the sun was trying to break through. The sky was red which I thought was very symbolic. All the scarves and rosettes were being thrown into the air. My friend chaired Joe Mercer off the pitch. Some of the players like Jimmy Logie couldn't get off the pitch. They just stood and chatted to fans. It was fantastic." Don Roper recalled: "Whenever I see re-runs of Liverpool v Arsenal in 1989, or Spurs v Arsenal in 1993, I always think our achievement was equally as dramatic. What a shame there were no TV cameras. I often think of what we achieved that night. I'm proud to be part of such a backs-to-the-wall display. To me, it summarises what it's like to play for Arsenal, and to do it in front of our own supporters too – marvellous." There wouldn't be another Highbury night like that one for another seventeen years'.

It was after that game that Joe Mercer finally decided his legs could run no more. At Everton years earlier Dixie Dean had already remarked to him that Joe's legs wouldn't last a postman a round. Each year Mercer would say "just one more season." At last he brought the curtain down on an illustrious playing career and announced, "My spirit is willing but my bandy old legs feel as if they have had enough." Even so he did yet another season, this time at Liverpool until a broken leg forced his retirement after which a career as a great manager followed.

Just a few weeks later, Frank Hill wrote about his experiences in football in a magazine article. He began with a mention for Arsenal. He must surely have had mixed feelings on the night when Arsenal clinched the title, disappointed to see his own team lose, but proud to see Arsenal triumph.

Frank Hill wrote: 'To have been associated with the Arsenal club at any time during the past two decades can be considered a complete football education. A sojourn at Highbury provides an invaluable background for any phase of the game, and particularly club management. Take a line from the influence of the late Mr Herbert Chapman, right through to the present day and Mr Tom Whittaker, and you have the full magic of soccer control and direction. Yet to go from the streamlined splendour of Highbury to the more grim realities which confront a club such as Crewe, which was the path I took, is a valuable experience too. For most people in football the journey lies along a middle road, somewhere between a Highbury and a struggling club. For me the harder sphere of a Crewe setting had considerable value. But the economics are different. The attractions for the likely stars of the future to join the staff are negligible by contrast; and to manage a Crewe is to learn how to make and mend. But to be equipped with a little knowledge of both ends of the scale in football control is to be prepared for the snags that confront the majority of clubs.

'When I took over at Burnley their finances were in a better state than had been their common experience throughout the club's long history. Nevertheless, the financial position was such as to enable wholesale buying of players of the ready-made type, to create a line-up of experienced performers. Here then was the middle road; and the aims of Arsenal and the necessities of Crewe which facilitated a logical outlook and produced a sense of proportion. With something to spend and something to mend, the main factor was patience while the development of young players began to show results. The latest reward to that endeavour has been the selection of four young players for the 'B' International teams of England and Scotland. All four of these youngsters as yet at the outset of their respective career have been brought to their present standard of efficiency in the course of three years.

'My best signing – probably my centre forward Bill Holden; Bill's value today would probably be anything in the region of a record fee. Here you have a player who has revealed a marked ability to learn, to remedy his faults, and develop his natural faculties. He is a clever and attractive footballer, possessing the graces of the game and none of the vices. But, again, from a club point of view; I might say that my most valuable signing was Billy Elliot. For Billy galvanised the good material I already had and added that special something that the team lacked before his arrival. By his enthusiasm Billy Elliot inspired the other lads with greater confidence in themselves and the ability of the team as a whole.

'The questions folk ask me? What was the most memorable thrill of my own playing career? Without a shadow of doubt my good fortune to be a member of the Arsenal team that won the League Championship three years in succession.

'My worst moment? Well that is a longer story and goes right back to my very first appearance as an Aberdeen player. We were due to play at Paisley on the Saturday and the team travelled from Aberdeen on the Friday. I had arranged to join the party at Forfar, but waiting for the train I found a friend who was also going to Glasgow. So, when the train arrived I was given permission to travel with the friend and join up with the party at Glasgow. It was at Glasgow that my troubles started. By the time I reached the portion of the train in which the Aberdeen party had travelled, I found that they had all gone off to their hotel forgetting all about me, their new team-mate. I had no idea where they were staying and after a vain round of enquiries found yet another friend who offered to put me up in Stirling for the night. Next morning I went down to the Paisley ground long before I was wanted. But I heaved a mighty sigh of relief – my worries were over.

'My most amusing experience? I would say this occurred while I was touring in Spain with Burnley. Two of the directors sallied forth along one of the Barcelona boulevards to have their shoes cleaned. Eventually they found a shoe-shine merchant and leaning against a tree they paid little attention to the proceedings as the shoe-blacks got to work. It was when the shoe-blacks stated their price that things began to happen. The language problem crept in and the two directors

31

walked off to their nearby hotel followed by the gesticulating shoe-blacks and an interested crowd. On reaching the hotel the interpreter carefully explained that, besides the shine, the shoes had also been soled.

'In conclusion – my advice to all players is be loyal to your club. At times there may be differences but it is my sincere opinion that no club worthy of the name will ever let its players down. Sometimes discipline has to be enforced for the good of the players as well as the club. But the great secret of success is self-discipline which always leads to close and happier relationships.

'To any prospective manager I would advise: Be prepared to talk to your players. Take them into your confidence and encourage them to confide in you. From time to time discuss with each individual player the aspects of his play as you see it. But allow him to explain his outlook, too. As to the player-manager post, without any hesitation I claim it is not the best arrangement. Playing and managing are two separate jobs, each requiring special and whole-time attention.'

2

Ian Lawson, an Astonishing Debut

Revie's Unsung Heroes by David Saffer
(Vertical Editions)
From Chapter 3: Ian Lawson

When 17-year old Ian Lawson burst onto the scene in January 1957 at Burnley, the impact he made was as dramatic as any player in Burnley's history. Four goals in the 7-0 demolition of Chesterfield in the FA Cup third round on his senior debut was emphatic enough but incredibly he also scored a hat-trick three weeks later in the fourth round as New Brighton were blitzed 9-0.

He was a schoolmate of another Burnley player, Jimmy Robson, and both players were to come under the scrutiny of the Burnley scouts. After outstanding performances for Durham Schoolboys, Lawson joined the Burnley ground staff, signing as a professional on this 17th birthday in 1956. The youngster set something of a record during the 1956/57 season, scoring goals for Burnley's first team, reserve team and the A and B teams. He was still not even a Central League regular when he made his debut and sensational entry into first team football. When the final whistle blew at the end of the Chesterfield game, the 27,000 crowd rose as one and gave the young newcomer a standing ovation.

All seemed set fair for a successful career at the top level at Burnley but in truth, after this spectacular start, it never really took off for him at Turf Moor although he won an England Youth Cap against Spain in 1957. But his next two years were in the reserves since this was a time when Burnley had an abundance of riches and great players. His next appearance in the First Team was in the Championship season of 1959/60 when he stepped up to deputise for Jimmy McIlroy. In the space of a week he scored three goals including the winner at Old Trafford in front of 63,000 people.

In March 1962 after yet more reserve games and hardly a sniff of a first-team place, he was sold to Leeds United for £20,000. He was a decent enough player but Burnley during this period had such a talented team it was near impossible for anyone to break through and with Andy Lochhead ahead of him in the pecking order it was sensible for Burnley to sell him. He was still not quite 23 and a new career at Leeds was not without its rewards. (*With thanks to Ray Simpson*)

* * *

There are times in a football club's history when key decisions have to be taken. Leeds United boss Don Revie illustrated this point with his team spiralling towards relegation from the Second Division in March 1962 when he signed three players in a bid to avoid the trapdoor into the Third Division.

Burnley centre forward Ian Lawson was first to arrive for £20,000 and immediately made his debut against Huddersfield Town in a game that signalled the end of Revie's playing days. Lawson, Cliff Mason and veteran Scottish international Bobby Collins lined up against Swansea Town at Elland Road in the next match. When Collins opened the scoring in a 2-0 win, the road to recovery had begun. Lawson went on to play his part in United's Second Division Championship success in 1964.

Born in Ouston, County Durham to parents Joe and Lily Lawson in March 1939, Ian was educated at Pelton Secondary Modern School where he excelled at athletics and tennis, but football was his first choice sport. Amongst his earliest memories was playing 20-a-side games near his home, and watching his father, an electrician by trade, play right half for Blyth Spartans in the North Eastern League.

Lawson recalled: "Football meant everything to me, so at every opportunity I'd be in the back yard hitting a ball against the wall into a false net, or playing on cobbled streets with coats for goals, long into the night.

"I started out as a centre half then moved into attack and couldn't stop scoring goals, so stayed as a striker. My school was small but our enthusiasm for football was massive and we became the best team in the region. From school, I progressed to our district team, Chester-le-Street, who won the Sunderland Hospitals Cup which was a big achievement."

As for following a club, there was only one choice for this football-mad youngster. "Newcastle United was my team and I'd watch them from the Gallowgate End at St James' Park. Singing 'Blaydon Races' was always a highlight and you could not believe the noise in the ground at each game. There was so much passion; it was just fantastic.

"Another reason for going was of course to watch Jackie Milburn lead the attack. Wor Jackie, as fans called him, was an incredible footballer because he was strong, direct and fearless. Newcastle were known for their attacking football and they had a fantastic forward line in Milburn, Tommy Walker, Ernie Taylor, George Robledo and Bobby Mitchell. Sunderland was the big game each season and as a derby clash it was a special occasion."

When Newcastle United won the FA Cup three times in five years during the 1950s, the Toon Army were in dreamland. "The FA Cup was the glamour competition every season, so we'd get up in the early hours to queue for tickets, and once you had one, it was brilliant. I didn't miss a home match during the '51 Cup run and was at the Hillsborough semi-final when we defeated Wolves to reach Wembley. I tried everything to get a ticket for the Final but it was impossible.

"On Cup Final day, we did not have a television so all the family crammed around a wireless listening to the commentary. At the final whistle after we'd won 2-0 against Blackpool we all ran out into the street celebrating. And when Newcastle paraded the Cup through the streets, I was amongst thousands of fans cheering them home dressed in black and white club colours."

Newcastle retained the trophy against Arsenal in 1952, and then won it again in 1955 when Milburn scored a bullet header against Manchester City in a famous 3-1 win. In the midst of these cup heroics, 15-year-old Lawson was attracting the attention of scouts across the country and within a fortnight of leaving school, Ian had joined the ground staff at Burnley FC. "I'd seen the set up at Newcastle and Sunderland but decided to get away from my home environment. Of course, playing for Newcastle would have been great but I knew that I'd be distracted. If apprentices went into town, I'd have gone and not concentrated on making it as a footballer, which was my goal. Burnley chief scout Charlie Ferguson had seen me play for the school team, met my headteacher and parents, then everything went from there."

After signing apprentice forms with The Clarets, Lawson lived in digs with Jimmy Robson and John Angus. Budgeting on £5 a week over this period was challenging, but Lawson embraced the apprentice lifestyle. "Of my weekly wage, £2 went on digs and the club put £1 in a post office account, so I was left with 18 shillings pocket money. Going out on the town was never going to be an issue!

"Ground staff duties included cleaning the first team players' boots and painting the goal stanchions. If we had a Saturday game, we'd sweep the terracing on a Monday morning then have a training session in the afternoon. We also helped look after the pitch at Turf Moor, which was not one of the best surfaces. Tommy Danns was groundsman and knew every swearword in the book. Tommy was a real character and had us in stitches if he had a strop. We rolled the pitch after every game, but in the winter if it was impossible to put a heavy roller on we had to hand roll it, which was not much fun.

"Alan Brown was manager but Billy Dougall coached the first team and was years ahead of his time with training methods. Billy Morris looked after the apprentices and was brilliant with us. In the early days, some of the lads seemed like world beaters to me, but when they went out in front of a few thousand supporters froze, whereas I felt fine."

Lawson had held his own in Burnley's reserve team and signed as a professional in March 1956. By now sharing digs with John Connelly, who would play for Manchester United and then England in the 1966 World Cup, Lawson made an astonishing first team debut against Chesterfield in an FA Cup third round tie in January 1957.

Scoring Burnley's first goal after four minutes, he completed his hat-trick nine minutes from full time and there was still time to hit a fourth as Burnley finished 7-0 victors. The teenage sensation was headline news in Saturday's evening sports paper. "Burnley's 14-man squad was pinned up next to the changing room door for the Chesterfield tie. When I saw my name, I thought it was just for the experience of being around our first team, but the manager had phoned my dad and invited him to watch the game. I had my boots with me when the squad met up and it was only at that point that I realised I'd be playing. I thought, that'll do me.

"Looking back, Brown handled the situation well because I was not too nervous, just excited to finally be involved and determined to make an impression. When the game kicked off, I just played my game and managed to put four goals away.

"There was a great feeling of elation afterwards and I knew I'd make the headlines, but there was no great celebration with a night out on the town. I went out with my girlfriend, Maureen, who I'd been courting for a while to see the World War 2 film *Attack!* starring American actors Jack Palance, Eddie Albert and Lee Marvin at the Odeon!"

Following his FA Cup exploits, Brown kept Lawson in the side and he continued his stunning form with a hat-trick when Burnley thumped New Brighton 9-0 in the fourth round. But the Cup run ended when Aston Villa won a quarterfinal replay 2-0 at Villa Park. "Villa knocked us out, which was ridiculous because we should have hammered them. I missed a couple of sitters that day and they went on to win the Cup against Manchester United."

Lawson made seven League appearances, aside of his Cup exertions, including a memorable match against his boyhood hero when Newcastle United came to town. "Jackie Milburn was the most exciting player I'd ever seen play football. I'd idolised him as a kid, and still did, but now I was playing against him for Burnley in a First Division fixture so there was no time for sentiment. If our paths crossed and I had to kick him, then I would, but on the day I couldn't get near him! Over the years, I was fortunate to meet Jackie numerous times and he was always a top man."

Lawson had shot to prominence, which brought him an England Youth appearance against Spain in a thrilling 4-4 draw at Birmingham City's St Andrew's ground in September 1957 but bizarrely, after his debut season for Burnley, he did not feature in the side for two seasons. "Playing for England was a proud occasion but the Football Association would not let players keep their shirt as a memento. We were allowed to take the badge with the three lions off the shirt, which seemed strange at the time, but I still have it along with my cap for playing. Both mean a lot to me."

Manchester United as League Champions had entered the European Cup in 1957/58, which was ground-breaking for English football. But tragically the world of football would soon mourn the loss of many talented players after the Munich air disaster in February 1958. "Everyone was stunned when we heard about the crash on the radio. When I started out at Burnley we played some tough teams and the 'Busby Babes' were by far the best side I'd faced with the likes of Pegg, Coleman, Taylor, Viollet and Charlton in their side. When the 'Babes' ran out to play we knew that we had a game on. There was something special about them and from the kick off they attacked at will.

"Duncan Edwards was such a nice guy, so modest and a magical player. They were an incredible group so it was a tragedy for the club and British football because they could have competed with the great Real Madrid team from that era."

Lawson's National Service at Chatham, which began in November 1958, was eventful. Apart from his marriage to Maureen the following April, he played his part in a remarkable First Division campaign when Burnley competed with defending champions Wolves and Tottenham Hotspur for the Championship in 1959/60.

Lawson played eight games at inside right as understudy to Jimmy McIlroy, scoring three goals, including the winner against Manchester United at Old Trafford. Burnley went on to stun English football when they clinched the title in the last game of an astonishing season (Tottenham would be the first 20th century team to win the League and Cup 'double' in 1960/61). "I trained with army sides during the week then had permission to play on a Saturday afternoon. Burnley had great senior pros and young players in a balanced side. We had a strong defence in front of goalkeeper Adam Blacklaw who was my best mate. Jimmy Adamson was an influential captain but McIlroy was the key player and you really respected him as a footballer.

"Going into the last game against Manchester City, only a victory would allow us to overhaul Wolves who had a one-point advantage with a superior goal average. We were dark horses for the title but had thousands of fans amongst a capacity crowd. Brian Pilkington scored then City equalised before Trevor Meredith, who was in for Connelly, clinched the title.

"I watched from the stands but back in the dressing room the champagne was flowing. Afterwards we went to Burnley Town Hall and Nelson Golf Club for a few sherbets! For little Burnley to win the Championship was incredible for the town and major news. Everything came together and it was an amazing achievement. I only played eight games that season, scoring three goals, but was always involved on matchdays so received a Championship medal, which I've been proud to own."

Lawson was out of the first team frame when Burnley made a spirited defence of their title, then progressed in the FA Cup during the 1961/62 season. Then out of the blue, Leeds United offered Burnley £20,000 in a bid for Lawson's services in February 1962. After 30 appearances and 15 goals for Burnley, Lawson had a big decision to make over whether to stay in the First Division and fight for a place in the team or drop down to a side struggling in the Second Division but with more certainty of playing regular football.

At this time, Leeds manager Don Revie had moved Jack Charlton into an emergency centre forward role with some success and Billy Bremner had hit nine league goals (and would finish top scorer on 11) but United's manager needed a centre forward to bring firepower to his ailing team.

Lawson explained: "Harry Potts was now the Burnley manager and made it clear I'd be in the reserves every Saturday. When he came round to my house it was a surprise, as it was our day off, but I was even more surprised when he told me Don and Les Cocker would be down at the ground by 2pm. Don had seen me play for Burnley's reserves against Leeds and was impressed with my attitude. It might have also helped that I scored a hat-trick that day!

"I knew nothing about Leeds, apart from Charlton being a Geordie, and they looked to be on their way to the Third Division. But Don had a clear vision for the club. He'd changed the strip to all white like Real Madrid and was determined they would make it back to the First Division and wanted me to be a part of it.

"Looking at the League table, Don's views seemed crazy, but he was so convincing that I went over on the Wednesday to have a look around, met the coaching staff and signed. I'd enjoyed my time at Burnley, our children, Sharon and Michael, were born there, but it was time for a new challenge and that meant helping Leeds survive relegation."

When Lawson met his new teammates at Elland Road there was no time to settle in to his new surroundings. He had to hit the ground running and was thrown into the first team three days after his arrival for a fixture at Huddersfield Town.

Huddersfield Town v Leeds United, March 3rd, 1962
Huddersfield Town: Wilson, Saward, Coddington, Dinsdale, McHale, Stokes, Massie, O'Grady, Atkins, Wood, White
Leeds United: Younger, Jones, Hair, Cameron, Goodwin, Smith, Bremner, Revie, Charlton, Lawson, Peyton

"Big Jack had been playing up front, which showed how desperate things were, and the game turned out to be Don's last game for the club. I had played against him in his Sunderland days, but he was now past his best, so it was not a surprise when he decided to call it a day.

"We lost to Huddersfield 2-1 and it was clear that we were in a real scrap for survival. I partnered Jack in attack against Town but it would be his last appearance as a striker."

A few days after the Town defeat, Revie pulled a masterstroke by adding Bobby Collins to the playing ranks at Elland Road. Cliff Mason also joined the fight for survival. Ten games remained for Leeds to avoid slipping into the Third Division. Relegation would be a shattering blow and could end Revie's tenure at the club before it had started. The trio of signings played against Swansea Town and recorded a first win in eight games.

Leeds United v Swansea Town, March 10th, 1962
Leeds United: Younger, Hair, Mason, Cameron, Goodwin, Smith, Bremner, Collins, McAdams, Lawson, Hawksby
Swansea Town: King, Purcell, Sanders, Johnson, Nurse, Williams, Jones, Davies, Webster, Donnelly, Griffiths

"Bobby was an incredible signing and his effect was immediate. The dressing room atmosphere changed when he arrived and I'd only been there a few days. It was no surprise that Bobby scored on his debut against Swansea. He led by example; it was a crucial win and built our confidence."

Lawson scored his first goal for the club in the next match against Southampton but the game is remembered for a goalkeeping crisis.

Southampton v Leeds United, March 17th, 1962
Southampton: Chadwick, Clifton, Godfrey, Huxford, Knapp, Mulgrew, Payne, Patrick, Penk, Reeves, Traynor
Leeds United: Sprake, Hair, Mason, Cameron, Goodwin, Smith, Bremner, Collins, McAdams, Lawson, Hawksby

"We went down 4-1 to Southampton when I got my first goal for Leeds, but we had been unlucky, because after traveling down by train our goalkeeper, Tommy Younger, fell ill so they had to fly down Gary Sprake, who was only 16, as a late replacement. Gary showed though that he could command his area, had class and the temperament to make it."

The coming weeks would see Leeds grind out an unbeaten run to give themselves a chance of survival. "Billy scored both goals in a win against Luton Town, then we defeated Middlesbrough which gave us momentum. From there the run-in brought a spate of draws as we scrambled for points, including a 0-0 draw with Bury which was my last game of the season because I'd picked up an ankle injury.

"It was all a bit desperate but we were at a stage of the season when points meant everything. Things were moving forward although there was a lot of work to do on the training ground because in games the lads had been so disorganised, but Bobby got into them. Big Jack was also his own man and did his own thing. He'd defend then suddenly join the attack but Bobby sorted that out too.

"Don knew what he was getting with Bobby and he made a difference in our approach to succeed. We feared Bobby more than Don at times. He'd yell at us, 'Do you want to be chuffing playing in the Third Division or do you want to get organised and avoid relegation?'

"Bobby was so determined and suddenly we were moving in the right direction."

With one match left, Leeds travelled to Newcastle United where a win at St James' Park would guarantee staying up. "Missing the game was really disappointing on a personal level but Billy McAdams came in and played his last game for the club. I travelled up with the lads by coach and we all knew how big the match was for the club. There was tension but we'd been on a good run and just needed to finish the job.

"On the day, we knew what we had to do and there was an overriding feeling that we were going to do it. Bobby was really fired up and made sure everyone was ready from the first kick. I was in the dugout watching the game with Don and Les. Don was quite calm but Les was kicking every ball and yelling at everyone. We had more to play for than Newcastle and by half time led 3-0 then saw out the game.

"There was huge relief that we'd done it and a feeling that we'd never be in that position again. It was a happy coach journey back to Leeds after the game."

Lawson was still struggling with ankle problems throughout the close season. To pep up his attack, Revie signed Airdrie striker Jim Storrie for £15,650, and sprang a surprise by bringing back former legend John Charles from Juventus to the club in a £53,000 transfer. "Big John was a superstar and arrived at our team hotel dressed in a well-cut Italian suit, looking like a Greek God. You could not get near him because every lady in the hotel was swooning around him! John was such a modest guy though and took it all in his stride.

"The first day he arrived for training, John asked where we wanted him to change, so we decided to wind up little Billy who was always late. Billy, all white and freckles, came rushing in and went straight to where he normally changed. Standing beside his peg, John was stripped and bronzed. Billy looked around at us, 'Jesus Christ, thanks guys'.

"It was brilliant; the banter was great. We were all mates on and off the field, and Don must take a lot of credit for the atmosphere in the dressing room. There was a tremendous feel-good factor and a determination not to endure another nightmare season."

Storrie began firing in goals when the 1962/63 season kicked off but, with the first team struggling for results, Revie blooded four teenagers in a league clash at Swansea Town on September 8th, 1962. Gary Sprake, Norman Hunter, Paul Reaney and Rod Johnson came into the side for the match which Leeds won 2-0, and results soon picked up. "My ankle was still causing issues, so it was no surprise Storrie and Big John got the nod. I played alongside both in a defeat against Rotherham United but was then out for a month. By the time I returned for a League Cup tie at Blackburn Rovers, John had played his last game for Leeds and he was past his best. Things did not work out for him, but John in his prime was up there with the very best players. In today's game he'd be alongside Messi and Ronaldo because John was that good a footballer.

"Don was right to bring in the kids as he did at Swansea with the first team struggling. I'd got my break at 17 for Burnley, so had no complaints. I've always felt that if you're good enough it does not matter how old you are for the first team. Hunter was a skinny kid but had that timing in his tackling he became famous for as a defender. Yet off the pitch he would not say boo to a goose, but clearly had bags of talent. Norman was professional from an early age, straight up, and you knew what you'd get with him.

"Reaney always worked hard and was so determined to make it. He wasn't naturally gifted like some of the other young lads but got the best out of his abilities.

"Sprake was a smashing lad and had already been in the first team, but this was his break, and he showed he was a terrific goalkeeper."

Following United's 4-0 defeat to Blackburn Rovers, Lawson would not enjoy first team action until late in the season when he teamed up alongside Storrie and recent signing Don Weston. But it was some return as he scored both goals in a 2-0 victory at Scunthorpe United.

Another brace followed at Chelsea in a 2-2 draw, but with his ankle playing up, Revie played Lawson sporadically in United's remaining five games of the season.

The season ended on a high with Leeds thumping Swansea Town 5-0. Storrie (2), Lawson, Collins and Johanneson scored the goals in a fine victory. "It was frustrating playing for the reserves but I was pleased with my comeback, however, that didn't stop Don resting me after scoring two goals against Chelsea and after my goal against Swansea when I ended the game playing centre half because Big Jack got injured. We finished in fifth place which was a remarkable turnaround from the previous season."

As the 1963/64 season approached a promotion push appeared on the cards. Revie, Les Cocker and Syd Owen had created a professional environment for players. There was a meticulous training and matchday routine but also a special atmosphere around the club. United were going places. "Pre-season was tough with the initial workouts then running round Roundhay Park. First though I had to get down to my target weight. The heavier lads, including myself, used to go in two weeks early to make sure we'd hit our weight, and once I hit mine I was fine throughout the season. There was also plenty of fun in between the sessions, especially cricket matches to lighten the mood. Confidence had returned to the squad and we had coaches who got the best from us in training. Cocker was so enthusiastic whereas Owen was a great organiser though a hard character. There was a sense among the lads that we'd be up there and were from the start. Promotion was the target and our bonuses were set for a win if we were top of the table and for attracting bigger gates.

"When it came to man-management, the boss was terrific and ran a tight ship. With Don, everything he did was for the players. Away from training we had regular golf days and at Christmas the young lads and staff behind the scenes would join us. The atmosphere was fantastic and you felt a part of something special. Before a game we'd meet up at the team hotel, have our pre-match meal then Don would go through his dossier on our opponents. We travelled to games by coach or train depending on where it was taking place. If we stopped overnight before a game we played carpet bowls and bingo to relax.

"Don was meticulous but also very superstitious. Some of the lads ran out in a particular position like Jack who was last out, however, Don was on another level. When a game came around we were prepared but Don would still have a quiet word with each player in the dressing room. There was no team warming up session as you see now, I did my stretches an hour before kick-off then ran out when it was time. Looking back, it's amazing there were not more muscle pulls.

"All the lads had a routine and whereas I'd take ages, Weston would walk in 15 minutes before the game and be ready in no time at all. Billy also seemed ill prepared but he'd go out and have a blinder! Before running out some lads would be shouting and balling while others would sit quietly but we went out as a team.

"The atmosphere was great behind the scenes where a lot of people were behind us and none more than chairman Harry Reynolds.

Harry was a larger-than-life character and loved being with the lads. On journeys to games he'd sit with us, not the directors. 'My boys,' he'd say, 'there is nothing better than having a beer with my boys, you do us proud.'

"Big Jack and Billy were also real characters. Jack was a fantastic personality, his own man and never deviated from what he believed in. On a club tour he'd say 'I'm going for a drink', so we'd say, 'Right you are, Jack, you do that.' We'd have a bet that after his second pint, he'd be back. And true to form, he'd come strolling in!

"I roomed with Billy who was not the tidiest of roommates and roped me into all sorts. We were always doing something crazy and, more often than not, Willie Bell would be on the receiving end. Willie, on occasions, would not go out on a night out so we'd ring him up and make out we were from the Water Board then get him to fill his bath which for some reason he did. Then if we got back late from a nightclub we'd run into Willie's room all dressed up. 'Willie, what are you doing man, it's time to go,' we'd scream.

"Poor Willie would get up dazed, dress and then we'd put him out of his misery. Willie got the brunt of our daft capers! On the field though, Willie was a crucial member of the team because he added balance."

Revie's line-up was taking shape, building from a settled defensive unit of Reaney, Charlton, Hunter and Bell in front of Sprake in goal. Midfielders Bremner, Collins and Johanneson were bolstered by the signing of Johnny Giles from Manchester United for £33,000 promising guile, strength and pace. Two of Storrie, Weston or Lawson would lead the attack. "Bobby Collins was number one in my book. For me, he is the most important signing in the club's history when you look at his impact on and off the field. Bobby brought in a winning mentality, even in five-a-sides he was so competitive and had to win. Giles had a winning mentality from his years with Manchester United but he could also play. Blessed with great vision, Johnny prepared well and could ping a ball anywhere around the park. When Johnny teamed up with Billy they were magic together, and on another level to other midfield partnerships.

"As for Albert Johanneson, he was a dandy fellow and loved to be smartly dressed. Back in Johannesburg where he grew up Albert experienced segregation, so despite his talent it took him time to settle at Leeds. Albert wouldn't shower with the lads at one time but we soon put him right. I also remember sitting with him at a plush hotel in Birmingham before a game when waiters served us. Albert laughed nervously, and when I asked him why he said he was wondering what it would have been like if white people had served him back in South Africa. Albert had to overcome racist chants from fans at some grounds, which was a disgrace, but he channelled his efforts into football, was exceptionally quick and could be a match winner."

Lawson was in the starting line-up when United got their league campaign off to a winning start against Rotherham, but would not feature again until opening the scoring in a 3-0 win over Northampton Town on October 1st, 1963.

Swindon Town were surprising early league leaders ahead of Leeds, Sunderland and Preston North End, but United were in the midst of a winning streak and headed the table for the first time on goal average following a 4-1 win at Southampton near the end of the month. Scoring four goals in the opening 33 minutes, Lawson bagged a brace in a memorable win.

Southampton v Leeds United, October 26th, 1963
Southampton: Burnside, Godfrey, Huxford, Kirby, Knapp, O'Brien, Payne, Penk, Traynor, White, Williams
Leeds United: Sprake, Reaney, Bell, Bremner, Charlton, Hunter, Giles, Lawson, Weston, Collins, Johanneson

Correspondent, James Hastings: "Seven coaches of a special train and a chartered aircraft took Leeds United fans to The Dell, and what a worthwhile journey it proved to be for the Yorkshire club who gained their fourth successive away win to emphasise their strong challenge for promotion. Southampton are a difficult side to beat at home but they were completely outplayed by the slick moving and direct Leeds attack."

Lawson was back in favour ahead of Storrie and continued his impressive form in wins over Grimsby Town and Bury.

Lawson recalled: "Don was always fair with the strikers if goals were hard to come by as he'd give you extra games to find your form, but it would come to a point when you would be out of the line-up. As things turned out, Storrie's goals dried up so I was back in the side and knew if I played well the attacking spot was mine."

United and Sunderland came up against each other in a double-header over the festive period. Anticipation in both cities was huge for the Boxing Day clash at Elland Road and return fixture at Roker Park two days later. The victors would gain a huge boost of confidence for the remainder of the campaign.

Leeds United v Sunderland, December 26th, 1963
Leeds United: Sprake, Reaney, Bell, Bremner, Goodwin, Hunter, Giles, Weston, Lawson, Collins, Johanneson
Sunderland: Montgomery, Irwin, Ashurst, Harvey, Hurley, McNab, Usher, Herd, Sharkey, Crossan, Mulhall

After Mulhall scored against the run of play, Leeds searched for an equaliser and eventually got it through Lawson's poaching ability.

By a special correspondent: "Leeds' efforts became almost frenzied but their directness seemed to desert them when it came to shooting at goal. Finally, however, they managed to equalise. It was a pity that such a long awaited goal should be so scrambled. Weston and Lawson challenged Montgomery, the ball dropped from his hands and Lawson scored. In spite of Sunderland's protests the goal was allowed."

Following the match, *Soccer Star* correspondent John Helm summed up Lawson's upturn in form in his Yorkshire Round-Up column titled 'Ian Is The Comeback Man'.

"Nothing delights the football fan more than a good comeback story, and a man who can undoubtedly claim to have done just that is Leeds United's bustling centre forward Ian Lawson.

"Remember Lawson, the 17-year-old youngster who first hit the headlines of the sports pages way back in 1957, when in two cup ties against Chesterfield and New Brighton, he slammed seven goals for Burnley in wins of 7-0 and 9-0?

"He was hailed as the greatest centre forward discovery since Tommy Lawton, but the reputation proved harmful to Lawson, who was never able to reproduce similar form in subsequent seasons. Finally, in February 1962, Leeds United decided to take a gamble, and Don Revie signed Lawson from Burnley, for a fairly substantial fee.

"But the fairy-tale did not materialise even then for Lawson. He had to fight his way back to the top, and it was not easy. He still found goals hard to come by, and the Leeds crowd did not take kindly to a costly flop.

"However, manager Don Revie was convinced he would come through with flying colours. For practically the whole of last season, Lawson had to be content with Central League football, as United's new signing from Scotland Jim Storrie was getting the goals regularly.

"But this time it is Lawson's turn to get the glory, and Storrie's turn to fight to recapture his form. Nothing has stood out more prominently in United's rise to the top of the Second Division than Lawson's ability to take the half-chance. So perseverance has paid off at last. Lawson is once again in favour with the crowds, and the goals are flowing fast from his boots.

"It was Lawson who got the point-saving goal in the Boxing Day clash with challengers Sunderland, just when it seemed the Roker boys were going to score a valuable success at Elland Road. Incidentally, the attendance that day of well over 40,000 was the best at Leeds since the golden era of John Charles. There was a fair sprinkling of red 'n white clad supporters there too, in one of the keenest fought matches I have seen this season."

Forty-eight hours on and the Wearsiders inflicted a 2-0 defeat on United, only their second in 25 matches, to throw the promotion race wide open. Going into the New Year, Leeds headed the way on 37 points with Preston and Sunderland a point back.

Lawson recalled: "The atmosphere in both games was fantastic but we did not perform because we drew 1-1 at home then lost 2-0 at Roker Park. The lads were so disappointed because you want to defeat your biggest rivals but there were plenty of games to go and we felt we could still achieve our goals. Don didn't go overboard about the Sunderland results, it's a cliché but you quickly move on to the next games. We vowed to send them a telegram after we won the title and did!"

Away from the promotion race, Leeds turned their attentions to the FA Cup. And continuing his run of form, Lawson hit his first FA Cup goal since his Burnley days when Leeds pushed First Division Champions Everton all the way during a fourth round clash when they drew 1-1 in front of 48,826 fans at Elland Road.

Leeds United v Everton, January 25th, 1964
Leeds United: Sprake, Reaney, Bell, Bremner, Madeley, Hunter, Henderson, Giles, Lawson, Collins, Johanneson
Everton: West, Brown, Harris, Gabriel, Labone, Kay, Scott, Stevens, Young, Vernon, Temple

"The ground was packed to the rafters against Everton and when crowds are massive you are more energised and want to perform. Big matches are why you play the game; you want to impress in front of full houses. Everton were a star team and Cup fever had really gripped the city of Leeds. Don really felt we had a chance because we were winning games and playing with confidence. And we should have won after I gave us a first half lead at Elland Road. I should have scored a second and then the referee made a terrible decision when Sprakie saved a penalty and he said that he'd moved. You think to yourself, come on ref give us a break."

Everton defeated United 2-0 in front of 66,000 spectators at Goodison Park three days later.

Everton v Leeds United, January 28th, 1964
Everton: West, Brown, Meagan, Harris, Labone, Kay, Scott, Stevens, Gabriel, Vernon, Temple
Leeds United: Sprake, Reaney, Bell, Bremner, Madeley, Hunter, Henderson, Giles, Lawson, Collins, Hawksby

"Everton edged the replay before another bumper crowd but it had been a great experience. Both games made us realise we'd be able to compete at a higher level, but first we had to make it out of the Second Division. Consistency was now the key and I knew that we could do it."

Sunderland held a two-point advantage over Leeds and Preston with 10 matches left. United's league form had dipped since the Boxing Day showdown with the Roker men, arguably due to their cup encounters, but Revie had strengthened his attack by signing Middlesbrough and former England centre forward, Alan Peacock, for £53,000 in February 1964.

Revie's hunch to link up Peacock and Lawson would bring dividends in the midst of consecutive 3-1 victories against Southampton, Middlesbrough and Grimsby Town. Leeds opened the scoring against Southampton with a fortuitous Lawson goal before skipper Collins ignited United's promotion push in early March.

Leeds United v Southampton, March 7th, 1964
Leeds United: Sprake, Reaney, Bell, Greenhoff, Charlton, Hunter, Weston, Lawson, Peacock, Collins, Johanneson
Southampton: Godfrey, Willams, Hollywood, Wimshurst, Knapp, Huxford, Payne, Chivers, Kirby, McGuigan, Sydenham

Correspondent, Ronald Kennedy: "The City of Leeds, hungry for success, breathed a sigh of relief in the 72nd minute of this rugged battle tinged with promotion glamour.

"Bobby Collins, a little chunkier and a little slower than in his heyday, swept away with the ball towards the left edge of the penalty area.

"Elland Road groaned because it looked a thousand to one that wee Bobby had thrown away a golden chance to settle The Saints' clash once and for all. But suddenly the little general's foot struck like the tongue of an angry viper, and the ball tore savagely into the net.

"Till then, United, once a goal ahead (through Lawson) and then level, had dangled the nervous fans on the end of a thread of suspense.

"Collins' goal restored the balance and was a tranquiliser for the fury that blasted from the terraces as United threatened to give the game away in a fit of casual inefficiency."

The Peacock-Lawson partnership then came up trumps against Boro' and Grimsby.

Seven games remained with Leeds on 51 points, Sunderland 50 and Preston 47.

"In all three games we were level at half time but Don was not the type to lose his temper. He made his points clear in encouraging us to win the game. However, Bobby was always fiery and made his viewpoint in no uncertain terms. He ripped into us all to get out there and do the business, which we did.

"Each game was so important because we edged in front of Sunderland and Preston. Peacock had really added impetus to the attack and I enjoyed playing alongside him. Alan was the best header of a ball I'd seen, so if he went up to head a ball, I knew he'd nod it down to me."

United now faced Easter trips to Newcastle United and Derby County before a return date with the Tyneside club on March 30th. Lawson helped Leeds win a tough encounter at St James' Park before sharing the spoils at the Baseball Ground. But United's 1-1 draw at Derby came at a cost with Lawson picking up a hamstring injury that would sideline him in the remaining games.

Leeds went on to clinch promotion at Swansea Town then the title at Charlton Athletic, courtesy of a Peacock brace, in a 2-0 triumph. Leeds topped the Second Division table with 63 points ahead of Sunderland with 61 and Preston on 56.

Correspondent, Phil Brown, *Green Post*: "Hail The Champions! Leeds United wound up a great season by claiming the crowning glory of Division Two at Charlton today.

"By rail, road and air, United supporters descended on this south-east London ground for the sight of United's final fling for the Second Division title.

"The win was completely deserved and it crowned the season ideally with the title again after 40 years."

With the title wrapped up, chairman Harry Reynolds made a special trip to the Potteries to collect the Second Division trophy from last season's winners, Stoke City, in order for Leeds to have it available for their victory parade at Leeds Town Hall and civic reception. Leeds United were back in the big time and Lawson had played his part in a historic season.

"I travelled with the lads to Swansea and had a fitness test on the morning of the game, but was not right so knew I'd miss out. It was a huge disappointment but there were no substitutes so the boss could not take a chance. If I'd pulled up after a few minutes then the lads would be down to 10 men. Of course, players get injured in games but going out knowing I'd not get through was too risky.

"We got the right result, which was the main thing, and it was so exciting to get promotion. There was a great sense of achievement, elation and relief that we had reached our objective because that was the main target. We'd got what we deserved after the effort we'd put in over the season and the overriding feeling was that we'd cracked it;

we were on our way. At the civic reception we knew this was just a start for the club."

Top-flight football was back in the city of Leeds and a competitive football team was developing. United's success had brought positive media coverage, including snippets on the club's youth academy. Peter Lorimer, Jimmy Greenhoff, Paul Madeley and Terry Cooper had made debuts. Eddie Gray, Rod Belfitt, Terry Hibbitt and David Harvey would soon make an impression.

"When I first saw Gray and Lorimer play at 15 years of age, I knew they were going to make it. Don asked a few of the lads to put them through their paces in a five-a-side game, so we put in some hard tackles to see what they were made of but they shrugged them off and played well. When Don asked what I thought about them afterwards, I looked at him with a wry smile. There was no doubt about it, both would be stars.

"Madeley was only a kid but his character was spot on. Don knew he had the talent but he could not have predicted just how good he'd be all over the park. Paul's build allowed him to move with ease around the pitch and there was something about him that stood out. Some players were good at getting forward, which he could do, but Paul could also turn with the ball and defend when needed. He was a fabulous footballer and would be worth an astonishing amount in the modern game.

"Cooper was another kid with enormous potential, yet so modest. Terry started out on the left wing then switched to left back and you knew he was going to make it to the top.

"Harvey was a good kid and as a rookie keeper clearly had potential, though had to bide his time for years before getting an opportunity.

"Of all the young lads, Hibbitt was cheekiest and the one you'd give a clip round the ear. As a prospect, he had a sweet left foot and could play but he never quite made it at Leeds. However, he was up against so many great midfield players it was always going to be tough. But Terry knew he'd be able to cut it somewhere, and did at Newcastle United when he teamed up with Malcolm Macdonald, sliding the ball through for 'SuperMac' to finish. Greenhoff and Belfitt also both had talent but like Hibbitt would enjoy better times at other clubs.

"Football is a harsh business where apprentices are concerned.

Barrie Wright captained England Schoolboys at Wembley but sometimes things don't work out. And then there were lads like Dennis Hawkins whom you felt sad for because he worked really hard and had a great attitude but did not make the grade. Unlike Dennis though, there were ground staff lads who thought they were far better than they actually were, so you didn't feel sorry for them when they came and went. Don had a huge array of talent to serve the club but that was for the future."

United were not predicted to make a big impression when the 1964/65 season got underway, but the mass media sat up when Leeds won their opening three games against Aston Villa, Liverpool and Wolves. Lawson came in for Collins in a 3-2 win against Wolves at the end of August, before leading the attack alongside Storrie in a 3-3 thriller at Sunderland a week later.

Leeds United v Wolverhampton Wanderers, August 29th, 1964
Leeds United: Sprake, Reaney, Bell, Bremner, Charlton, Hunter, Giles, Weston, Storrie, Lawson, Johanneson
Wolverhampton Wanderers: Davies, Thomson, Harris, Goodwin, Flowers, Woodruff, Broadbent, Knowles, Crawford, Melia, Wharton

Correspondent, Edgar Turner: "I'll be the first to stick my neck out and say it, Leeds United for the Championship! I know that this was only the third game of the season, and I know there's a long way to go. But you can take it from me, Don Revie's boys will be no pushover's for any team in the First Division. Far from it. They're soccer's new glamour boy's challenging the best in the land for a crack at that European jackpot."

Sunderland v Leeds United, September 5th, 1964
Sunderland: McLaughlan, Irwin, Ashurst, Harvey, Hurley, McNab, Usher, Mitchinson, Clough, Crossan, Mulhall
Leeds United: Sprake, Reaney, Bell, Bremner, Charlton, Hunter, Giles, Lawson, Storrie, Collins, Johanneson

Correspondent, John Dunn: "The symphonic sweetness of Leeds United's rhythmic soccer movement sent the far-travelled Yorkshire fans home in rhapsodies from Roker Park yesterday. And well it might have done for this United outfit have bridged the gap between Second

Division clog and First Division finesse with admirable ease."

Sadly for Lawson, a 4-0 loss against Blackpool at Bloomfield Road would be his final game of the season due to a knee injury, and while United went close to winning the 'double', Lawson underwent an operation and wondered about his future. "Something had been wrong for a while with my knee but you just soldier on in games. Against Blackpool it gave way and I ended up hobbling through the match because there were no subs. By the Friday it was diagnosed as a cartilage problem and I had the operation a few days later.

"The injury was a real blow and there were complications after the procedure so it took ages to get close to match fitness. I was fine running forward but turning was a real issue, so I realised my knee would not be right again. It was soul-destroying but all you can do is battle away and hope for a chance to get back into the first team. Don was great though because even though I was not involved on the pitch, he wanted me to be with the first team squad for away games and on short breaks after cup games.

"Watching from the sidelines was not easy, especially seeing the lads lose the First Division title on goal average. But I was in the crowd at Nottingham Forest when Billy headed us into the FA Cup Final with a late winner against Manchester United. The atmosphere in the dressing room after was amazing and historic because it would be United's first Wembley final.

"For every footballer, to play in an FA Cup Final was a major ambition, and I missed out twice, which was the biggest disappointment of my career. Burnley let me go leading up to the 1962 Final against Tottenham Hotspur and now I was injured at Leeds. At least this time I was a part of the build up to Wembley when we recorded 'The Leeds United Calypso' with Ronnie Hilton. There were plenty of bad voices but it was all part of the experience, and it was top of the chart sales locally at Schofields and Lewis's department stores.

"I was at Wembley for the big day and hoped they could do the business. Unfortunately we did not play well against Liverpool, which made the banquet afterwards at the Savoy Hotel tough on all the lads. We'd gone really close to the 'double' so to lose out on both was heartbreaking but it had been an incredible season."

Lawson, who scored 21 goals in 51 appearances for Leeds United, joined Crystal Palace in a £9,000 transfer during the close season.

After one season at Selhurst Park, where he made 17 league appearances, Lawson played briefly for Port Vale before moving to Barnsley in 1967. However, he never made an appearance for the Oakwell side as persistent knee problems forced his retirement from the game at 29 years of age.

During a career in the steel industry, the Lawsons, who have four grandchildren, moved around the country from Congleton to Stanley in County Durham, and later Tamworth, where they continue to enjoy retirement.

"Before the FA Cup Final in '65, I realised it would be tough getting back into the first team, and not long after it was obvious I'd have to drop down a division to continue my career. When Palace came in for me I was determined to give it a go, but my knee was still an issue.

"One of the highlights during my spell at Palace was England captain, Bobby Moore, dropping in to our local pub on a Saturday night after a game for a drink. With the World Cup coming up it was great chatting with Bobby who was such a modest guy. Charlie Woods, Tony Millington and Keith Smith, like myself, also lived in Brighton, so we drove in together each day to training. We also watched the World Cup Final, and after England won, I did think about contacting Big Jack to join the celebrations, but there was no way after toasting the success we could have driven to London!

"After Palace my knee kept swelling up, so after a season not kicking a ball I hung up my boots. Retiring was tough though. You can only play football professionally for a short period and it was deflating to call it a day but I had plenty of memories and I would not change anything.

"The highlight at Leeds was winning the Second Division title. There were not that many players under Don who won a title, so to achieve it with that group was really special. I played with three of the greatest footballers of any generation in Billy Bremner, John Charles and Bobby Collins. Playing with those guys, you can't help but think how great was that."

3

1975 A Wimbledon Disaster

Underdog! *by Tim Quelch is a personal story of years of watching football, and in particular following the fortunes of the 'small' struggling clubs. He loves nothing better than seeing such clubs cause upsets and achieve improbable successes. If you could turn back the clock and seats had been available for the David versus Goliath fight, Tim would have been there in a close-up ringside seat. Now retired, he moved north from Hampton and lives in Skipton.*

Supporting Burnley, the classic underdog, for the last 40 years he has followed Brighton, Brentford, Aldershot, Kingstonian and the original Hastings United. He has watched games all over England from Grimsby to Norwich and from Newcastle to Southampton. Most of us have eyes only for the club we support. Tim is perhaps a genuine student of football's wider world.

Underdog! *looks at teams who have punched above their weight and have briefly excelled in the game, usually only to sink into anonymity again; the likes of Hereford, Wimbledon, Oxford, Northampton, Workington and Carlisle. The themes are improbable successes and abject failures, inspired leadership and dogged hope, all set against a backdrop of changing times and Tim's personal experiences in football, including how he first came to be a Burnley supporter even though he hails from the south.*

It's all too easy to write about the great games in a club's history; the ones that bring fame, glory and great victories. In Underdog!, *in the case of Burnley, Tim describes games that are the opposite, infamous defeats and inglorious failures; a mind-numbing home defeat against Hull City in the early '70s, a humiliating defeat against non-league Wimbledon in the FA Cup in 1975 and then the game at Blackpool in January 1976, again in the FA Cup, that saw Burnley defeated and provoked manager Adamson's departure.*

The introduction tells us how football took hold of him. His opening line sums up his whole football philosophy. DT

***

Underdog! Fifty Years of Trials and Triumphs with Football's Also-Rans by Tim Quelch (Pitch Publishing)

I have never been attracted by easy, vicarious glory. Even as a kid I rooted resolutely for the Indians (sorry, Native Americans). Southern Dixie stole my affection for no better reason than they were underdogs in the US Civil War. So, it was destined that my choices of favourite football teams should follow a similar pattern. I do not drool over failure, though. I simply believe that success should be hard-earned. What sets my pulse racing is a team of doughty competitors punching well above their weight, determined to beat their retreat when the going gets really tough.

Although I have remained largely faithful to one team, Burnley, for over 40 years, I am no monogamist. I have always had an unstoppable urge to lend a struggling club my Jonah-like support. Ironically my life as a football supporter began in the First Division, at Stamford Bridge, in the late fifties, but in those days Chelsea were a cash-strapped, faltering First Division side en route to Division Two. As soon as Tommy Docherty had transformed them into swish King's Road slickers my interest began to wane. By that time I had developed affections for two local sides, Brighton and Hove Albion, and Hastings United, and they immediately dropped like stones.

I came haltingly to football. My dad first tried to kindle an interest when I was five. He presented me with a birthday gift of a leather ball. We tried it out on a soggy surface in a deserted recreation field on a glowering autumn afternoon. The ball became impossibly heavy with excess moisture, barely trickling away from my flailing kicks. This did not seem like fun.

A year or so later I had to move to a new school in a distant town. Here, I discovered that Chix bubble gum cards were hard currency. Staring at their crudely coloured images I couldn't imagine what the fuss was about. Most of the footballers were captured in stiff, perfunctory poses, their faces devoid of expression. They didn't seem to be having fun, either. However, the faraway places they represented – Huddersfield, Sheffield and Burnley – seemed as exotic as the Black Hills of Dakota. Gradually my curiosity increased but it wasn't until I came across a 1957 football annual – *The Big Book of Football Champions* – in a local Woolworth's store, that my interest took hold. Seeing that I was absorbed by that book, my father seized his Jesuit moment and bought it for me. The pictures were quite different from those on the cards. Here was drama aplenty. There were shots of the ball yanking the goal-net amid broken-toothed celebrations. There were lunging, muscular tackles by beefy defenders with furrowed expressions, while slight forwards writhed at their feet in pain. There were ballistic Brylcreemed goalkeepers, clad in thick jerseys, their flat caps dislodged by their frozen acrobatics. Thick, cloying mud was everywhere as if football was trench warfare. Unlike the cards these snapshots conveyed excitement, action and suspense. I was so entranced by the seized moments of high drama that I tried emulating them in our shared orchard. Perhaps dad was alarmed by my grimacing, clawing, twisting tableaux for he decided to take me to my first game.

(*That game was Chelsea versus Wolverhampton Wanderers on 30 August 1958. He saw Jimmy Greaves score five times when the man could do no wrong. Greaves himself used to say that some days he just knew he would have a good game before he had even set foot on the pitch and every touch would be perfect. Ten years later Tim saw Burnley for the first time at Brighton. But Brighton was the team he had gone to see. Allegiance to Burnley was still a long way away. DT*)

28 January 1961 'Poetry in Motion': Burnley were the current Football League champions. They had just beaten a very strong Hamburg side, featuring German international Uwe Seeler, 3 – 1 in the first leg of the European Cup quarter-final. Alan Ridgill of the *Sunday Pictorial* described Burnley thus: 'Here was the almost perfect soccer machine – as smooth running as a Rolls Royce and yet packing the punch of a Centurion tank.' Yet Burnley was only a small-town club supported by a population of just 80,000. This was a third of the size of Brighton with its population of 246,000. Burnley also spent less on assembling its title-winning side (£13,000) than Brighton had in creating a middle-of-the-table Second Division team (over £30,000). But this contest was billed as a contest between the 'giants' of Burnley and the 'minnows' of Brighton.

January 28th was a wild, wet day. The train had to almost pick its way through the sodden, sagging, sullen marshes and the grey, grubby, foam-flocked sea. Shrouds of rain were driven across our path by the gusting wind. Already saturated in our walk to the station, our clothing gently steamed inside the carriage. A further soaking awaited us on the open Goldstone Ground terraces. Fortunately the rain became patchier once we arrived. It was just as well because the glistening pitch was already pitted with small pools of water, particularly in the grassless goalmouths. Here, the groundsmen set about their forking and sanding duties industriously. As they moved in our direction, each prod of their forks emitted a hiss of earthy complaint. Despite the awful weather, a large crowd of 28,672 congregated. Many fans, like us, occupied the East Terrace, but discomfort was soon forgotten as the game got underway. The match was a corker, in the very best traditions of FA Cup ties.

It was expected that the boggy conditions would sap Burnley's pace, and yet the ploughed field did not appear to incapacitate them. The Clarets started strongly with their fast raiding wingers, Connelly and Pilkington, making early inroads, and their quick, mobile centre-forward, Ray Pointer, pulling Brighton's centre-half, Roy Jennings, all over the place. But it was their powerful left-half, Brian Miller, who struck the first blow after 25 minutes. He beat Brighton's young keeper, Charlie Baker, with a typically emphatic effort. As the game progressed the pitch churned up, enabling Brighton to compete more equally. They began to stall Burnley free-flowing moves and attack with greater menace. With just two minutes remaining of the first half, wing-half Jack Bertolini broke through the Burnley defence to equalise. The roar was incandescent.

Lifted by their success, Brighton began the second half boldly, but their momentum was upset when Joe Carolan headed into his own net after 52 minutes. Undaunted, Brighton's right-back, Bob McNichol, seized his moment, atoning for his partner's error. Having run 50 yards with the ball at his feet, he decided to let fly from 35 yards. McNichol had never scored for Brighton before but no-one would have known. Having made perfect contact, the ball flashed into the Burnley net, leaving their 'keeper Adam Blacklaw a helpless spectator. It was one of the most sublime goals seen at the Goldstone Ground. In trite harmony, the leaden sky parted, briefly allowing a shaft of wan sunlight to filter through.

So, with an hour gone Brighton were back on terms. Now hope turned to belief. Driven on by the excited crowd, the Albion pushed forward resolutely. Seen minutes later, the much maligned Dennis Windross put Brighton ahead. Having been written off by some as the centre-forward who 'couldn't hit a cow's arse with a banjo', this was a particularly sweet moment for Windross. Even manager Billy Lane had conceded that 'Dennis has taken a little time to settle down.' In their frenzied delight, the Brighton fans had wholly forgiven Windross. However, Burnley were not yet beaten. For all their silky skills, Burnley were a resilient bunch. They responded immediately, pouring forward in numbers. With the Brighton defenders losing their footing in the oozing mud, Burnley's arch-poacher, Jimmy Robson, slipped in to snatch an equaliser. For the remaining 17 minutes both teams slugged it out toe to toe. But despite close calls at either end, the deadlock could not be broken.

Ultimately this splendid 3 – 3 draw would have little significance for either side. Burnley progressed to the semi-final, where they lost to 'double' winning Spurs. They also failed to defend a two-goal lead in Hamburg. And, to complete the hat-trick of woes, Aston Villa eliminated them from the newly-introduced Football League Cup competition after a semi-final replay. But that wasn't all. The Football League also fined Burnley £1,000 for fielding a reserve side against Chelsea prior to their return game with Hamburg. As for Brighton, they held on to their Second Division status thanks to a late surge, but following Billy Lane's much-lamented resignation, troubled times lay ahead.

(Tim left the south in 1968 and headed to Lancaster University,

then more a building site than a seat of learning. Friend number 1, Baz, acquainted him with Preston North End and Willie Irvine. In deference to his pal Baz, and in homage to Irvine, Tim went to Deepdale to see him after he had moved from Burnley. Prior to this, Irvine's leg had been broken in a tackle by Everton's Johnny Morrissey. They say you could hear the crack at the back of the stand. Everton manager Harry Catterick distinguished himself by telling the stricken Irvine he had got what he'd asked for. He didn't do too badly at Preston and ironically then went to Brighton, Tim's erstwhile favourite team. But in truth his shattered leg had pretty much destroyed the glistening career that lay ahead. DT)

Willie Irvine had enjoyed two and a half successful years at Burnley, his parent club. Taking on the mantle of the immortal Ray Pointer, he made his first-team breakthrough in 1964. In next to no time, he proved himself to be a top gun. In 144 starts in all senior competitions, Irvine scored 97 goals for Burnley. He was smart on the ground and strong in the air. He put himself about with a strut, insinuating himself into the tiniest spaces to get a shot away, heaving himself above defenders with perfect timing to produce a flashing header. He would get up the noses of his opponents with his cocky, sometimes brash, 'gobby' manner. It was all part of the contest. The mind games matter as much as the quick feet. Like the very best strikers he was always ready to pounce on the half-chance, eyes keenly alert, primed, nerve ends sparking, leg muscles twitching in readiness, coiled to make that explosive spurt, just enough to put him ahead of his markers. It didn't need to be much. At this level the slightest margins are decisive.

(Still at Lancaster, it was another friend Dave that took Tim for his first ever visit to Turf Moor in 1970. It was a life-changing event. Things would never be the same. We all have our Damascus moments and for Tim this was his. DT)

21 March 1970: I had mixed feelings when Dave interrupted my abbreviated sleep, offering me my first trip to Turf Moor, Burnley. Dave was a West Brom fan. He wanted some company. That's why he dangled, no, prodded his invitation. Besides he had his newly-acquired Vauxhall Victor to show off. The V-bomber was a chic vehicle when the

Z-Cars crews hit the road in 1962, but Dave's rusted wagon obliterated the memory. On the motorway we were well off the pace. Other traffic hissed by derisively. The heater was knackered and the smearing wipers weren't any better.

It was a foul day. Dirty, ragged clouds rolled in from the Irish Sea, dragging with them curtains of rain. Stepping out onto the greasy, cobbled streets, a blustery wind propelled stinging, spiteful rain into our screwed-up faces. All around us were the scars of industrial blight: the derelict mills, the oily canal, and the weed-strewn, rusted marshalling yards. Yet beneath the drab and rain-darkened moors, stone-terraced Burnley appeared welcoming. The inviting light falling from the latticed windows, the flickering front room fires, did not mock our discomfort as much as draw us in, making it possible to feel at home here.

The football club, like its town, was a declining force. A newly-constructed, all-seated stand had been built at the western end but the southern flank was a cordoned-off demolition site. Post-war austerity characterised the remaining parts of the ground. Rusted girders dripped with the penetrating rain. In step with their surroundings, the kids exuded nonchalant toughness. It wasn't so much their bovver boots or their scuffed scarves tied to their wrists. None of them wore coats. They seemed oblivious to winter's late riposte. I was deeply impressed ...

... It wasn't just the club management that was in a state of flux. The team was beginning to change markedly, too. Only full-back John Angus remained from the 1959/60 championship-winning side. But still young hearts ran free. Steve Kindon and Dave Thomas were the newish kids in town, complementing established home-grown stars like Ralph Coates and Brian O'Neil and astute signings like Frank Casper and Martin Dobson. Kindon and Thomas had graduated from the youth team that had won the FA Youth Cup in 1968. Before the Albion game Adamson purred about the performances of his gifted youngsters who had done him proud in the midweek 3 – 3 draw at Old Trafford. Two-goal Thomas was singled out for special praise.

Not that Adamson's pre-match euphoria inhibited West Brom. A skidding strike from a midfielder, 'Bomber' Brown, fizzed over the glistening mud to give the visitors an early lead prompting the Burnley Longside fans to chant inanely, 'Zigger, zagger, zigger, Astle is a n*****.' Jeff Astle was the Baggies' white, free-scoring centre-forward.

At this time, football had a dismal record in combating racism. This didn't just apply to what was happening on the terraces. Many football coaches had little compunction about writing off black British players peremptorily, often castigating their alleged lack of commitment, mental toughness and work rate. Few black players managed to break through this stultifying discrimination. It is perhaps worth speculating whether, as a young hopeful, Pele would have been offered terms by a British club. Those who did break through had to contend with racist abuse, even from their own colleagues and fans. When the black Bermudan striker, Clyde Best, made his mark in West Ham's front line during the early seventies, the home fans greeted him with the chant 'We bought Clyde Best and covered him with chocolate, ooh!' It was an adaptation of the reggae-style Cadbury's Fruit and Nut TV advert. Although meant affectionately, the chant seemed to suggest that Best's blackness was just a veneer, as if he was an honorary white. But perhaps that's reading too much into it.

Meanwhile Burnley had worries about their top-flight status. A point at Old Trafford had not relieved their relegation woes. Stung by the early setback, they set about wresting control from the Baggies. Eventually Tony Brown, Len Cantello, Graham Lovett and Bobby Hope were forced to concede the sodden midfield to the flitting Coates, the twinkling Thomas, the terrier-like O'Neil and the steadfast Bellamy. Increasing pressure became applied to West Brom's suspect defence.

Steve Kindon was in 'runaway wardrobe' mode. Making light of the heavy conditions, he continually powered in from the left, uninhibited by surface water, spattering mud and despairing tackles, to launch muscular assaults on the opposition's goal. Warming to his efforts, the 12,000-plus home crowd set aside their groaning, moaning and heckling and threw themselves into the fray, belligerently bellowing their side on. Suddenly the promise was fulfilled. Kindon broke through on the left side of the Baggies' box, lashing home a fierce, rising drive past the Albion keeper, Osborne. The visceral force of Kindon's shot unleashed a leaping, straining tumult on the Longside. The sullen away support was treated to their jabbing gestures of derision. The Clarets fans vociferous joy pierced the afternoon's dank greyness.

The rain grew in intensity as a premature dusk descended. The glare of the floodlights flashed and sparkled in the muddy pools appearing all over the pitch. As the second half progressed, the game became, quite simply, a trial of strength. It was one in which Burnley's youngsters were the more determined. By the time that Bellamy's slithering long-range effort had evaded a thicket of legs and found goal, neat football had been abandoned. The objective was now to propel the ball as far forward as possible and set off in dogged pursuit. Hacking it clear of the mud and puddles seemed to require herculean power. We felt exhausted by association. The crowd continued to urge Burnley forward, hurling encouragement and invective in equal measure. But the Clarets could not find another way through. It didn't matter. By then, West Brom had lost their way entirely.

And soon would I. Little did I realise this, then, but a claret and blue potion had been injected into my veins. Life would never be the same again.

(Tim was well and truly hooked, even though this was a time when it was a club that was hardly succeeding. Harry Potts had been moved to an 'upstairs' position of little consequence, supporters were clamouring for Adamson's head and the team was now in Division Two after a humiliating relegation.

There had been a bleak mid-winter with daily power cuts as Prime Minister Heath slugged out a losing battle with the miners. Industrial action was widespread. Flying pickets wreaked havoc. Arthur Scargill planned the warring miners' strategy against the government. The NUM had never been a militant organisation but their conditions of work had become intolerable. Three-day working weeks became commonplace. People were urged to heat just one room in their homes as power became a scarce commodity. Sales of candles and paraffin lamps surged. After several weeks Heath was defeated. Enter Margaret Thatcher to quell the troublemakers and destroy an industry. And alongside all this there were 'The Troubles' in Northern Ireland where one year – 1972 – saw the deaths of 72 innocent civilians, 43 soldiers, 11 policemen and 5 members of the Ulster defence regiment. You could have argued that football was an irrelevance. There was certainly no good cheer in Burnley be it industrial or football related, so that by the time of the Burnley versus Hull City game, supporters were disillusioned and not a little angry. DT)

12 February 1972 Burnley versus Hull City: After a promising start to life in Division Two, Burnley's subsequent performances did little to lift the glum mood. Welsh winger Leighton James had emerged as a major talent, though, scoring seven times in his first 11 games. He was twice on target as visiting Middlesbrough were thumped 5 – 2 on 13 November, although, arguably, Burnley's star performer that afternoon was 'super-sub' Steve Kindon, who created so much havoc in Boro's defence with his bullish power and thoroughbred pace. Jimmy Adamson told James Lawton of the *Daily Express:* "There is no more powerful runner in English football than Steve Kindon. When he is feeling good in himself he frightens opposing defences right out of their skins." And yet a few weeks later, following a succession of fitful performances, an exasperated Adamson told his young striker, "You are either brilliant or rubbish. I cannot afford to gamble with you at the moment." It was reported that Bert Head of Crystal Palace and Malcolm Allison of Manchester City were prepared to offer £180,000 for the unsettled Kindon although nothing transpired …

… February 12 was another grisly day. Grubby clouds squatted overhead, spattering the town with insistent, icy rain. Traffic hissed passed past Turf Moor, leaving momentary trails on the road's sheen-like surface. Some people had better things to do. Cowering under their rain-darkened headwear and glistening brollies, a crowd of only 11,751 made haste for the shelter offered by the Longside and the Cricket Field Stands. Surely, only the hated power cuts could have driven so many people from their cold homes. The derelict Brunshaw Road Stand remained boarded up – an unsightly accusation – while the chairman, Bob Lord, glumly contemplated its indigestible replacement cost, then said to be around £500,000.

At the Bee Hole End, where the uncovered terraces were glassy with excess water, there was a scattering of ascetic misanthropes folded over their pet barriers, stoically defying the elements. A distorted version of T. Rex's 'Telegram Sam' emerged erratically from the club's PA system. Nobody seemed in the mood for electric boogie. Some stared into space as if afflicted by combat fatigue. With personal warmth a distant memory, others stamped and blew into their hands. Much of the pre-match talk focused on work shortages and home discomforts. Competitive deprivation was the rage, if lugubrious mutterings could be so described. Once the game was underway those gripes receded, leaving embattled Jimmy Adamson to face the music …

… Burnley were in the midst of a goal drought, having managed just three goals in their last five games. But lifted by their feisty victory over Norwich, Adamson selected an unchanged side, including the attacking talents of David Thomas, Frank Casper, Paul Fletcher, Steve Kindon and Leighton James. In the first 45 minutes, they created just one chance. It came soon after kick-off. Fletcher – normally so ruthless in the air – unaccountably headed wide from Alan West's perfect cross. While James continued to impress on the left wing, Dave Thomas had a wretched game. Just two minutes after the restart, the Tigers showed they could bite as well as tame. Neill played a free-kick to Wagstaff, who quickly relayed the ball to the advancing full-back, Banks. Banks instantly sent over a low skidding cross which eluded everyone except Hull City's left-winger, Butler, who slid the ball in at the far post.

Burnley tried to raise the tempo. Despite their spluttering form, chances came but went, with Casper, Kindon and James the worst culprits. However, Fletcher was unlucky with a goal-bound header which beat Hull's keeper, only for the full-back to head the ball over the bar. Not that Hull were restricted to all-out defence. They were able to exert a bit of pressure themselves, using long passes to good effect. Stevenson had to make athletic saves from Pearson and Lord and was at full stretch to prevent Colin Waldron scoring an own goal. But he was helpless when Wagstaff scored Hull's second goal two minutes from time. With Burnley committed to a final all-out assault, Wagstaff seized upon Casper's misplaced pass just inside the Burnley half, and raced through for a fine individual goal.

The Longside supporters immediately began to chant 'Adamson out! Potts in!' Their demonstration lasted for several minutes after the game. Adamson offered no excuses. He told *Burnley Express* sports editor, Keith McNee: "It was a poor game and one we shouldn't have lost. Generally, we had too many players below par. When Hull City scored our players got anxious, the crowd got anxious and we couldn't recover. Our supporters were fully justified in their criticisms. We can't put on an exhibition like that and hope to get away with it. We are entertainers and we must do a heck of a lot better than this … But this is part of the hazards of being a manager and I have got to take it on the chin.

Adamson had been in charge for 88 games. He had won just 27% of them. The *Daily Mirror* football correspondent reckoned that 'Burnley needed someone like Jimmy Adamson out on the park … Someone who can take stock, point the way and calm their hell-for-leather approach.' The *Daily Express* football reporter thought that Burnley's problems were due to a lack of mental toughness. He wrote: 'In short, Burnley's prodigies look hurt and surprised if their dazzling footwork fails to bring goals. Lesser players than Terry Neil and Ken Wagstaff smack their lips when they see that.'

Burnley supporters' letters to the local newspaper were unequivocally critical. One wrote that 'the booing of Jimmy Adamson has been on the cards for some time. In my opinion, Mr Adamson could bring internationals to play at Burnley and within a month they would be unrecognisable. The youth policy is a dead loss. I am honestly worried we will finish in the Third Division. What a disappointment this team is.' And yet another commented that: 'Players valued at half a million pounds are giving Central League performances. What a disaster for the 'team of the Seventies.' Just before their relegation from Division One, Adamson had boasted that his young side would become the *Team of the Seventies.'*

But chairman Bob Lord was having none of it. "It's not Jimmy's fault," he retorted. "It's the players who are not getting the results … The fans will not get their own way." Keith McNee reflected in his *Burnley Express* column: 'The manager and the team must expect to share a bitter reaction. Where the Clarets go from here, especially in their strained relationships with their own followers, remains to be seen, but the mood at the moment is black indeed and only a massive improvement on the field of play can move that monster cloud onto someone else's patch of sky.' After a subsequent defeat at promotion-bound Birmingham City, Burnley dropped to tenth place.

(But things would get better and McNee would get his wish that things would improve on the field of play; but not before they got worse. After a defeat at Blackpool the cries for Adamson's head were even more vociferous and after the game police were needed to quell the ugly scenes. But, by the end of the season, at last, Adamson had found the blend of players that would lead them back to Division One the following season. What followed were three seasons of delightful

football that might indeed have seen the emergence of 'The Team of the Seventies,' but for the sales of key players. It was a great time to be around Turf Moor with some wonderful performances but just every now and then one or two defeats left us deflated, such as the FA Cup semi-final defeat against Newcastle; or utterly stunned when a defeat was totally unexpected. One of the latter was the FA Cup defeat against non-league Wimbledon at Turf Moor in January 1975. DT)

Wombling Merry Christmas 4 January 1975: Burnley's boss, Jimmy Adamson, began the new season (1974/75) in a morose mood. It wasn't just Mick Docherty and Frank Casper's long-term injuries that troubled him. He had been right in what he had been told by Paul Fletcher. Club chairman Bob Lord was prepared to sacrifice the team to build the stadium. The price of the new stand rested on Martin Dobson's head. With the season barely underway, Dobbo went to Everton for a Burnley club record fee of £300,000. 'The only classical wing-half left in the country,' stated the *Football Digest* in 1974.

Burnley's bottom line made grim reading. The balance sheet showed a loss of £224,000 for the previous year. The wage bill was becoming an increasing problem. Eleven players earned more than £10,000 during the 1973/74 season. An annual wage, then, of £10,000 was more than £8,000 above the national average wage. With Premiership players now earning over 20,000% above the national average that seems a trivial difference. But a £10,000 wage was a lot for little Burnley to find in 1974. Although Willie Irvine earned more at Second Division Preston than he did at Burnley, Bob Lord continued to believe, rightly or wrongly, that his players were among the best paid in the country. Of course, his pay policy meant that there was a price placed on each of his players' heads. Necessary ground renovation increased his problem. When Martin Dobson was sold, Bob Lord defended his decision by stating: 'It will cost us £450,000 to run this club this season and we could not turn down £300,000. Four years ago people were fed up with a three-sided ground and we wanted a new stand. So we built one' …

… Although the average gate remained around the 20,000 mark, on a par with the 1973/74 figure, it was clear that the club were looking for another good FA Cup run to swell its dwindling coffers. A third-round home draw with a Southern League side, Wimbledon, offered a perfect start …

… The Wimbledon board had turned to Allen Batsford, the successful Walton and Hersham manager. The man was a winner. His Walton side had won the FA Amateur Cup in 1973 without conceding a single goal, a unique feat. Three of his players, Dave Bassett, Willie Smith and Roger Connell, had represented the England non-league side. To cap it all, Batsford's Walton & Hersham had shocked the football world by winning an FA Cup replay at Brian Clough's Brighton, by 4 – 0. A highly embarrassed Brian Clough was forced to concede that Walton 'were better than us in every aspect of the game, better technique certainly, and better organisation.' Right-back Bob Stockley was already a Wimbledon player when Batsford arrived and said in a *Back Pass* magazine article of autumn 2009: 'We were run like a Football League club. We stayed in a hotel the night before away games and were well-drilled and organised. We practised free-kicks, corners and set pieces religiously before every game. We knew exactly where every player should be – both attacking and defending. And we knew how the opposition would play, especially Burnley.'

Wimbledon made it to the third round of the FA Cup the hard way, having to extricate themselves from the four qualifying stages before reaching the first round proper. With money too tight to mention, a successful FA Cup run was imperative …

… Typically thorough in his preparations, Batsford had Burnley watched prior to the Turf Moor game, producing a 15-page dossier on their strengths and potential weaknesses. 'We reckoned that Burnley were rather predictable,' he remarked. What he meant was that Burnley were over-reliant on Leighton James' strong running and piercing crosses. During that season 60% of Burnley's goals came directly from James' strikes or his 'assists.' It was well known that if Burnley were to be neutralised, James had to be stopped. In his pre-match briefing, Batsford detailed Bob Stockley and Dave Bassett to double up on James. 'Dave was not the most cultured footballer or a great passer of the ball,' admitted Stockley. 'But he had a huge will to win and loved to break up play. He was a fantastic player to have in front of you. Several times I got a tackle in or Dave did and Leighton

James wasn't too happy. He also got plenty of banter from Dave. But he was quick and got past us a couple of times but overall we handled him quite well. I'd had more difficult games.'

Despite the Dons' effective shackling of James, Burnley monopolised possession, pushing forward relentlessly. But the Wimbledon outfield players, from front to back, grafted incessantly to close their hosts' players. And behind the Dons defenders, there was Dickie Guy, the London Docks tally clerk, who was in inspired form. I failed to recognise him as the hapless loanee who had gifted Barnet victory at Hastings eight years before. His transformation was extraordinary. He had not missed a game for Wimbledon in four years. His positioning seemed spot on, his handling so assured and as for his reflexes, they were simply astonishing. In the third minute he comfortably grasped Fletcher's cross shot. On the half-hour he easily collected Ray Hankins's header after James had made a rare escape from his jailers, Bassett and Stockley. But Guy surpassed himself just before the break when he pushed over a scorching volley from Keith Newton. It was a stunning, lightning reaction save that drew applause from all quarters of the ground.

Four minutes after the break, the unthinkable happened. Wimbledon scored with only their second effort on goal. Burnley centre-back Jim Thomson, was slow to close down Ian Cooke. The Dons striker managed to get a shot away that keeper Stevenson could only parry. Mick Mahon recalled: 'The ball came to me on the edge of the box. I just hit it. There wasn't a lot of goal to aim at … before I knew it I was flattened. Everybody was on top of me celebrating wildly. It wasn't the staged celebrations you get nowadays … it was pure joy.' Mahon told Niall Cooper, 'It wasn't the greatest time to score, but we had a plan and stuck to it. Normally I would play on the right wing but with Dave Bassett playing there I was pushed into the centre of midfield. I didn't like playing there. On the flanks you only really had to concentrate on what was ahead of you. In the middle you had to look everywhere.

Although Burnley upped the tempo, laying siege to the Wimbledon goal, they could not find a way past the brilliant Guy. He made a breathtaking stop to deny Fletcher's point-blank effort but was indebted to Collins' lack of composure as the midfielder blasted the rebound over the bar with the goal gaping. This was not one-way traffic, though. Revelling in the extra space granted by Burnley's hurried advances, the Don's bearded strike partners, Connell and Somers, had several excellent chances to finish off the game. Between them, they managed to send three shots skimming just wide of the Burnley goal.

After the game, Jimmy Adamson muttered tersely that his 'players gave everything, but their skills were off.' An ecstatic Allen Batsford said: 'In many ways Burnley had only themselves to blame and once they fell behind they panicked.' Burnley captain Colin Waldron admitted: 'We played ignorant football. Right from the first minute we kept hitting these long, high balls into their goalmouth in the hope that someone would make a mistake. This made their centre-halves look like crosses between Jack Charlton and Jairzinho.'

The press were as generous about Wimbledon's magnificent victory as they were scathing about Burnley's abject defeat. Paul Wilcox of the *Guardian* reported: 'The expected Wombling taunts from the crowd faded with Burnley's reputation. And little wonder. The only rubbish that Wimbledon picked up on Saturday was the First Division team's errors.' Local reporter Peter Higgs wrote: 'Hang your heads in shame after this defeat Burnley. The match they said was a free pass into the next round of the FA Cup provided arguably the most humiliating result in the history of Burnley.'

(It was humiliation indeed and those who were there still recall the memories and cringe. This was the same side, although minus the departed Martin Dobson, that had smacked Leeds United not much more than six months earlier at Elland Road. It was the same side that would win the next three league games to mount an improbable challenge for the title. It was a challenge that would last until March and a game against Liverpool, that had they won, might have seen them take the top spot if other results had gone their way. Alas it was only a 1 – 1 draw at Turf Moor, and after that the club's prospects faded away and it would face relegation the next season. But the win at Leeds is another game that is still remembered and talked about – but this time with reverence rather than Wimbledon mortification. Paul Fletcher scored what is arguably one of Burnley's all-time top ten goals after Leeds had equalised Burnley's opening Fletcher prodded goal. DT)

* * *

Almost directly from the restart, Noble made progress along the right flank. Nulty and McQueen contested his high centre, the ball flicking off both their heads towards Fletcher, who had his back to goal. Despite Hunter's indecent close attention, Fletcher performed a stunning bicycle kick. The ball flew past Harvey in a blur. The cacophonous clamour that had greeted Clarke's goal was instantly silenced. It was as if a Neutron bomb had taken out the entire home support. The eerie silence that followed was surreal. The ecstatic celebrations of the Burnley players made it even more so. We watched, but did not recognise. We saw, but did not comprehend. It was left to an unusually audible tannoy announcer to confirm the reality. 'The scorer of Burnley's second goal was number 9, Paul Fletcher.' The adjacent Leeds fans glared at me maliciously; not that my thoughtful response helped. For having regained my faculties, but taken leave of my senses, I chirped, 'I bet you don't see a better goal than that in the next ten years.'

(After the jubilation of that stirring win at Leeds, just seven days later Burnley lost a near one-sided FA Cup replay against Newcastle United. Who knows what the ensuing history of the club might have been had they won that game and appeared at Wembley. You could argue that this game marked the watershed of any Burnley hopes of continued success. There were more wins but in truth it was an uphill battle on an uneven and unfair playing field as the last of the 'little' Lancashire clubs fought on in the top division. Just a year after the Wimbledon defeat there was another Cup defeat and this one would have huge consequences. DT)

4 January 1975, Blackpool versus Burnley (FA Cup third round): After making an awful start (in 1974/75), Burnley managed a brief revival during the early autumn. League Champions-elect, Liverpool, were beaten in the League Cup. Frank Casper signed off with a late, scorching free-kick that defeated Queens Park Rangers, who were then heading the table. Another stunning drive, this time from Leighton James, saw off Coventry at Highfield Road. Although Fletcher was crocked, the versatile Peter Noble filled in admirably as Hankin's strike partner until November, when he too, succumbed to injury. In the summer, Jimmy Adamson had been allowed to spend £50,000 in bringing Mike Summerbee, and old boy Willie Morgan, to bolster his slim first-team resources. But, they couldn't cover the widening gaps left by injuries to Burnley's leading players. After the QPR game, Casper made only three more starts, Fletcher, Collins, Brennan and Noble were also missing for significant periods. James' inexplicable loss of form added to Adamson's woes. Burnley's strength in reserve was not good enough. Hankin, Flynn, Rodaway and Brennan had graduated successfully from the youth system, but few others seemed capable of stepping up. After relegation rivals Wolves had stuffed Burnley (1-5), James left to join ambitious Derby for £300,000. Burnley desperately needed the money. Besides, James was unsettled. Adamson noted how much better he had performed for Wales. However, up until New Year, Burnley clung to a wispy hope of salvation. On Saturday 3 January this hope was whisked away in a Blackpool storm.

The previous night was wild. A violent gale rampaged across the country causing 26 deaths and £100million worth of damage. In some parts of the country gusts reached 80mph. My wife Liz and I were staying with friends in Bristol. Throughout the night the wind buffeted their windows and growled in their grate. In the neighbouring gardens loose gates and shed doors groaned and slammed.

We rose early on that bright Saturday morning, unrested and irritable, with a long drive ahead of us. The debris of the night's torment lay everywhere: fallen trees, torn branches, collapsed fences, overturned dustbins and scattering litter. The deep-blue morning sky seemed free of impurity but soon the clouds gathered.

Holding the car on course was a struggle in the buffeting wind. We arrived in Blackpool just before midday. With my eyes gritty from lack of sleep and concentrated driving, I left Liz in the car and took to the prom. There I stood, braced against the rusted railings, taking in the sea's fury. The towering, wrinkled, grimy grey waves lurched in and out of the flitting sun, their frenzied race for the shore wall urged on by the icy nor'wester. Only the sea wall arrested their charge, each repelled wave clawing back its glinting hostages with seething resentment. I normally loved days like this. The west wind would usually stir my torpid spirits. But on this day I felt out of sorts. I returned to the car and slumped in the driver's seat, staring dully through the saline-smeared windscreen. The wind had been briefly refreshing but now my eyes smarted with salt as well as fatigue. My skin was tacky and my hair tugged on the comb. I felt a mess. Liz prescribed a pint and a hotpot. She sensed we would need fortification for what we were about to receive.

As we approached the ground, snippets of 'Bohemian Rhapsody' were wafting erratically towards us on the gusting, eddying wind. The chanting, too, was whisked above the rooftops in waves of variable volume. It seemed as if there was mass celebration of 'seaside air.' It took me a little time to twig that the chant was 'Seasiders.' I loved the pre-match routine, particularly on smarting cold winter days such as this: the chirpy banter, the put-downs, smoky pubs, heaving with unsegregated supporters, the banter, the grotesque caricatures, the surreal tales and the outrageous gossip. Then, there was the walk to the ground to stir the senses. I recall an Evertonian, describing the time his grandfather took him to his first game. Excited by the noise of the crowd as they crossed Stanley Park, he wanted to press on. But his grandfather held him back, refusing to increase his slow measured step. Reflecting on his formative experience, this Evertonian reckoned that his grandfather had the perfect grasp of foreplay. On this stormy Saturday only foreplay was on offer.

On the day of the Burnley FA Cup tie, Blackpool were in 14th place in Division Two. No-one at the club was satisfied. Goals had dried up; Harry's team managed only 40 league goals all season with Micky Walsh netting 17 of these. Only Middlesbrough loanee Malcolm Smith gave him support, after scoring five in his eight games. It was Blackpool's failure to land Smith in a permanent deal that helped seal Harry's fate. As Harry prepared to face his old club he was under intense pressure. Blackpool had drawn a blank against relegation-bound York City in the previous home game, 0 – 0. Harry was desperate for a cup run to revive the club's spirits and fill its coffers. He knew that only a good run of results would save his job.

With so much at stake and both teams in such poor form, this was never going to be a fluent game. In fact it was truly grim. The players had huge difficulties contending with the wind which twisted, swirled and gusted, carrying away fluttering programmes, crisp bags and sweet wrappers. The wind howled ghoulishly under our rusted, corrugated stand roof, tugging also at the furiously flapping club flag. Long balls became a hostage to fortune. Ball control was an embarrassment.

Chances were fewer than hardy beach boys. Before the floodlights eclipsed this fading day, the sky began to clear. Only torn fragments of clouds remained, fleeing from the north-west approaches, their crimson reflections of a raw sunset entirely unappreciated by the anxious 20,573 crowd.

Liz and I had settled for a 0 – 0 draw. Then, Burnley's game fell apart. Hankin, Burnley's only striker of substance, was dismissed. Immediately afterwards, Blackpool defender, Bill Bentley, crashed in a free header from a corner. We bowed our heads as the home fans leapt around us. With Waldron's late equaliser ruled out, there was no way back.

Harry Potts was understandably jubilant. He dismissed the reporters' comments that it had been a petulant game littered with niggling fouls and reckless challenges. With his club £4,500 better off from the victory; Harry had good reason to feel chuffed. Besides, he had just put one over his former Burnley rival. 'We always seem to be playing uphill,' said a disconsolate Jimmy Adamson. 'We've been waiting for the tide to turn in our favour for weeks. But everything still keeps going against us.' The *Burnley Express* reporter's verdict was less forgiving: 'Scraping the barrel,' he wrote.

It was a lugubrious journey home. Liz drove. We hardly spoke. The branches of the overhanging trees still thrashed wildly in the stiff wind. The dead leaves were whipped up into twirls by the passing traffic. Outside, there was an irrepressible energy but inside we felt flat and empty.

(Adamson was dismissed; his heartache and subsequent sufferings well documented in the biography Jimmy Adamson: The Man Who Said No to England. *In came assistant Joe Brown to replace him. With a sort of grim inevitability, relegation came at the end of the season and during the following season out went Joe Brown and Bob Lord turned to a willing Harry Potts to take over at the club he loved. He steadied the ship from sinking yet further and the signing of Steve Kindon was a masterstroke. There was a night of glory when Celtic came to Turf Moor and their fans caused bloody mayhem. But Burnley won 1 – 0 and for good measure won the second leg in Glasgow as well. It looked like Potts might inspire a degree of upward mobility but it was progress that was ultimately doomed. Towards the back end of the 1978/79 season Tim Quelch noted that Burnley were due to play at Brighton.*

Of course he went to the game to see the team that had once held his interest, against the club to which he now owed his allegiance. DT)

Brighton and Hove Albion versus Burnley, 3 March 1979: Burnley won the Anglo-Scottish Cup that season but their over-riding priority – promotion back to Division One – eluded them. As with so many other clubs, Burnley suffered from the ravages of one of the harshest winters for 16 years. They managed one game in January, a 2 – 0 FA Cup victory at baleful Birmingham City. Their backlog of league fixtures was horrendous. When Burnley arrived at the Goldstone ground on an overcast Saturday 3 March, this was their fifth game in 11 days …

… On Saturday 3 March, Brighton were in second place, one point behind Stoke City, but a point ahead of West Ham and Crystal Palace, who both had games in hand. Burnley were in 13th position, nine points behind Albion but with four games in hand. They had already met twice that season – both times at Turf Moor. Brighton had won the League Cup game 3 – 1 when full-back Chris Cattlin had contained Burnley's 'Welsh Wizard' Leighton James. But Burnley had won the league game shortly afterwards (3 – 0).

Burnley were continuing to sell their young talent. Three members of their squad had been sold in the last nine months, netting the club around £240,000. Tony Morley would also shortly leave for Villa for £220,000 raising the club's post-war sales to £3million. Whilst Burnley's younger talent was on the move, former stars were returning. Steve Kindon had come back for £80,000, as had Leighton James for £165,000. Martin Dobson would re-join the club, too, in the summer for £100,000.

It was a sombre day. As Liz and I strolled along the empty promenade, fine rain wafted in on a stuttering Channel wind. It left a dull sheen on the tarmac and the green, thickly-painted benches. Despite the damp, ruffling wind, there was an indolent feel to the day. Mucky waves emerged out of the creased, swishing swell and staggered listlessly to the shore, their soiled surf collapsing on to the shingle with resigned sighs. We had little enthusiasm for the game. With the club apparently selling its future in order to commemorate its past, we felt as if we'd been invited to the *Last Waltz* for the Team of the Seventies.'

Actually the team paid due respect to its estimable past. Shaking off the fatigue of the punishing schedule, Burnley immediately turned on the heat. They mounted one attack after another on Eric Steele's goal. Had he not been in such superb form, denying headers from Fletcher with breathtaking agility, Burnley would have been deservedly two goals in front at the break. If Cattlin had been James' master in the League Cup tie, the tables were turned here. Linking well with Burnley's attacking left-back, Ian Brennan, James roasted the Brighton full-back, jinking one way, only to flash past him on the other. One cross after another arrived in the Brighton box. Even the combative Horton seemed powerless to prevent the incessant aerial bombardment. With the spring-heeled Fletcher frequently outjumping his markers and Kindon acting as a shuddering battering ram, Rollins and Lawrenson were unexpectedly at sixes and sevens.

As the teams left the field at the break – Burnley in sprightly fashion and Brighton pensively – we were relieved that our lads had done us proud. We were concerned, though, that they hadn't made their domination count. While Debbie Harry's tinkling voice took us through 'Heart of Glass' Alan Mullery was tearing strips off his team. He berated them for not heeding his warning. He had impressed on them beforehand that Burnley were a tough nut to crack. Smarting from their first-half chasing and from Mullery's half-time lashing, Brighton began the second half fired up. Adopting a higher defensive line, Horton and Clark began to express themselves in the centre of the park. Ryan and O'Sullivan had more of the ball and as a result Maybank and Ward were able to push up more against Burnley's slow-moving central defenders. Now it was Burnley's turn to feel the heat. They were unable to commit so many men forward. Their suspect defence became sorely stretched.

Within five minutes of the restart, a penalty was conceded which Horton put away decisively. But Burnley didn't buckle. Within one minute they were back on terms as Ingham stole into the box, unseen, to poke home a loose ball all at close range. The game then turned into a nip and tuck affair, but one that began to tip increasingly Brighton's way. The contest was settled in the 69th minute by a goal of sublime quality. Lawrenson began to make probing runs. It was no wonder that Mullery was so keen to snaffle him. His sublime technique and composure were underpinned by throbbing power. He proceeded to turn the game. Seizing the ball in midfield, he strode forward effortlessly, gliding through the Burnley defence as if it was an apparition. Upon reaching the edge of the box, he easily evaded Jim Thomson's desperate lunge and sent a skimming shot past Stevenson's helpless dive at the speed of light. A huge roar greeted his effort. After the commotion had dimmed, Liz and I agreed reluctantly that a goal as good as that deserved to win any game.

Since I saw Burnley play at Brighton in January 1961, the clubs' prospects had completely reversed. Brighton were destined for a four-year stay in the First Division while Burnley were to embark upon a slide that would take them to the trapdoor of oblivion. The 'Team of the Seventies' was a shattered dream.

With a child shortly on the way we found quickly there was less time or money for football. Saturdays became consumed by morose meanderings around heaving supermarkets, packed shopping centres or, worst of all, MFI where we sought affordable flat-packs to bless with our incompetence. For the first time in my life football became expendable, subjected to financially constrained choice rather than obsessive necessity, often only heard or seen peripherally, until our daughter became old and wise enough to want to go. The addiction doesn't expire though. It is merely suppressed by the weight of parental duty, waiting for the moment when the trailing guilt of parenthood thins sufficiently for it to pop up again. That prospect was hard to imagine, sat on those penal MFI benches, waiting to collect our chipboard ensembles. There, my unseeing eyes would be fixed on the cartoon channel but my attention would be elsewhere, possibly speculating on events at the Shay or Spotland, or wherever lonely Burnley were then playing. I would have to wait. The radio was always a car park away. Setting aside the contradictions in warmth, I felt like a beached expat, comatosed by Spanish wine and the Tenerife sun, indulging maudlin home thoughts from abroad.

4

1975 And Brian Flynn Joins Burnley

He is one of the great names of Burnley Football Club and rightly so. Not only that but Brian Flynn is hugely respected at Swansea and throughout Wales, the latter for his untiring work in helping to establish the successes the modern Welsh side has had after some years in the doldrums. He played for Burnley over two spells, was at Leeds United from 1977 to 1982, played for Cardiff City, Doncaster Rovers, Bury and Wrexham. He managed Wrexham, Swansea City, the Welsh U21 side, the senior Welsh side in a caretaker capacity, and then Doncaster Rovers. He made a staggering 568 first team appearance over his career and earned 66 Welsh caps.

Today he still lives in Burnley and is a familiar figure around the town. Like so many Burnley players he married a local girl and put down firm roots. With his total effort and commitment, total involvement in any game he played in, his bravery and combative spirit, he has earned respect and affection wherever he has played. He was once described as being exactly the kind of man you would like to have alongside you in the trenches. To many Burnley fans it has always been a source of mystery that he has never undertaken any kind of role at Burnley FC, either managerial, coaching or scouting.

The two chapters from Leon Barton's fine book Little Wonder *cover his boyhood and joining Burnley Football Club. There are many more references to Burnley throughout the book, a worthy addition to any Burnley fan's bookshelf. DT*

***

Brian Flynn: Little Wonder, Leon Barton
(St David's Press)
From Chapter 1: Steeltown

The first time I spoke to Brian Flynn he was … actually; I don't know what he was doing. It was quarter to nine in the morning and, as usual, I was struggling to get my four-year old son to *kindergarten* on time

When I did phone him later that morning he was at an Accrington Stanley youth game. Rochdale were the opponents I think. Knowing that he had been employed to scout young players for Everton, I asked if that was why he was there.

"No, I left Everton when Ronald Koeman came in as manager; I'm not working at the moment. Just keeping my knowledge of players up; you have to really."

Christ, I thought I was a dedicated football lover. This guy is something else. I suppose when you've had to fight to play football in an area obsessed by another sport, it leaves an indelible mark.

"You don't know what to make of Port Talbot when you drive past the first time. I'd never seen anything like it," says Londoner Leon Britton in *Jack to a King*, the film that documents Swansea City's incredible rise from the depths of the Football league to the heights of the Premier League; a rise precipitated by Flynn's appointment as manager in 2002.

There is nowhere like it really. As you drive the stretch of the M4 motorway between Wales' two biggest cities, Cardiff and Swansea, the sight of the sprawling steelworks, the coke oven quench towers, sinter plant stacks and vapour-exhuming cooling chimneys, dominate the horizon as you look down towards the coast.

Often thought, perhaps erroneously, to be one of the inspirations for the look of science fiction films Brazil and Blade Runner, the town is dominated by the steel industry, both economically and physically. Local academic and historian Angela V John describes it as 'in some respects a Valleys town that slips down towards the seaside.' The mountains that hem the town to the coast produce a dramatic vista. All of Wales is there in that skyline: the beauty and the industry, the smoke, the sea, the shades of grey cutting through the green, the drama and the melancholy, fire and danger.

There are certain industrial towns the world over, that produce an inordinate number of sportspeople, given their relatively small number of inhabitants. The former coal mining town of Ashington in Northumberland has a population of less than 30,000 but still produced a Footballer of the Year, no fewer than three times: Jimmy Adamson 1962, Bobby Charlton 1966 and his brother Jack, 1967, as well as Newcastle United goalscoring legend Jackie Milburn and a host of other top flight players.

The lead, copper, and zinc rich conurbation of Mount Isa in Queensland, Australia, population 22,000, is the birthplace of golfer Greg Norman, tennis player Pat Rafter and a slew of notable Aussie rules and rugby league stars. The theory usually put forward to explain this, is that sport is the means of escape from a life of industrial drudgery; a way out of the darkness. Port Talbot is different. The town and its surrounding villages has produced an extraordinary number of professional actors.

The most well-known pair, Richard Burton and Anthony Hopkins, share a staggering eleven Academy Award nominations between them with one win, Hopkins for *Silence of the Lambs* in 1991. More recently, the big screen exploits of Michael Sheen, who might himself have pursued a football career, and television star Rob Brydon have maintained the town's thespian tradition. But those are just four amongst many. Angela V John's book *The Actors' Crucible*, lists 50 stage and screen professionals from the area, a huge number considering the population of the town has never exceeded 52,000.

By the time Brian Flynn was born, at home on the sprawling Sandfields council estate, on October 12, 1955, Richard Burton, son of a coal miner from the local village of Pontrhdydfen, was already a huge Hollywood star and the construction of a third steelworks had been completed just two years earlier. Port Talbot was about to enter its heyday. Flynn's father, Jim, went straight from school to steel, working in the industry for the next four decades.

"He did continental shifts, which was Monday afternoon and Tuesday afternoon, then he'd work nights which was Wednesday night and Thursday night, then he'd have two days off. When he went back he'd do the afternoons again, and so on. He did that for forty years at

the blast furnace. Talk about the frontline. That's the frontline. That's molten steel coming down in front of you. That was the so called coalface – forty years."

Although work was hard, wages were relatively high for manual labour and jobs were plentiful. Nearly 20,000 people worked at the three steelworks and the town could boast close to full employment in the 1960s.

"My character is basically my dad," Brian Flynn proudly states of the man he quite clearly and unreservedly admires. This despite the fact that Jim Flynn, "never kicked a ball." Cricket was the only sport he played as a young man, a batsman in the local leagues around Port Talbot.

"My mum always said 'the milkman was a good footballer Bri,' with a little wink. She loved winding my dad up." Joyce Flynn, barely five feet tall, worked as a cleaner, a nanny, an ice cream lady and various other part-time jobs alongside raising her two boys. It was a household full of love and warmth.

Flynn remembers his childhood as a happy time. "I had loads of good mates who I am still in touch with." Older brother John wasn't particularly sporty but Brian was obsessed with ball games from an early age. "I played rugby first. We had to play rugby at primary school. We all played football at break time but PE was rugby."

He was taken to see the local rugby union side, Aberavon RFC, play much more often than he was to see any football. He does remember Swansea Town's epic run to the semi-finals of the 1964 FA Cup though, and attending a 4-0 fourth round replay demolition of Sheffield United. The Swans overcame Bill Shankly's Liverpool in the quarters before losing out to fellow Second Division side Preston North End, 2-1, in the semi-final at Villa Park. The West Ham United team of Bobby Moore and Geoff Hurst won the final 3-2.

In June 1965, the Queen visited Port Talbot to open the Afan Lido Sports Centre. Cultural historian Peter Stead describes it as 'the first modern building of its type in Wales. It represented the beginning of a new age and was seen very much as a turning point.' It was also a turning point in the life of the nine-year-old Brian Flynn. "They used to have five-a-side tournaments. I was never away from there, was I?" Indoor football was a godsend. Not just somewhere to go in the event of inclement weather during the dark winter nights, but a chance to play on a fast, true surface which would hone the technique of the most dedicated frequenters.

The first manager of the centre was Richard Burton's younger brother Graham Jenkins. Richard had changed his name when his teacher and mentor Philip Burton became his legal ward, and the thespian superstar would visit when back in Wales. He'd usually head straight for the Sportsman's Bar and would very kindly "put a couple of bottles in my cabinet in my office so that the next time he called, I'd have a bottle there for him," remembered his brother. Jenkin's son Richard also played regularly at the Lido. "A decent winger," Flynn remembers. The new sports centre was a symbol of the town's industrial prosperity.

In 1966, the World Cup was held in England and Flynn remembers watching the tournament on television, enraptured by events from over the (then under construction) Severn Bridge. One man in particular stood out during England's triumph. The winning team's smallest player, Alan Ball, became Flynn's boyhood idol, with his all-action display in the Final, a particular inspiration.

"He was probably the best player that day and if it had not been for his impact the result could have been totally different," said Ball's more celebrated team-mate Bobby Charlton. Less than five years earlier, Bolton Wanderers had broken the 5ft 6inch Ball's heart when he was told: "Sorry, we don't think you are good enough to make the grade as a professional. You're too small."

Unsurprisingly, those are words that have never been uttered by Flynn in nearly 20 years of management and coaching. "There's no such thing as 'too small.' Is Peter Crouch 'too tall?' It makes no sense. It's a cop-out."

"So I go to Sandfields Comprehensive School and get picked for the school rugby team. At the same time, at 12 years old, I first officially joined a boys' club to play football, Neath Boys' Club. I don't know why I didn't join Aberavon Boys' Club but one or two of my mates were going to Neath. It was five miles away but renowned as one of the best boys' clubs in Wales. Football took over then. But, I regularly got picked for the rugby team which played at 11 o'clock on a Saturday morning, the same time as the football team played, so I didn't turn up. For a period of about three months my dad had to come to school with me

every Monday morning.

'Where was Brian on Saturday? He should have been playing rugby for the school team.'

'No he wants to play football.'

'No, no, school comes first, if the school picks you, you have got to play for the school.'

'But he doesn't want to play. Brian wants to play football.'

"*I loved playing rugby. I was a scrum half. I loved it in PE, but it was amateur wasn't it? I didn't care about money but I always wanted to be a professional sportsman. After three months the school gave up when I was starting to have Welsh football trials for the under-15s, when I was only 12 or 13. So, when I got my Cap, it caused a fuss as they then had to introduce football into PE and all the PE teachers were rugby men. They didn't know a thing about football.*"

The story sums up Flynn's character in so many ways; bloody-minded, enthusiastic, with a genuine love and voracious appetite for competing, but most of all a fierce determination to succeed; the kind that anyone needs to get to the top in any sport, but especially so when you are the smallest kid in the class. Flynn didn't follow his father into the steel industry but the steeliness was certainly on display throughout his playing career.

Lack of height was never really an issue. "I had a good first touch and I was quick; quick to get out of the way as well. That was probably from playing rugby. I learned how to get out of the way, how to fall. You think to yourself, 'If I don't get out of the way I'm gonna get tackled here.' Playing rugby definitely helped me. If you know you are going to get hurt you do something about it. Even at 10, 11, and 12, rugby was full on. Those kids were fierce.

Flynn's goal-scoring exploits at that young age were impressive. "I think I got over 40 one season, for the under-13s. And then his combative displays in the Neath Boys' Club midfield caught the eye of the region's local professional clubs.

"*I signed for Cardiff when I was 12. At the time this was illegal although I didn't know that. I went up there twice a week, Tuesdays and Thursdays, on my own, on the train at night. Then I walked from the station to Ninian Park, finished at about half past eight, to catch the 9 o'clock train, getting home about quarter past ten. Twice a week for two years, but one night, we had a knock at the door at home. It was a Swansea scout.*

'We're interested in Brian coming to train with us.' My dad says 'nah he's sighed for Cardiff.'

'He hasn't. He hasn't been signed by Cardiff.'

'He has. He signed a form.'

'He might have signed a form but he's not registered. So in effect you haven't signed a form.'

Cardiff then realised they had made a mistake. Because I'd got to the final round of trials for the Welsh schoolboy team and my profile's been going up but I'm a year underage. I'm 13, going on 14 but I'm playing with 15-year olds. My profile was getting high within Wales.

So Jimmy Scoular was the manager and he phoned us and tried to persuade me to re-sign.

My dad said, 'no, sorry, it's your mistake, you'll have to live by it.'"

When he was 14, the Afan Lido established 11-a-side teams, so rather than play for Neath Boys' Club along with training with Cardiff City schoolboys, Flynn joined his local leisure centre side for a year. His insatiable appetite for the game was further sated when he was picked to play for his country. Pulling on the red shirt of Wales made him "feel like I was 7 feet 8 inches tall."

Welsh football historian Ceri Stennett can remember being taken, aged 10, to see the Welsh schoolboys play England at Ninian Park in March, 1971. "Playing for Wales that day was Brian Flynn and I can still see him in my mind's eye, a small diminutive central midfielder, involved in everything." Wales lost the match 5-0. Later that spring, Wales went to Edinburgh to play Scotland at Tynecastle and put in a much better performance. Flynn scored in the 1-1 draw, but the goal wasn't the most significant moment of the evening for the youngster.

"The Burnley chief scout Dave Blakey was there for one particular reason. After the game he said, 'follow me,' so I followed him to his car. I signed the contract there and then. 'When are you coming up?' he asked. I said, 'End of the season,' but he said, 'No the manager wants you in now.'

"So I went straight up to Burnley and left school at Easter aged 15. You could do that then. I'd been to Arsenal, Leeds and Chelsea for trial matches but as soon as we went to Burnley, I said, 'Dad I want to

85

come here.' My mind was made up already. The training ground was fantastic, the best in the country, and I knew I'd get my chance there."

Although Flynn enjoyed school, with geography and maths particular favourite subjects, by that point the desire to become a professional footballer had become all-consuming. The final year of formal education was sacrificed. Flynn had a new place of learning to attend in the north of England.

For those of us who have never lived in South Wales it is perhaps hard to understand just how much rugby union permeates the culture of the region. Certainly it dominates sports media coverage, and for years Welsh politicians have chosen to use the game as a prism through which to view the country as a whole (much to the annoyance of many, especially in the north where football has always been more popular). But, as the actor and film-maker, Jonathan Owen, explained in a piece for the BBC ahead of Cardiff City's FA Cup Final appearance in 2008, the great and good, the establishment basically, in Wales have always been aggressively protective of their beloved sport "and nothing could be seen to take their precious jewel."

Flynn's future Wales team-mate, Terry Yorath, was immediately banned from the rugby and cricket teams at Cathays Grammar School when he told the sports master that he was going to play football for the Cardiff schools team. When Yorath won his first full Wales cap in 1969 the school did not put a picture of him on the wall, as they had done when former head boy, Billy Raybould, first played international rugby two years earlier. The stubborn, future Wales captain and manager never forgot the slight, and always refused invitations to go back to present prizes. It is telling that many of the top South Wales footballers of the time who emerged at this time, Yorath, Flynn, Leighton James, all share similar single-minded temperaments. Those three also felt the need to move across the border to realise their ambitions. For Flynn that involved a seven to eight hour car journey, in the days before extensive motorway networks significantly reduced travel time from the south of Wales to the north of England.

"I know the A49 like the back of my hand." So it was goodbye to Port Talbot, to the sea and the steelworks and the oval ball.

"The rugby team in Port Talbot is Aberavon, and then down the road you've got Neath. We also had Aberavon Quins who used to play

in the second tier. Then you had clubs like Cwmafan and Tonmawr, so in a radius of 10 miles you must have had eight decent rugby teams. There must have been another four in Swansea. Competition was fierce. At that time, when the All Blacks used to tour, they'd play against club sides across South Wales but because they couldn't play against all of them, Neath and Aberavon combined to play them. They were good games. I always went to see them as it was only once every four years. Rugby was huge. I enjoyed playing but I always much preferred football."

In 1972, just to the west of Swansea, club side Llanelli famously beat the All Blacks 9-3; the last Welsh team, club or country, to beat New Zealand. But Brian Flynn, having just turned 17, was in Lancashire by then, 250 miles to the north.

***

Chapter 2: Milltown

As Brian Flynn chomps down on a bacon bap at the Tickled Trout Hotel just outside Preston on a drizzly March Monday morning, he tells me how he usually spends his Fridays at around this time. Up to six old Burnley team-mates, Paul Fletcher, Colin Waldron, Jim Thomson, Mick Docherty, Frank Casper and Flynn, all meet up for coffee; a natter and to "wind each other up worse than we ever did when we played."

A lot of ex-clarets stayed in the area after their playing days were over, Thomson is Glaswegian and Casper is a Yorkshireman. They love the town and it seems the town loves them. For an urban centre of only 70,000 or so to have sustained such a successful football club, one that has spent so much of its history in the top flight, is truly impressive.

"It is punching above its weight," Flynn states. "It always has done."

He is not wrong. Twice the champions of England, 1921 and 1960, and three times FA Cup finalists, winners in 1914 and runners up in 1947 and 1962, Burnley are one of English football's famous names. After starting life in the 1870s as a rugby club, by 1882 they had swapped the oval ball for round, and two years later were already attracting crowds of over 12,000 to their new home, and home ever since, Turf Moor. The popularity of the club led to them becoming one of the 12 founder members of the Football league in 1888. Although Burnley FC has always had its fair share of local Lancastrians, Fletcher is from Bolton, Docherty was born in Preston, where his famous Scottish father played, right from the start their success has always been contingent on importing talent from elsewhere. As far back as 1883 the team fielded nine Scots.

Their production line was world famous, and superstar George Best was amongst those fully aware of it when he said: "Although Burnley were never a 'big club' in terms of money and attendance figures, they were big in footballing terms and had a super youth system that was a conveyor belt of good young players." The north-east of England and South Wales were two traditionally fertile regions for their extensive scouting system to mine for talent to take back to Lancashire.

Flynn's first professional manager and biggest influence in football was Jimmy Adamson. In 1946, aged 17, he was spotted by Burnley scout Jackie Dryden playing as an inside forward for East Chevington Juniors and was whisked across the north of England for a trial. The club was impressed and in early 1947 Adamson signed his first professional contract. No testimony exists as to whether he was homesick or not but fellow Geordie, Jimmy Robson, who made the same move a few years later, certainly was: "I came from a small mining village and hadn't seen much of life outside. A lot of us were like that. Those first three months were hard." It is easy to imagine that Adamson might have felt similarly.

Although travel had become much easier and cars more affordable by the early 1970s, it is likely that the experience of arriving in that similar alien environment over 20 years earlier had made an impact on the manager when he stated: "As soon as a youngster arrives at Turf Moor he is made to feel part of Burnley Football Club. And, just as importantly, he knows that he is not going to be tossed out after just a short spell. Every young player arriving at Turf Moor is guaranteed four or five years on the staff. In that time he gets the chance to learn the game. He is not tossed out if he fails to live up to expectations in one season. If he wants, the lad can be apprenticed to a trade. Or he usually goes on the ground staff doing all the odd jobs around the ground."

When I asked Flynn if he ever suffered from homesickness, he immediately responds: "Oh yeah." But his determination to make it was the overriding factor, though. Besides, most of the youngsters at the club were in the same boat having come to East Lancashire from Tyneside, the English Midlands and Wales. In those days, apprentices were housed by local people, usually elderly, paid by the club to look after the teenagers brought to Burnley. Flynn lived with Dora Whitefield, a retired milk-woman who had delivered door to door using a horse and cart. Another young south Walian, Ian Lewis from the Afan Valley village of Glyncorrwg, who'd played alongside Flynn in the Welsh schoolboys' team, also lived at Dora Whitefield's house on Parkinson Street, a short walk from Turf Moor.

According to Flynn: "Ian was shaving by the time he was eight," but never made it as a professional, suggesting he was one of those players who peaked too soon, a youth star unable to transition to senior level. There also appears to be a difference in the level of focus displayed by the two youngsters. Future team-mate Peter Noble described Flynn as "very single-minded, he didn't get himself involved in a lot of the silly stuff." Whereas Burney fan Brian Barker recalls that, "Ian was a good lad but his main hobby seemed to be helping us wind up the park rangers in Thompson Park."

"As a teenager I used to get busses everywhere; I couldn't drive. There was a bunch of us teenagers, boys and girls, and we used to congregate in the bus station, in the café or the Hasty Tasty chip shop. It was good to get to know the local lads and lasses. It was great. That's what Burnley is about. In our day, Burnley players had to live in Burnley. Today it's all different. They all live in Manchester. Nobody lives in Burnley now but in our day you had to. Chairman Bob Lord put it in the contract."

One of those local lasses was called Elizabeth Oddie. Flynn and Oddie were part of the same crowd of youngsters who gathered in the town centre cafes and bus station. They have been married since 1976.

Developed in the 1950s, Gawthorpe Training Ground was one of the major factors in drawing talented youngsters to the club. During the reign of highly respected and innovative manager Alan Brown, in charge from 1954 to 1957, and under the auspices of ambitious new chairman Bob Lord, the training facility was conceived with the intention of keeping Burnley ahead of their much richer rivals. Club legend Harry Potts described Gawthorpe as being "the sort of spot to make even the most reluctant footballer feel good to be alive." Considering that for decades after its opening, many bigger clubs continued to train in their stadiums, often leading to an awful deterioration of the playing surface over the course of a season, Gawthorpe with its all-weather pitch set in the grounds of an Elizabethan mansion was the envy of much of the football world.

Then there was the training. Midfielder Geoff Nulty had struggled at his first professional club, Stoke City, and credits his breakthrough to the quality of the coaching he received upon moving to Burnley in 1968.

"What really impressed me was the training sessions were always well planned," he told writer Tim Quelch. "Adamson and his assistant Joe Brown always worked out our training schedules in advance. This was quite unlike what I had experienced at Stoke. There, only the first team received any real attention, and even their training sessions didn't seem that well prepared. The reserves were largely left to their own devices. But at Burnley, the senior players, the reserves and the youth team players trained together, at least for most of the week. Adamson and Brown would divide us into mixed groups and, typically, these groups would be made up of four first-team players, four reserves and four apprentices. Jimmy wanted everyone to be inducted in the Burnley style of play."

Regular contact with the bosses when the youth team players trained with the first-team was to prove a key factor in encouraging Flynn's development. "It was blatantly obvious the manager liked me, the other players used to say it too. 'He loves you Flynny.' You know when a manager likes you." The feeling was mutual. Respect for Adamson flows from Flynn with only the slightest prompt.

"He was so many years in advance, fitness wise. Nowadays, everything is new, or so they tell you. All these fitness people saying 'this is scientific and this is new. You won't have done this before. You are going to do a Fartlek run.' But a Fartlek run is just a horseshoe run. You start on the halfway line, go round to the dead ball line behind the goals, back to the halfway line, then jog across – so that's your resting time. It will take you 35 seconds. Do six of them and it's hard going.

We used to call them '35-seconders.' Sports scientists say they have invented this stuff. We were doing those 40 years ago.

"As a coach Jimmy Adamson was miles ahead. Training sessions were always straight to the point, sharp and quick, not laborious. Say, you've got three key points you want to coach in a day. In a session you come prepared as you've got three key points you want to achieve. If Jimmy Adamson didn't get to point three, he'd stop and say, 'We'll get to that tomorrow. I'm not going to keep going and going for an hour. Let's stop at point two and tomorrow we'll go from point two to point three.' But the players were eager to learn and loved his coaching and we'd say, 'Can we come back this afternoon boss, can we do a bit more?' Honestly it was like that all the time. We were asking because the sessions were that good. He was so influential for so many of us.

"Jimmy Adamson introduced 4-3-3 to British football. Everyone else was playing 4-2-4. But Jimmy always wanted three in the middle of midfield. 'You've gotta win the middle of the park,' he'd say. 'All the fights are in the middle of the park. Defend for your life, take your chances. But the midfield is the most important part.' That's what I was brought up on."

It's the work with the ball that stands out the most when ex-Adamson players recall their former manager. Former England midfielder Martin Dobson remembers:

"Everyone was training with a ball, the international players and the young players. There was two-touch and shadow football played without opponents, something Alan Brown had brought to Burnley when Adamson was a player. Players were going through pass and move drills; what impressed me immediately was that so much of the training centred on developing ball skills. There was instruction in what to do, not only in technique but in making runs, positioning and so on. I had never seen anything like this at Bolton. And at the heart of the activity was Jimmy Adamson. He seemed to know exactly what he wanted from his players, blowing his whistle to stop the play when the exercises weren't being executed as he wanted, praising his players when they got it right and demonstrating what was missing when they didn't. There was much practising of building attacks from the wings. Once again Jimmy was meticulous about the type of crosses that were being supplied. We would go through a series of routines involving whipped or hanging crosses. He paid so much attention to detail."

It's a crime to lose the ball, was one of Adamson's favourite sayings. That he valued skill and intelligence over physicality was music to Flynn's ears: "Jimmy Adamson never mentioned my size. Or, you've gotta do this or that to compensate. Never, ever, not even once did he mention it. He might have sarcastically said 'Look I'm not expecting you to be picking up players at corners or set pieces, I'm not expecting you to win balls in the air Bri.' But that was it."

Goal-scoring legend Jimmy Greaves considered Adamson to be the best English footballer never to win an international cap. He did go to the 1962 World Cup in Chile though. It seems strange considering that he'd just been named Footballer of the Year, but Adamson wasn't taken to South America to play; instead, manager Walter Winterbottom wanted the respected Burnley captain to be his assistant. After losing to Hungary, beating Argentina and drawing with Bulgaria, England were knocked out by Brazil in the quarter-final with the great Garrincha scoring twice. But Adamson had impressed the players with his knowledge and coaching ability.

Bobby Charlton, who started life on the very same street in Ashington, Laburnum Terrace, before his family moved across to Beatrice Street, spent the long flight back from Chile discussing all things football with his fellow Northumbrian. It was a conversation that made a lasting impression and the two would visit each other for years afterwards. Winterbottom was so impressed with Adamson's training pitch work that he recommended that the Football Association should employ him as his successor. The 33-year old turned down the chance to talk to the FA about the role feeling, quite understandably, that his playing days were still far from over. Of course, there is no way of knowing, but he, rather than Alf Ramsey, could have been the manager to win the World Cup at Wembley four years later. It was not a decision he came to regret, at least not publicly. A one-club player, his relationship with Burnley FC was a love affair he had no desire to break off and he could see a clear pathway to the top job at Turf Moor.

Harry Potts was Burnley's manager when they won the league in 1960, with Adamson playing as the midfield anchor in support of playmaking star Jimmy McIlroy. The club nearly won the double in 1962, finishing one point behind Ipswich Town in the league and losing the FA Cup Final 3-1 to Spurs. The following season, McIlroy was sold to Stoke City for £25,000. It was a transfer Adamson came to see as the beginning of the end of Burnley's position as a major force in English football. He started to take on more responsibility for training the team following his experiences at the World Cup and he officially became coach in 1965. Over the course of the late 60s he gradually, but noticeably, to Burnley's players, began to usurp Potts as the main man.

In February 1970, Bob Lord made the changing of the guard official. Adamson took over as manager with Potts moving 'upstairs', a course of events that left the former title-winning boss bitter and resentful at the treatment dished out to him by the club he had brought such success. Potts' final game was a 5-0 thrashing of Nottingham Forest. It wasn't a move he saw coming. Certain players, such as midfield star Dave Thomas, were sworn Potts loyalists and never really warmed to Adamson in the manner that later signings like Paul Fletcher or apprentices such as Flynn did.

"Not everyone's cup of tea," is Paul Fletcher's subtle way of describing Adamson's character. Although some of his mannerisms annoyed certain players, he would beckon people towards him by crooking his index finger, and his habit of asking anyone who answered back to go and shine his Player of the Year trophy also wound a few up; virtually everyone who played under him agrees that in terms of tactics and training he was way ahead of his time.

Then he had his disciples. "He was a master of communication," is Flynn's opinion.

"He was a genius," states Stan Ternent, briefly a player for the club in the late 1960s.

Knowing the level of young talent being developed by the club, Adamson made a bold prediction that Burnley would become the "team of the seventies." It was a statement that made the manager look a little foolish when his side were relegated at the end of his first full season in charge. Bob Lord wasn't keen on hiring and firing though, and had full faith in his manager getting the club back up to the highest level. The club finished a disappointing seventh in 1971/72, in the days before the play-offs were introduced in a successful attempt to increase the end of season excitement.

That summer, the Burnley U19s team had featured in a five nations youth tournament at Sunderland, beating the hosts at Roker Park to win the trophy. In the Final, Flynn was named man-of-the-match and received the award from the Burnley chairman.

"He's a good little 'un," said Bob Lord suggesting it wasn't just the management team, but also the Burnley hierarchy, who had high hopes for the diminutive midfielder. The following season was much more successful with Burnley taking the Second Division title to regain their place in the top flight.

Another Turf Moor legend from the north east of England, right back John Angus, was awarded a testimonial in May 1973 after failing to recover from injuries following 17 years of stellar service. A large crowd of over 16,000 attended, to see the Burnley 'millionaires' team, all players sold by the Clarets, versus the newly promoted first team; with a 'veterans' side against the youth team as the warm-up. So, the 17-year old Brian Flynn first played in front of a big crowd at Turf Moor directly up against the legendary midfield of McIlroy and Adamson. The close relationship between player and manager was in public view that evening, with Adamson encouraging Flynn to nutmeg him, before picking the youngster up, twisting round and depositing him back on the pitch, before getting on with the game.

"He also told me to sit on the ball in the centre circle. I don't know why, but if the manager tells you to do something, you do it." The crowd were thoroughly entertained by the evening's frolics.

"Adamson always used to say you should play with a chuckle in your feet," Flynn told the *Lancashire Telegraph* in 1997. "And I think he was right."

First team football was now within reach for Flynn. Burnley were an excellent side though, so making a breakthrough was never going to be easy. George Best is on record as saying, "As far as we were concerned at United, a match against the Claret and Blues was one of our biggest games of the season. The fixture had added spice in that it was considered a 'derby game' and consequently had a highly competitive edge to it. In the seventies the team included the likes of Frank Casper, Martin Dobson, Paul Fletcher, and as Denis Law used to call them, the Battling Baldies, Ralph Coates and Peter Noble. When United met Burnley, the fans were always assured of a game in which the level of skill and entertainment would be out of the top drawer."

By the 1973/74 season George Best was on the wane and Burnley had built up a momentum gained by their promotion. Although Liverpool and Leeds United had opened up a gap to turn the title battle into a two-horse race, subsequently won by the team from Yorkshire in Don Revie's final season before taking over as England manager, Burnley were very much part of the chasing pack.

It was into this highly competitive environment that Flynn was thrust in to first team action on the first Saturday of February 1974. Up against his football idol Alan Ball and Irish friend Liam Brady, both trialled at Arsenal at the same time and captained their respective nations at schoolboy level, the Clarets salvaged a 1-1 draw against the Gunners when Paul Fletcher shot through a crowd of players late in the game at Highbury. Flynn caught the eye of the *Observer* reporter Peter Corrigan: 'At 18 years old and 5 feet 4 inches he might have been expected to take it gently. But this pugnacious and thoroughly self-confident young man has learned maturity as captain of the youth teams of Burnley and Wales and looked a real Billy Bremner. Three times in the first 20 minutes he earned himself a lecture from that demonstrative referee Roger Kirkpatrick but his only fault was that of exuberance; and it was only in the final stages that his seniors caught up with the pace of his contribution.

"Before the game, Captain Colin Waldron said to me, 'Alan Ball will try to disturb you, disrupt you, there may be some verbal abuse Brian, so expect it.'" The abuse never came but it speaks volumes for Flynn's focus that he impressed on his professional debut despite the prospect of his hero giving him a mouthful of expletives.

With left-sided midfielder Dougie Collins injured, Flynn kept his place in the side, immediately impressing the fans at Turf Moor with his skill and tenacity. "I can remember seeing him for the first time, the images of what he did in that game are vividly imprinted. It was a stunning performance from a pint-sized kid who sprayed passes around long and short, ran the midfield, scurried here and there, and slotted into the team as if he'd been there for years. We kept looking at each other open-mouthed as this preciously talented kid showed no nerves, hesitancy or shyness," states Dave Thomas, author of over a dozen books about his beloved Clarets.

Burnley finished that season in sixth place, the highest position of all the Lancashire clubs. Manchester City were fourteenth. Manchester United were twenty-first and relegated, with Denis Law scoring a famous back heeled goal to help send his former club down while playing for their City rivals. Perhaps there was still time for Burnley to become the 'Team of the Seventies' after all.

* * *

(No, they did not become the Team of the Seventies. That was always an improbable dream and Adamson's forecast would haunt him for years afterwards. One by one the best players were sold to pay the costs of running Burnley Football Club; costs that always included high wages for players and expensive accommodation in the best hotels. Martin Dobson went, Leighton James went, Adamson was as good as sacked in January of 1976, and with him gone Burnley soon slipped into Division Two. With deteriorating gates it became even more crucial that players were sold. In November, 1977, after 115 games for Burnley, it was Flynn's turn to go and he was sold to Leeds United. DT)

5

2000 Peter Swan, an Uncompromising Hero

Peter Swan played in over 500 games and worked for some of the biggest names in football including Howard Wilkinson, Neil Warnock, Billy Bremner and Peter Shilton. Equally at home as a centre-forward or centre-half, Swan signed for Leeds United in 1984 and broke transfer records at two of his next three clubs – Hull City, Port Vale and Plymouth Argyle. He played at Wembley twice but never made it into the top flight. His book is the story of a journeyman pro playing just below the big time and the big money.

With a reputation as a hard player who lived a hard life, Swan's football days were littered with twists and turns. Before the Autoglass Trophy Final at Wembley in 1993, he partied until dawn, staggered out onto the pitch and was named Man of the Match. Nine days later, he followed the rules and went to bed early in preparation for the Division Two play-off final – and ended up getting sent off as his side were defeated by West Bromwich Albion. While at Plymouth he suffered a torrid time, shunned by his fellow players, despised by supporters and living alone in a haunted house.

During his time at Port Vale he met a young local lad by the name of Robbie Williams. The two soon became firm friends and incorrigible drinking partners, with often hilarious results. But no matter how hard he partied off the field, he still set himself the highest standards in his professional life.

Falling foul of several managers along the way, he was often in trouble with referees, too, picking up 10 red cards and countless bookings. But on the other side of the coin he is a caring man who always took time out at various clubs to visit children in hospital. After retiring in 2000, Swan initially struggled to come to terms with life outside football, but he has since become a cult figure in Hull where he now commentates on Hull City's matches.

A larger than life character with no regrets, in his book he tells of all the adventures and confrontations of his 16-year career. He experienced joy at Wembley but the agonies of a chronic knee condition that forced him out of the game and almost saw him confined to a wheelchair.

Desperate to get away from Plymouth, it was Jimmy Mullen who first brought him to Burnley and then Chris Waddle who released him. After a spell away from Turf Moor, Stan Ternent brought him back. Like so many other players, he regards his time at Turf Moor as amongst the most enjoyable and happiest of his career.

He first met Stan Ternent up close and personal at Hull City. Colin Appleton had just been replaced as manager and in came Stan Ternent after Appleton's assistant Tom Wilson had taken over for a couple of games. DT

***

Swanny: Confessions of a Lower-League Legend by Peter Swan (John Blake Publishing) From Chapter 6: Wilko and Out

'We didn't have to wait long before Appleton's replacement was named: Stan Ternent, who'd been number 2 to Steve Coppell at Crystal Palace. We learned straightaway that life under Stan was going to be a very different kettle of fish. He called a team meeting on his first morning and came straight to the point. "Right, we're in the shit. If we're going to get out of the shit, we'll all have to piss in the same pot. If you don't want to piss in the same pot, come and see me and you can piss off. See you on the training ground in 10 minutes!" It was the kick up the arse we desperately needed.'

***

From Chapter 7: The Dog of War

Stan Ternent was up front, in your face. He knew exactly what he wanted and anyone who didn't buy into it found himself on the outside looking in. The strong characters fell into line, the results improved and Hull eventually finished in mid-table. We won 14 and lost 10 of the 30 league games after Stan moved in. His philosophy was simple – and it never changed during my three spells as one of his players; if you were prepared to run through a brick wall for him, he'd back you all the way. Anything less and he didn't want to know. That was where I came from, too.

I got on well with Stan and he went on to sign me twice, for Bury and Burnley, later in my career, but we didn't get off to the best of starts. Tom Wilson, who'd been caretaker since Appleton's departure (from Hull) had picked the team for Stan's first game at Bradford City and named me up front with Billy Whitehurst.

Stan was sitting in the directors' box, supposedly to have a look at the players he would be inheriting on the Monday. But after about 15 minutes he appeared on the touchline. Up went the linesman's flag to indicate a substitution and my No.4 was held up. I couldn't believe it. I stormed off, had a shower, got changed, walked straight into the bar and supped three pints, one after another. As soon as the game finished, we won 3-2, I walked up to Stan and said, "Can I have a word?" he said he'd see me Monday morning, end of conversation. Now somewhere down the line, don't ask me how, I'd discovered that Stan didn't like dogs. And it just so happened that we had a dog and a half back home in Wakefield. Zee, our Great Dane, weighed in at around 13 stones. So, on the Monday, I decided I'd take Zee across to training and get one of the kids to give her a run round while we were working.

I'd calmed down a bit from Saturday but I was still simmering as I walked down the narrow corridor to Stan's office. Zee was out in front on her lead. I knocked on the door. Stan shouted, "Come in," so I opened the door, let the dog in and shut the door again. I could hear Stan yelling at the dog and when I opened the door again, Stan was pinned to the wall with Zee's paws on his shoulders. She only wanted to play, but Stan didn't see it that way. He looked absolutely bloody terrified.

After a few seconds, I called off the hell hound, but made a point of telling her to sit outside on guard – just in case. Stan sat down and we started to talk about Saturday, but I could see he was a bit wary, wondering whether I might set Zee on him again at any moment. He explained why he'd taken me off and how he didn't think it would work with me and Billy up front. In the end, I accepted his reasons and the ice was broken. We still have a laugh about Zee when we meet up.

The atmosphere at the club was a million miles better under Stan. To help things along, he decided we needed a bit of team bonding, as they'd call it today. So one morning, after he'd been around for a few weeks, he breezed into the dressing room and said, "Right you're doing well lads; time for a day at the races." He fished into his pocket, drew out a wad of notes and handed the dosh to Billy Whitehurst. "OK, Bill, you organise a bus and take the lads for a day at Cheltenham next week." So far, so good.

The day before our trip, Whitehurst issued strict instructions. "I want you all here at half-past eight in the morning, suited up because I've ordered tickets for the posh enclosure." We were all on time, but when the clock ticked round to 8.45am with no sign of Billy or bus, we started to get a bit twitchy. Nine o'clock, no bus, ten o'clock, no bus, no Billy. We tried to contact him but no joy. It was obvious our trip was off, so we decided to cut our losses. After a few pints in the boozer, we went to the bookies in town and watched the racing from there – in our suits, with our binoculars at the ready.

Whitehurst's status in the dressing room meant that no-one was willing to take him on about it the next day, but we soon found out from Stan that although Bill's intentions had been honourable, he finally succumbed on the afternoon before the trip and put Stan's brass on a dead cert at Huntingdon or somewhere. It went belly up, and so did our trip to Cheltenham.

(Peter Swan signed for Burnley on 4 August 1995, the manager was Jimmy Mullen. He eventually ended up at Plymouth but after a torrid time at Argyle he was utterly relieved to get away from there. He felt he'd got out of jail. He would later meet up with Stan again at Bury. DT)

* * *

From Chapter 15: Home Sweet Home

I sat on a bench in the dressing room at Burnley's Gawthorpe Hall training ground, letting the gritty northern accents, the jokes and the banter wash over me. I leaned back, rested my head against the wall and smiled to myself. It seemed a very long time since I'd smiled in a dressing room. I was home, back where I belonged in the North of England. I was back among friends.

Moving clubs is like starting a new school or a new job. You can never be quite sure about the players around you. They all have different personalities and have to be approached in a different manner, and just as a player assesses his new team-mates, they are assessing him. Twelve months earlier at Plymouth I'd sensed straightaway that something was wrong. But here I knew almost immediately that I was going to be welcome. I felt relaxed.

After a few minutes a voice shouted, "Come on lads. Let's be having you." I was fastening my boots at the time and there was a table between me and the man behind the voice, so I could only see him from the waist down. I noticed straightaway that one of his knees seemed to bend inwards. I raised my sights and saw a middle-aged guy wearing shorts and a club tracksuit top. It was Clive Middlemass the first-team coach. I was used to coaches being younger than the manager but Clive looked like something from another era and I couldn't imagine him sprinting round the training ground.

But what a lovely bloke, what a good coach; he made me feel involved straightaway in the first training session. And, I soon realised that while Clive might not have been in the first flush of youth, what he didn't know about coaching probably wasn't worth knowing, and he knew how to put it across. I seemed to slot into the dressing room from the word go, although I soon discovered that some of the pranks that had become my stock in-trade at Port Vale were out of date. I'd spent a year more or less in isolation at Plymouth and you can't take the mickey out of yourself can you? I didn't like them, they didn't like me, so there wasn't much to laugh about. So, I was a bit ring-rusty at first and discovered that cutting the end off people's socks and moving cars in the car park were yesterday's jokes. Instead, I started to learn how it felt to find my underpants on the teapot or Swarfega in my shampoo bottle.

When I signed we were still living in Stone, but I decided that from then on, I was going to stay in the north. We soon started looking for a house back home in Yorkshire. Our first stop was a converted barn in a village called Barkisland in the hills above Halifax. Richard Jobson, my former team-mate at Hull, who played nearly 700 games for 10 clubs, lived opposite. He went to work for the PFA before retiring in 2003.

We took out a six-month lease but, after three months, found a place of our own in Holmfirth, the village where *Last of the Summer Wine* is filmed. Harry, our second son, was born while we were there and we're glad he and George have been able to grow up amongst their own kind. We sold the place in Holmfirth after I moved to Bury in the summer of 1997 and found a house near Wakefield. We've been in and around the area ever since.

I used to joke that I only crossed the Pennines to Burnley and Bury to take the Red Rose money, although I've always got on OK with Lankies. But living in Yorkshire meant we could see more of our parents and the rest of the family. It was good to be on the doorstep as they were growing older. And, after a gap of four years, Mam and Dad were able to come and watch me play on a more regular basis. It hadn't been easy for them when I was at Vale, never mind Plymouth.

Usually, the three of us based in Yorkshire, Liam Robinson, Ian Helliwell and me, travelled over to Burnley in one car. The most direct route was over the top from Hebden Bridge. It wasn't far as the crow flies, but involved climbing up a narrow, steep, winding road called Mytholm Steeps. It more than lived up to its name. Then there was the rollercoaster ride over the tops between places with weird and wonderful names like, Blackshawhead, Kebcote and Cliviger, before dropping down into Burnley, right by the ground at Turf Moor. On the journey back we had a competition every day to set a new record for freewheeling. We'd flog the car up to around 70mph at the top of the final roller-coaster hump, just past a pub out in the middle of nowhere called the Sportsman's Arms. Then we'd bung the gear lever into neutral and head off through Blackshawhead and down the Steeps. If we met anything coming up the Steeps, the record bid was knackered. And when we hit the main road in Hebden Bridge, we prayed for a gap in the traffic so we could sweep straight out without having to halt. The all-comers record stood at 4.4 miles, or, to the technically minded, the second lamp post heading into Hebden Bridge.

It could be a tough trip in winter and once I had a lucky escape. Liam was doing the driving, but I'd arranged to stay overnight in Burnley so I didn't make the return trip. Soon after setting off, he clipped another vehicle on a bad bend and his car turned over. The whole of the nearside of the car was caved in on the passenger side, just where I would have been sitting.

I actually signed for the Clarets on loan to begin with and my first match was the final pre-season game against Manchester City. Burnley's manager Jimmy Mullen had signed me as a central defender and I was desperate to impress to make sure the deal was made permanent. The other 21 players were treating the game as just another friendly, but not me. I was marking Niall Quinn and he must have thought he was playing in a World Cup Final. I kicked lumps out of him from the first minute and I was taken off midway through the second-half. I might easily have been sent off, had it been for real.

To be honest it was a relief when my number went up. I'd hardly done any serious pre-season work at Plymouth and I was completely knackered. But the fans liked what they saw and gave me a massive ovation. Before long I was known as 'Godzilla' or 'The Incredible Hulk' in the local press, who seemed to be looking for a positive angle. It was a completely different world from my nightmare in Devon. I signed a two-year contract before our first game against Rotherham. As it happened, Jamie Hoyland, the club skipper, was suspended for the first two games and, the day before the Rotherham match, Jimmy Mullen called me into his office. He said I'd be wearing the captain's armband. I'd only been around five minutes, so it gave me a real lift. Twelve months earlier at Plymouth, I'd led out a team of strangers, feeling I was on my own. Here, I knew I was among friends and that the other players were supporting me, not stabbing me in the back.

After we'd won our first two games, I thought I might have a chance of keeping the armband. Then Jimmy called us both in. He said he'd promised Jamie the job for the season and would stand by that. He added that it had been a tough decision. I really fancied it, but shook hands with Jamie and said, "Right, let's crack on with it." We were good mates from then on.

I played in central defence alongside Mark Winstanley, strong, quick and a good left peg, right foot – non-existent. Jamie and I sometimes used to wind him up by passing the ball at pace to his right foot. He used to get into all sorts of contortions trying to run round the ball so he could use his left instead. Jamie and I would be in stitches. Afterwards, Mark used to ask why we'd done it. "Because it's funny," I'd reply. And before games he'd plead with us not to mess him about. We never did it when there was any danger, of course, but one day his lack of a right peg backfired badly. A cross came in from the left and the ball skidded past me and headed straight for Mark, who was covering behind. It was on his right foot and he just smashed it first-time towards his own goal. The idea was to concede a corner but instead, the ball flew like a bullet into the top corner from 15 yards. Marlon Beresford, our keeper, never had a chance.

Warren Joyce used to play in midfield. We used to call him 'Weirdo' … but don't get the wrong idea. He was a lovely lad and, like me, had spent a season at Plymouth before joining Burnley in 1993. He's done well since retiring and, in 2006 was appointed manager at a Belgian club, Royal Antwerp. At times Joycie seemed to live in a little world of his own. Sometimes one of the lads would report early and go to the gym to loosen up. The place would be in darkness but when the lights were switched on, Joycie would be in the corner doing his yoga. He didn't seem to notice that the lights had gone on and that someone was working out on the treadmill or the weights.

David Eyres was 31 at the time and little did any of us know he'd still be going strong 11 years later. By the time he quit league football at Oldham in 2006, he'd played over 700 games in an 18-year career. He possessed a great left foot, spent 7 seasons at Turf Moor and was a good man in the dressing room, always up with the banter.

Kurt Nogan scored 26 goals in my first season. Like Andy Payton and Bernie Slaven, two more of my former team-mates, he was a penalty box predator and only interested in scoring goals. But even though he became a bit of a folk hero and won the Player of the Year award, he never settled at Burnley. He once went on local radio and said he wanted to get away and go back to Wales. This caused a bit of a stir, but after my experience at Plymouth, I knew where he was coming from. Even though he might have been doing well at Burnley, he couldn't settle and wanted to get back home. Instead he ended up down the road at Preston.

Marlon Beresford, our 'keeper, was a great shot stopper, but we used to call him 'Gorgeous George' because all the women loved him. He lived in Sheffield and used to wheel his family over the Pennines for home games. There seemed to be hundreds of them. He ended up with a £500,000 move to Middlesbrough in 1998, although with Mark Schwarzer around, he didn't play much first-team football. He still picked up decent money playing in the reserves, money that would probably have set him up for life.

The physio was Andy Jones, another top man and a real favourite with the fans. He had a curious style of running, with his arms down by his sides, and if there were two players down from opposite sides, he hared on to the park, desperate to beat the other team's physio to his injured player. He was a dumpy little chap, so the crowd loved seeing him come out of the blocks like an Olympic sprinter and go dashing onto the pitch. When he ran on to treat a player he had this strange habit of sliding the last couple of yards on one knee. In one game, Gerry Harrison, one of our midfield players, was pole-axed and lay prone on the turf, dead to the world. Andy dashed on and slid in towards Gerry on one knee, but he'd overcooked the slide and his right knee went straight into Gerry's bollocks. I've never seen anyone come round so quickly.

Andy used to work one-to-one with injured players and sometimes he'd take us to a nearby sports club at the Dunkenhalgh Hotel. I went along with him one day and when we arrived there was a women's keep-fit class going on in the gym. Most of them were young and they were all wearing highly-coloured leotards and, all in all, they looked pretty fit. Andy was obviously keen to impress. We were both working on the treadmill with our backs to the keep-fit girls and after a while I said, "Hey up Jonah, your lace is undone." Even though the treadmill was going fairly quickly, he stopped and looked down to check. Mistake! The treadmill didn't stop and Andy went hurtling backwards into the group of women. He picked himself up, muttered a few sheepish apologies and headed straight for the changing room. We never used the Dunkenhalgh again.

We started well enough with four wins and a draw in our first five league games and league cup games, but were a bit hit and miss after that and it wasn't long before Mullen started to come under pressure. He'd been in charge since October 1991, succeeding Frank Casper with the Clarets standing eleventh in the old Fourth Division and apparently going nowhere. Six months later they were promoted as champions and, after a season of consolidation, went into what is now the Championship via the play-offs. They were relegated after one season. I arrived at the club after relegation for a change.

But after our patchy start, we were knocked out of the cup in the first round, beaten 3 – 1 at home by Walsall, and although we had a decent December, the alarm bells were ringing for the gaffer. A run of four successive defeats between 20 January and 10 February signalled the end. I hadn't been around for long but I'd got on well with Mullen. In my early days the lads used to tell me he could be a bit unpredictable. There were tales of how he'd fallen asleep in the toilet before one game and another time he'd announced a 12-man team in the dressing room before kick-off.

Once, when we were playing Carlisle away, we stopped for a pre-match meal. The players ate their food, had a stroll round the hotel grounds and then climbed back on the bus to wait for the manager and directors. We waited and waited, and by the time the top brass returned to the bus, having obviously had a good lunch, we were behind schedule. When we arrived, we had to get changed in a rush while Jimmy gave his team talk; or tried to do against stern opposition from the PA system, which was broadcast into the dressing room through a loudspeaker.

One day I took a rugby ball out for our warm-up before a practice match. It was a frosty day and we were working on the Astroturf pitch. We had a few minutes of touch and pass before Jimmy arrived. He put a ball in the centre circle and walked to watch from the touchline. While his back was turned, I swapped the football for my rugby ball and we kicked off. You can imagine how a rugby ball behaves on Astroturf so we were obviously all over the place. Jimmy was ranting away on the touchline and eventually he blew his whistle and shouted, "Here, give me that ball." We chucked the rugby ball across and he was just about to show us how it should be done when he spotted what was going on.

Not long before he left, we lost 3 – 0 at Shrewsbury, a third league defeat on the bounce. I'd been thrown up front to try and snatch a goal and get us back in the game, only to be substituted five minutes from time. I muttered something under my breath in Jimmy's direction as I stalked off down the tunnel. Afterwards, I was chatting to my dad in the players' lounge when one of the lads told me the gaffer wanted to see me. I sensed another bollocking was on the way and went back to the dressing room. He wasn't there. So I went out onto the pitch and spotted Jimmy sitting in the dug-out. I walked over and saw he was in tears. I tried the humorous approach. "Come on gaffer, we weren't that bad." He turned and told me he'd had enough, that he was going to see the chairman there and then and resign. He said the pressure was getting to him. I told him not to rush into anything, to think about it over the weekend, to have a chat with the missus first and make a decision in the cold light of day.

We went back in on the Monday morning and Jimmy was right as rain. I walked passed him in the corridor and he never said a Dickie bird. I was sure he'd call me in to say he'd listened to what I'd said, and thanks. But nothing, it was as if the conversation had never happened.

After he left, Clive Middlemass took over as caretaker manager while the board found a replacement. One of the first names in the frame was Adrian Heath. He'd made his name with Stoke, won a championship with Everton and established himself as a big favourite with the fans after joining Burnley in 1992. Two or three months before Mullen left, Heath had moved to Sheffield United as assistant manager to Howard Kendall, his mentor as a player at Stoke, and his championship-winning manager at Everton. Heath was obviously going to be a popular choice with the fans if he came back, but he sounded like bad news for me. We'd never hit it off from the day I joined Burnley.

At the time we both lived in the Potteries and travelled north together. We shared the driving but that was about all. He used to go droning on about all the big names he'd played with and against while he was at Everton, about how he was going to be a manager one day and how he'd do the job. One day I said, "Look, if you ever get a manager's job, I wouldn't want to play for you." I couldn't be arsed with him anymore, so every morning, I used to buy half a dozen daily papers. If he was driving, I'd start reading the papers as soon as we set off. If I was behind the wheel, I'd hand him the pile of papers.

So, when he was appointed to succeed Mullen in February 1996, I feared the worst. There was an uneasy peace between us for the rest of the season as we hauled ourselves away from trouble and finished in 17th place. In the summer, Heath appointed John Ward, who subsequently managed Bristol City, Cheltenham and Carlisle, as his number 2. He brought a lot of new ideas to the training ground and when we set off for a pre-season trip to Northern Ireland I was feeling pretty optimistic. But Northern Ireland was the setting for my first major run-in with Heath. As a player, he'd been known as 'Inchy' but after taking over he made it clear he wanted to be called 'Boss' or 'Gaffer.' Not by me, he wasn't. I carried on calling him 'Inchy'. One day in Ireland he pulled me to one side and asked why. I said, "Because I don't respect you. You know I don't. I've told you often enough."

Surprise, surprise, I didn't really feature in the senior side in pre-season and, Sod's Law, I was suspended for the opening game against Luton. He had the perfect excuse not to involve me, and with Vince Overson, an experienced defender who'd started his career with the Clarets back in 1979, back at the club, my prospects looked pretty bleak.

And so it proved. We won that first game and, even though Overson was injured, I didn't get a look-in during the opening weeks of the season. It wasn't long before I was knocking on the manager's door. He told me there was an opportunity for me to go on loan to Hartlepool or Hereford, both in the bottom division. No chance. I asked for a move and went on the transfer list in mid-September.

However, before long, the side started to go through a dodgy spell and I knew the fans wanted to know why I wasn't playing. A piece in the *Lancashire Evening Telegraph,* the local paper, in which I asked Heath why he wasn't selecting his best centre-half, kept the pot on the boil. On 29 October, we drew 1 – 1 in a midweek game at Preston. Mark Winstanley and Overson picked up knocks and, afterwards, Heath told me I'd be in the line-up at York the following weekend. It was a chance I wasn't going to miss. We lost 1 – 0, but I played well. Heath admitted as much in the press and kept me in the side. We won our next four games and, after a 1 – 0 win over Bournemouth at Turf Moor, the *Evening Telegraph* carried the headline HEATH HAILS PETER THE GREAT. He'd given me the armband at half-time after Nigel Gleghorn was injured and in the article he enthused, 'Peter is a tremendous leader and he's done brilliantly since he came back into the side. His performances have inspired the people around him. I can't praise him highly enough.' Pass me the smelling salts!

Our next game – Plymouth Argyle at Home Park; the papers in Burnley and Plymouth went to town. In the *Evening Telegraph*, the Incredible Hulk had turned Ghostbuster and was going back to bury the memory of his Home Park House of Horrors. And the *Plymouth Evening Herald* gave Warnock a chance to air his views: 'Peter is his own worst enemy. He's one of the best defenders in the league or one of the worst, depending on his mood. But he's done ever so well for Burnley lately. I didn't have any problems with Swanny. It's just that when I came to the club, he'd already made his mind up that he wanted to go.'

I'd told the lads about my time there and warned them what to expect. But even so, my reception surprised them. There were far more fans around than usual when we went out for the warm-up 40 minutes from the start. They'd come early just to have a go at me and the booing started as soon as I appeared. They were going mad. The rest of the boys couldn't believe it. When we got back into the dressing room, I joked, "It was like that when they were ON my side, never mind playing for the opposition."

We agreed that if I scored, I'd run back to the centre circle and stand with both arms raised. The Burnley lads would form a circle round me and go down on their hands and knees and pay homage. And it so nearly happened. There were chants of, "Greedy northern bastard," throughout the match, but late on, I had a shot cleared off the line that would have given us a 1 – 0 win – if only.

The following day's *Sunday Independent* summed up the mood in the South-West. 'For much of the second half with the game remaining goalless, the script appeared written in advance for Peter Swan to mark his Home Park return by seizing the decider from a Burnley set-piece. Such a miserable outcome didn't bear thinking about for the Argyle faithful who, judging by the boos that regularly accompanied every movement by Peter Shilton's record signing, still hadn't forgiven him for the derogatory comments he made about their club and city after bitterly regretting his West Country move. But even the most uncharitable had to admit that he commanded his territory with a masterly dominance that was singularly lacking when he wore an Argyle shirt.'

But even though Heath had gone public to say how well I was playing and I had said all the right things too, there was no real chance of us burying the hatchet behind the scenes. I was still on the transfer list and made no secret of my desire to get away. I also knew that Stan Ternent was keen to take me to Bury. They'd come up from Division three as champions and were in the process of winning back-to-back promotions. After I'd collected the Man of the Match award in a televised win over Bury in January, I bumped into Stan in the corridor. I pretended to be talking about the good old days at Hull, but when we were out of earshot, I said, "For fuck's sake Stan, get me out of here." He replied, "I'm trying Swanny, I'm trying."

On one occasion, I almost made it easier for him. We were getting ready to board the bus after an away game and I'd stashed two bottles of wine and six cans of beer in my Adidas bag as sustenance for the boys on the way home. All the bags were lined up outside the players' entrance waiting to be loaded as hand luggage and I was just about to collect mine when Heath beat me to it and picked it up instead of his own. I can't think how he didn't spot how heavy it was and take a look inside. I dashed over, explained that I'd got the wrong bag and made the switch. We were barely speaking at the time and if he'd discovered what was in the bag, I could have been on my bike.

Soon after the end of the season, Burnley and Bury agreed a fee of £50,000. I went to see Heath to check that Burnley would pay me the rest of my signing-on fee, something like 20 grand. He said he didn't think there'd be a problem. Compared with my previous moves it seemed a bit too straightforward and I wasn't entirely happy. I gave Stan a call. He wasn't interested in lengthy negotiations. He told me what was on offer, adding, "If you're not happy with that, don't bother coming." Like I said, Stan doesn't mince words. The money wasn't brilliant but I wanted to play for Stan again and even though Bury was a smaller club, they were going to be in a higher division. So, I said yes. When I got home, I switched on the teletext. Heath had left for Everton as number 2 to Howard Kendall.

Next day my first port of call was with Frank Teasdale, the Burnley chairman. I said, "You'll know I'm going to sign for Bury, but I just want to make sure that everything I agreed with Inchy is still OK." He had no idea about the transfer or paying the rest of my signing-on fee. The deal was off.

Chris Waddle took over, his first, and to date, only job in management. He was a hell of a big name and his appointment was seen as a coup, but it didn't work out and he left after one season. I spoke to him as soon as I could and told him I'd fixed up a move to Bury. He said we'd talk after a practice match between the first team and the reserves. I was half tempted to toss it off and not really bother, but instead I went out and had a blinder. I scored twice from centre-half. After that, I thought there was no way he'd let me go but he called me in and said, "Right, get yourself away." I signed for Stan soon afterwards.

Thankfully it was au revoir and not goodbye to one of the best clubs I played for and I'd be back at Turf Moor 12 months later.

***

From Chapter 16: Silence in Court

Stan Ternent was the reason I joined Bury. Most people saw it as a nothing club and, from the outside, there wasn't a lot going for it – except Stan. I had a lot of respect for him after our time at Hull City and he'd guided Bury to two successive promotions, so I reckoned it was worth a go. Stan was a strong character who wanted strong players around him. A lot of managers don't like forceful personalities in their squad; they're afraid their own authority might be undermined, but not Stan. He actively sought out strong players. Even though they might cause one or two problems off the field, he knew they'd always do the business once they crossed the white line.

And, there were some very forceful personalities at Bury, men like Ronnie Jepson, Gordon Armstrong, Andy Gray, Paul Butler, Chris Lucketti, Dean Kiely, David Johnson and Lenny Johnrose – and me. But Stan trusted us and while there may have been a few bust-ups, there was never any real bother.

His man-management was different class. I'd discovered that for the first time after I'd torn my cruciate ligament at Hull. Stan lived in Burnley and used to travel over to Humberside every day. Obviously I couldn't drive because of my knee, so twice a week he picked me up in Wakefield and took me over to Hull. I can't think of many managers who would do that. A lot of them prefer injured players to be out of sight, out of mind. But he knew I was desperate to stay involved with the boys, even though I couldn't train, and because he'd been prepared to go out of his way to help me, I was always ready to do the same for him. Maybe I would play with an injury when really I should have been sitting it out.

Stan didn't have a problem with his players having a drink the night before a game. He wanted the ones who enjoyed a pint to feel they could drink in front of him rather than go behind his back. On away trips at all the clubs I played for under Stan, he'd sometimes call us together in the hotel foyer before dinner. If there was a pub nearby, we'd pop out for a pint; if not, we'd use the hotel bar. Quite a few players didn't want alcohol and just had orange juice or a soft drink, but the important thing was that we went out together as a team. Then we'd go back for our evening meal and Stan would say that anyone who wanted another half, then or afterwards, there was no problem. He knew that if he played ball with us, we'd go out and give everything for him.

But, woe betide any player who crossed him or failed to give him 100%. His bollockings were legendary and if anyone didn't buy into his 'we're all pissing in the same pot' philosophy, they were out the door. Like any manager, he made one or two enemies over the years, but he's the best gaffer I've worked for. I always respected him and still do. A lot of his former players feel the same. I once called in at his home on my way to Burnley, where I was working for Radio Humberside. While I was there, Glen Little who'd played for him at Turf Moor, popped in for a chat and there was a phone call from Ronnie Jepson, another of Stan's ex-players …

… Every Friday morning, Stan held a court in the dressing room. He was the judge and stood up at the front of the courtroom. The players were the jury and we dealt with any petty offences that other players or staff might have committed during the week. We'd all troop into the dressing room and Stan would stand in judgement. He'd announce

Frank Hill took over as Burnley manager in 1948 and almost took the team to the first division title in the 1952/53 season

Picture courtesy Burnley FC

The team that came close to the 1952/53 title

From the author's collection

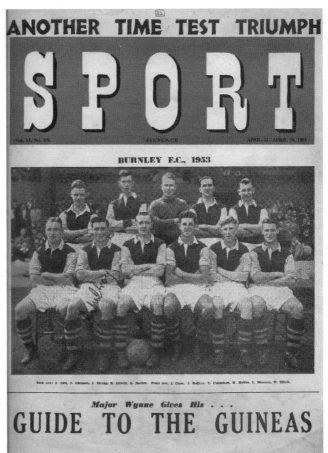

Harold Mather, a regular from 1946 to 1954, played 36 games in the 1952/53 season

Picture courtesy Burnley FC

Jimmy Strong, making a save in training, played for Burnley from 1946 to 1953

Picture courtesy Sandria Burkinshaw

Ian Lawson made an emphatic start to his Burnley career scoring four goals on his debut

Picture courtesy David Saffer

Brian Flynn at a book signing session in the club shop
Picture by Brian Speak

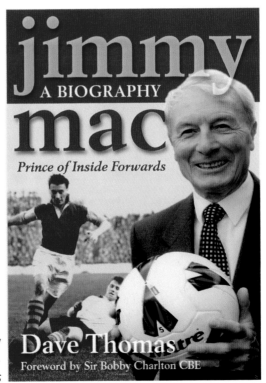

The Great Jimmy McIlroy
1931 to 2018.
Book cover by David Eaves

The young Jimmy Mac, destined for greatness

Picture courtesy of the McIlroy family

Jimmy Mac relaxes before a game with teammate Brian Pilkington

Picture courtesy of the McIlroy family

The author and Jimmy Mac during work on the biography and scrapbook in 2008

Picture by David Eaves

Paul Fletcher pictured on the cover of his autobiography *Magical*. A thoroughly entertaining book filled with great stories

Book cover by Vertical Editions

'Fletch' posing for a pre-season photoshoot in his playing days with Burnley

Clarke Carlisle. On the football field a true warrior and a Wembley hero
Courtesy of Burnley FC

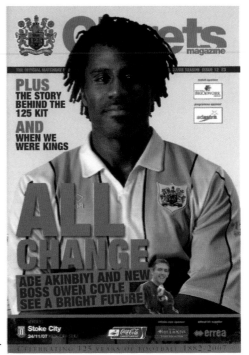

Ade Akinbiyi, a cult hero who scored a magical goal at Chelsea
Courtesy of Burnley FC

Champions!
Picture by Ron 'Rocket' Jenkins

Robbie Blake. A great
favourite at Turf Moor
and remembered for his
wonderful goal against
Manchester United.
Picture courtesy of Burnley FC

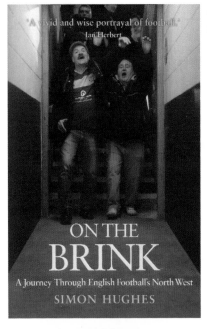

A superb Sean Dyche chapter
Courtesy of Simon Hughes

Burnley town and Turf landscape, the
stereotypical view of cobbled streets and mills
long gone
Picture by Mick Warn

Sean Dyche's Claret and Blue Army in London for the West Ham game
Picture by the author

that the court was in session and from then on, no-one was allowed to talk without the judge's permission. Anyone who did was fined. He had a handful of papers, each containing an offence committed by one of the lads. The accused would be asked to plead guilty or not guilty and could appeal against the sentence. A failed appeal might mean double the fine. We'd fine people three or four quid for things like wearing someone else's training kit, wearing flip flops in the car park, moving another player's car, bad haircuts, bad sense of fashion, and an offence created by Stan – being a complete pillock. That covered any minor offence not on the official hit list.

One of the players wrote down all the fines and they had to be paid within a week – or doubled. There'd be about £50 worth of fines each week and all the money went into a pool towards a day out at the races or a trip off somewhere else. I've never known it happen at any other club. It was great for team spirit and Stan loved every minute …

(When Stan Ternent left Bury to join Burnley as manager, it was Neil Warnock who took over at Gigg Lane. Peter Swan's last encounter with him had been at Plymouth. Swan's departure from Bury was therefore predictable enough. Within three weeks Stan Ternent took Swan to Burnley for his second spell there. DT)

∗∗∗

Chapter 17: The Beginning of the End

I returned to Turf Moor in time to play against Millwall on 1 September 1998. I felt as though I'd never been away. The fans gave me a standing ovation before the kick-off, we won 2 – 1 and I picked up the Man of the Match award. It was a false dawn … for both Burnley and me.

I'd been looking for a two-year deal, but Stan would only give me one. He liked to keep his players hungry; not a bad idea on balance. A three or four-year contract spells comfort zone to a lot of players, but the knowledge that you might get kicked out at the end of the season tends to focus the mind. It certainly did for me. I was only three weeks away from my thirty-second birthday.

After using me as a striker at Bury, Stan now wanted me to play at the back. I didn't have a problem with that but the season went pear-shaped more or less straightaway. In all, I only started 11 games and made six substitute appearances, but it was an on-off business all season long. I was sent off in my third game at Reading and it took the best part of a month to complete the three-match ban. Sometimes it can be over in a week. Then I missed a couple of games with a chest infection and seemed to struggle with one niggling injury after another.

The team never got off the ground, either. Stan had brought three of us with him from Bury, me, Ronnie Jepson and Gordon Armstrong, but he wasn't happy with the squad he inherited from Chris Waddle. And there wasn't much money to strengthen. At one point he sacked four players he believed were not pulling their weight and, by the time he turned on the town's Christmas lights, Burnley sat nineteenth in the table and Stan was public enemy number one.

When we travelled down to face Wycombe Wanderers on 20 February, we'd won just three of the last 14 games. We were heading for the relegation zone. Wycombe might easily have been the beginning of the end for Stan. Instead, it was the beginning of the end for me. And it started with a little pop in my right knee. Just like I'd felt at Hull nine years earlier. I started the game on the bench. Stan sent me on up front early in the second half. I went for a harmless 50-50 ball with a lad called Jason Cousins. His knee caught my knee. Pop, my knee buckled. I collapsed. Agony. Andy Jones ran on. "What's up?"

"My knee – just went pop."

"Get off and we'll have a look in the treatment room." Already I feared the worst. The St John's Ambulance team ran on with the stretcher and started trying to lift me on board. Stan wasn't having any of that.

"Fuck off you lot, leave my player alone." He called everyone off the Burnley bench and they carried me into the dressing room on the stretcher. My knee was numb. Andy put a compression bandage around it and, after the game, which we lost 2 – 0, I was lifted on to the bus for the journey back to Turf Moor.

I couldn't drive home so the club put me up in a hotel in Burnley for the night. The knee was heavily bandaged and I was due to have a scan the following morning. When I got to my room, the pain had eased a lot so I took off the bandages and went for an exploratory trot along the corridor. The knee felt fine. I convinced myself that I had got away with it. But the next morning's scan confirmed my worst fears. The cruciate had snapped.

It couldn't have happened at a worse time. There were three months of the season to go and it would be nine months before I would be fit again. My contract was due to expire in the summer; I had a wife and two kids to support and I was knackered. I went back to the ground with Andy. Stan sent for me. He asked if there was any particular surgeon I wanted to do the op. A consultant called David Dandy from Cambridge had done the same operation on Paul Gascoigne eight years earlier so I said I'd see him. The club made an appointment. I was also booked in at Lilleshall for some rehab work in the hope that an operation might not be necessary. After all, I'd got away with it at Hull in 1990, why not now?

I drove to Cambridge from Lilleshall on my own. The appointment didn't last long. I climbed on the couch. Mr Dandy took hold of my heel and foot, lifted my leg, twisted and pushed at the same time … POP… operation. He was going to take a section of my right hamstring and staple it to my kneecap as a replacement ligament. I walked back to the car and rang Stan. As I started to speak I began to cry. That doesn't happen often, believe me, but all of a sudden the reality had hit me. I believed to all intents and purposes my career was over. I turned the phone off.

When I thought I was OK to talk, I switched it back on and rang again. Stan said he'd been trying to get back to me. He must have noticed there was a catch in my voice. "Are you down there by yourself?"

"Yeah."

"WHAT! Right, leave that with me. Get yourself back up here and we'll talk as soon as you arrive."

I suspect someone at Turf Moor was about to cop for a massive bollocking for letting me go to the appointment on my own. I saw Stan as soon as I arrived. He said, "Get yourself booked in and have the operation." Then he shook my hand and looked me straight in the eye. "And I'll look after you until you're fit again."

"But my contract expires …"

"Don't worry about that. I'll look after you."

I had to wait for the swelling to go down before Mr Dandy could operate, so it wasn't until the last week of the season that I caught a train down to Cambridge. I was in for four days, on my own and with no visitors, but that didn't bother me. On the third day, I had a call from the lads. They'd just arrived in Northampton for the last game of the season and wished me all the best. To rub it in, I had another call later to say how much they'd miss me at the end of season piss-up that night. The following day, Bex drove down and took me home.

At least the boys had something to celebrate: survival. After the Wycombe defeat, Burnley had lost their next three games, 5 – 0 against Gillingham, 6 – 0 against Manchester City and 1 – 0 to Preston, all at home. We were in the drop zone and a 1 – 1 draw at Wrexham hardly looked as though it was going to save Stan. If he'd gone then, there would be no-one round to look after me, but the board held their nerve and Stan stayed. We beat Macclesfield 4 – 3 next up and didn't lose again all season, finishing fifteenth.

We all knew there were going to be big changes in the summer. Barry Kilby, who'd taken over as chairman midway through the previous season, was prepared to put a bit of money in and I sensed there was a feeling among some board members that I wasn't going to be much use to the new-look Burnley. Swanny was coming up to 33, was out of action and out of contract. In their minds, it was time to move him out. But Stan stood by me and fought my corner. There was no way he could give me a one-year deal, but he set me up on a month-to-month basis until I had a chance to prove my fitness.

I spent hours working on my own, on the track and in the gym that was part of a new leisure complex behind the Longside Stand at Turf Moor. It was a long and boring grind. When I'd finished I used to nip into the café and have a coffee with anyone who happened to be around. I became pals with a chap called Jim Fallon. He was blind. He and a mate used to come and play indoor bowls and worked out in the gym as well. And with Jim around I was never short of a laugh.

I was always trying to wind him up but he obviously had a sixth sense that I was around. If he was on the treadmill, I'd sneak up behind him. I'd be about to move it up a gear when he'd call out, "Swanny I know you're there." Or if he was doing weights I'd try and move the pegs so he was lifting a heavier weight. But I never got away with it.

Because he was blind I suppose people were afraid to take the piss out of him. Not me: what's more, he used to have a go back.

I finally came out on top when he was playing in a bowls match against a pair of women. Jim and his mate were bottom of the league and I used to rib them about it. One day, Jim told me his pal wouldn't be around for the game the following week so did I fancy taking his place? I turned up for the match and asked him what I was supposed to do while he was bowling. "You line me up right and tell me how far the jack is from the end of the mat."

"Ok." I guided Jim to his starting position, told him where the jack was and then lined him up … facing the wrong way. He was three feet away from the concrete wall instead of 45 feet away from the jack. When he let go of the ball, it hit the wall with a crack and then rebounded into Jim, sending him flying backwards onto the mat. Our opponents didn't see the funny side of it, but Jim was killing himself and it took five minutes before we settled him down and he was ready to start for real.

Three months after the op, I had to go back to Cambridge to make sure everything was OK. It was. I could step up my schedule but pre-season had come and gone without me. Jeppo and the rest of the lads did their best to involve me in the banter, but until I could train properly I was just an outsider looking in. I had to see the physio every Monday morning, first Andy and then Paul Lake who took over when he left to check how things were going. They wanted to see if my movement had improved, if the knee was stronger, if there was any unexpected swelling. And each week I was able to step up my workload a little bit. It meant less time in the gym and more on the training ground.

Every week I was told that if I had any pain I had to stop and take it easy for a while. That was vital. If it hurts, stop. They told me time and time again but I'd never worried about pain before. I'd always reckoned that pain was a temporary thing to put up with, so I took no notice. Even though my body was yelling at me to slow down and take it easy, I ignored the warning signs and insisted I wasn't in pain. So, every Monday, I told a load of half-truths and was given the go-ahead to move up another gear. And, there was another reason to rush back ahead of schedule. I'd felt all along that I had to repay Stan. He could easily have let me go when my contract expired. But he hadn't. He'd kept his word, and in November, after 7 months of what should have been a 9-month rehab, I said I was OK to give it a go in the reserves against Oldham. It was madness. Jeppo was also playing and he kept chivvying me along. I played for 45 minutes and then called it a day.

To be honest, I could have come off after 10 minutes because I knew straightaway that I wasn't ready. I spoke to the local reporter afterwards and told him that it had gone really well but I'd decided enough was enough at half-time. That was a signal for a summons from Stan the next day. He told me in no uncertain terms that he made the decisions at Turf Moor, not his players. Then he asked how it had gone. "Fine," I lied. "Yeah, it went really well."

But the knee wasn't fine and the more I pushed myself, the more it complained. I was living with pain 24 hours a day and firing down the painkillers every three or four hours. It was the only way I could get through training. In the end, my stomach rebelled against the constant bombardment from painkillers. I started passing blood. I'd be standing at a bar, sitting in the car or walking around town when I'd feel the tell-tale signs in the seat of my underpants. Did I heed the warning? Did I fuck! All I was interested in was a new contract or a move and another years' football.

So, instead of the tablets I used suppositories, four a day, just to train. Obviously I couldn't get them from the club doctor because he would have reported back to Stan. So, I went to my own GP and managed to convince him that everything was above board. Incredibly, nobody found out. I used to flush the empty suppository tubes down the bog but sometimes I needed two or three attempts before they went away.

Once, one of the lads followed me in and spotted the empty tube. "Who's sticking these things up their arse?" Nobody answered and I never said a word. If anyone had told Stan, I'd have been flushed out, as it were.

It was hopeless. Because I was coming back from such a long-term injury, other parts of the body started to play up: ankle, Achilles, calf. I used to go to the sauna or have a Jacuzzi to try and loosen up the joints. I'd stay in for hours at a time. I got up early to do extra gym work before training, just so I'd be reasonably loose.

It was around then that I had my first real bust-up with Stan. I'd put a bit of weight on while I was out of action and I couldn't lose it because I wasn't training properly. I cut down on how much I ate. I even cut down on the booze but no joy. After I'd played a couple of reserve games, Stan called me in. "Look Swanny, you've got to lose some weight. If you don't, I'll have to get rid of you." I thought he was just looking for an excuse.

"Right, fucking well get rid of me then!" And I stormed out of his office.

I came off the bench in a couple of first-team games in January, but I knew it wasn't right. I'd done everything and it hadn't worked. One day at the beginning of March, just over a year since the injury, I was late for training. Stan saw me arrive, which would normally have meant an automatic fine. Instead he just said, "Morning Swanny, all right?"

"Yeah fine Gaffer … you?"

"Yeah," but I sensed something was wrong. After training he said, "Can I have a word?" I knew what was coming. We went into his office.

"I'm going to have to let you go," he said.

I stood up, shook hands. "OK, thanks for keeping your word and standing by me. That's meant a lot. I'm fit again. I've got a chance."

"I'll make a few phone calls; try and sort something out for you," he said.

"Thanks, I appreciate that." We shook hands again. I walked away from Burnley for the last time. It was a lonely drive home and my knee was killing me all the way. For me, the Turf Moor party was over.

But for Burnley it had only just begun. And the man who lit the spark was a football legend: Ian Wright, who'd arrived not long before I left. The boys had been up with the front runners all season without attracting too much attention, but when news leaked out that Wright, Arsenal's all-time record goalscorer with 33 England caps to his name, might be on his way to Turf Moor, the football world sat up and took notice. He'd joined Celtic from West Ham in October 1999, but it hadn't worked out. Stan heard on the grapevine that he might be available but it looked a long shot. Wright was 36, a London legend, and the word was that if he was going anywhere he'd be on his way back to the smoke. But Stan didn't give up and on Valentine's Day 2000, a month before I left the club, he pulled his rabbit out of the hat. Wrighty joined the Clarets – lights, camera, action!

Wrighty had an incredible impact at the club and in the town. He had an aura about him, and at a stroke, Stan convinced people inside and outside Burnley that he meant business. The media came calling and over 20,000 fans rolled up for his first game against Wigan, an increase of 7,000 on the previous match against Bristol Rovers. It was a goalless draw. Wrighty started only four games, made 11 substitute appearances and scored four goals. But his presence set the dressing room alight and sparked a successful promotion challenge. After losing the next two games, Burnley won nine of their last 13 games and clinched promotion at Scunthorpe on the final day of the season.

I was long gone by then, of course, but I'd still had time to write my name into Wright's legend. I'd always admired him. He was a fantastic player, a natural goalscorer and a great personality. And I wanted a slice of the action. Needless to say, the YTS lads were queuing up to be his boot boy, but they reckoned without me and Jeppo. On his first day we strode into the boot room. "Who's doing Wrighty's boots?" One of the kids put his hand up. "Right, fuck off!"

Jeppo took the right foot and I took the left. We cleaned his boots, trainers, rubbers, the lot. We were like two big kids. I can still see Jeppo, fag in the corner of his mouth, giving Wrighty's right boot an extra shine, talking about his impact on the training ground and how good his sessions with the strikers were. I'm sure Ian had no idea who his boot boys really were. He certainly didn't offer us any tips. But to this day, Jeppo and I can sit back over a pint and tell anyone who's prepared to listen that we were once Ian Wright's boot boys.

Burnley was a great place to be. Even though I was playing at the third level of English football, I always felt the club belonged much higher up the ladder. The facilities were good and you could almost smell the tradition behind a club that had been a founder member of the Football League way back in 1888. It always felt like a big club waiting to happen.

And, the fans were something else. The ground is surrounded by terraced streets where everyone seems to be a Clarets supporter. I used to do some coaching in local schools and all the kids would be wearing the claret and blue of Burnley, not Premier League strips belonging to clubs based somewhere over the horizon. These were Burnley kids; they supported their home town team and they were proud of it.

I was chuffed to bits when news came through that Burnley were back in what is now the Championship. They've been there ever since. Will they ever go back to where they belong in the top flight? It won't be easy but I for one would love to see them do it.

6

A Game and a Player to Remember

Luton 2 Burnley 3 and Ade Akinbiyi, from *Something to Write Home About,* the magazine of the London Clarets. Article by Dave Thomas

Is it possible that there has been, over the years, a player more popular at Burnley than Ade Akinbiyi; a player who left the club possibly both a legend and a cult figure?

What is a legend; is it a particular long-serving character famous for their skills, deeds or talents maybe? Or is it a story or set of stories about someone that have grown over the years? It is possible that both these definitions apply to him.

What is a cult figure? Perhaps we all have our different interpretations. Is it someone, not necessarily hugely talented or even long-serving, but who has made a great contribution to a club, uniquely entertaining us, and for whom we feel deep affection and has left an indelible mark on our memories?

Ade certainly had a talent and that talent was scoring goals. The story that he was utterly bad at this is totally inaccurate, but that is the legend that developed, at one club in particular, Leicester City. The band of Burnley supporters who were at Luton on November 5th, 2005, would disagree having seen at first-hand what an in-form Akinbiyi was capable of. It will be a day that neither they nor he will ever forget.

In truth, at Burnley on other occasions, he missed sitters that Harry Redknapp might say his wife could have scored, but then so do all other strikers on a bad day. In many other games he displayed all the things that he was good at, and the attributes that he had in abundance.

If he left Burnley a legend and cult hero, just how then did he do this? Here was a player of no great finesse or technical ability. He had no great elegance either in the air or on the ground; he couldn't shoot with unerring accuracy like a Malcolm Macdonald or head a ball like an Alan Shearer, and he moved from club to club with clockwork regularity.

But he had talent and it was based on running, strength, power, size, pace and muscle and very often being in the right place at the right time. On this he founded a lucrative career and his popularity at Burnley will remain undimmed.

Burnley fans will remember him for moments of glory – the hat trick at Luton when Burnley were reduced to ten men and goalkeeper Jensen had been replaced by midfield player John Spicer. This was a game that belonged to Ade Akinbiyi first and then John Spicer second. And then there was the never-to-be-forgotten night at Chelsea when his superb strike levelled the score and set up extra-time and the penalty win. He was not in the starting eleven, but when he came on he changed the pattern of the game and Chelsea feathers were seriously ruffled.

If those are the two events that secured his legend and cult figure status they contrast hugely with the impact of his debut. Within three minutes of coming onto the field as a substitute he was sent off for the perfect head-butt on Sunderland defender George McCartney. Debuts don't come more spectacularly than that and it still makes us shake our heads in disbelief. It was so unexpected, so outrageous, so daft, that contrasting with the inherent goodness and honesty in him, it instantly made him a cult figure.

In between the head-butt and the goal at Chelsea he ran and ran, tried and tried, was totally honest and fair, and behind the scenes we were told he was a thoroughly nice guy, a great clubman who went out of his way to mentor people like Jay Rodriguez. His celebration after the latter's goal against Tottenham in the Carling Cup semi-final was almost as memorable as the goal itself and he clearly shared Rodriguez's joy.

In his first spell at Burnley, 2005 to 2006, he played superbly well and his arrival was the result of a game for Stoke City at Turf Moor when he and Noel Gifton-Williams ran Burnley ragged. He scored twice. Manager Steve Cotterill clearly memorised the two names and eventually brought them both to Burnley. At Stoke he had asked to see the chairman and made it clear to him that he didn't think the club was going forward. Sheffield United reputedly matched the asking fee but Akinbiyi chose Burnley. In spite of his 'protest' at the running of Stoke City, paradoxically he did not really want to leave, he said, and the move to Burnley took a while to sort out. He had already played with Frank Sinclair at Leicester, and it was Sinclair who helped persuade him that Burnley was a fine club to join.

"I just like working hard," he revealed in club programme notes, "You're always going to get me running round like a headless chicken, but that's what I'm all about."

His debut was delayed because of a thigh strain and the TV cameras were there for the game when he made his first appearance. "That's the game I'm aiming for. I need to settle down and get back on the pitch doing what I do," he said beforehand; keen to kick-start his career with his new team. Head-butting someone within minutes was in no way what he usually did.

In that first period at Turf Moor Akinbiyi's career seemed revitalised. He ran, chased, covered every inch of ground and scored goals. He was almost prolific, 16 goals in 39 games, a more than excellent return for a modern-day striker. Warnock at Sheffield United, by then in the Premiership, was thus tempted to take him to Sheffield for £1.75million but there he did little of note other than incur the wrath of the manager who allegedly berated him on one occasion for not deliberately going down under a penalty area challenge. He preferred to be honest and stayed on his feet. He did not score and thus Neil Warnock was not best pleased.

In his second spell at Burnley, 2007 to 2009, brought back for a much smaller fee, looking more like Hercules than a professional footballer after all his weight training, he was less impressive, sometimes assuming the mantle of the old Ade (Leicester City) who on some days seemed incapable of hitting a barn door with a banjo. And yet we smiled, continued to give him our respect and just accepted his shortcomings. "Well that's Ade," we would say, and shrug with a sort of wry, benign acceptance. With other players we would be far less charitable.

Into the early months of 2009 and it was clear he had lost many of the qualities that made him what he was. The running and chasing decreased and the acceleration was gone. Now aged 34, the heart might have been willing, but the legs were older. Some players with a more slender, wiry physique might continue far longer than that, but big players whose games are based solely on power and running, seldom do.

We will not forget Ade, that is a certainty and it is perhaps that one goal at Chelsea that finally sealed and confirmed his place in Burnley hearts. Ironically it was at a time when his powers were certainly declining; he was used from the bench as an impact player. How it paid off.

***

Sixteen years earlier his career began at Norwich in 1993 where he made 49 appearances, scoring three goals. The son of Nigerian parents, he was brought up in multicultural Hackney in London. Gang culture was rife. He was an Arsenal supporter and in his early teens was more interested in athletics than football, the 100m and the 200m his best events. It was a PE teacher who nudged him towards soccer. The teacher said they needed a striker for the school team so he volunteered. He then played for Senrab, an East London team that also produced Ledley King and John Terry. Muzzy Izzet played alongside him there and Lee Bowyer was a year younger. He wanted to stay in London and sign for Arsenal but with the choice of Arsenal or Norwich, his parents wanted him to get away from London teenage street-life and all its attendant pressures and problems.

Moving to Norwich at the age of 16, in digs with an elderly lady in the middle of the countryside, was a great culture shock. Looking back he thinks they both found it difficult. Not the least of the difficulties was the food she made. From a Nigerian-based diet of rice and chicken, his landlady made potatoes and roast dinners. He returned home as often as he could.

His racial difference in Norwich was very apparent. 1993 might not seem that long ago, but it was far back enough for skin colour to stand out in a predominantly white place like Norwich. He found it a relief to see another black face. Standing at bus stops waiting for the bus for training was not easy. To avoid this he would often walk rather than wait in a queue. He was only 16, ill at ease, feeling vulnerable and worried.

In his early days he remembers that the abuse, both racial and non-racial, was endemic. His mother never liked seeing him play because of the swearing and the shouting.

His background and culture is clearly important to him. At one club another black player referred to him as "African this" and "African that." It was banter but it was clear that the other player had no concept of his roots until Akinbiyi pointed out to him that they were all from Africa. At another club, young kids wanted to touch his hair. He let them do it seeing it as an important step in their learning. Learning is important to him, reading about history and other cultures and passing these on to his own son.

In his very early days at Norwich the team was doing well in Europe. Under Mike Walker they were a force to be reckoned with. During training one day, Walker called him over, told him one of the strikers was injured and that he would be in the squad for the Bayern Munich game at Carrow Road. He was only 18 and had never played a game for the first team.

"It was a bit of a shock to make my debut coming on against Lothar Matthaus and Bayern Munich. I couldn't believe it.

"So I got in the team, scored some goals but then Norwich said they needed some money so they offloaded me (after loan moves to Hereford and then Brighton). I went to Gillingham for £250,000 where Tony Pulis did a lot of work on my finishing."

From there, 29 goals later in 67 games, no mean return for a modern day striker; it was a £1.2million move to Bristol City. 23 goals came in his first season. And this prompted the first really big money move – £3million to Wolves. Fulham and Birmingham were reportedly also pursuing him but Akinbiyi was swayed, and understandably so, by the history and tradition at Wolves, the big stadium, the ambition and the training ground. All these made him feel this was the right club.

"I could see it happening for me at Wolves, they are a massive club. I settled in well." He thought he would be there for years, scored 16 goals in 37 appearances but then it was the next move. Again he says it was the old story. Having missed the play-offs by one place, Wolves needed money so that when Leicester and Peter Taylor came knocking on the door, a £5million deal took him to Filbert Street.

Things here did not go well and he looks back at this period with no real fondness. A return of 11 goals from 58 appearances earned him poor reviews and much criticism. At the end of his second season Leicester were relegated. The outstanding Martin O'Neil had left, and under Peter Taylor Leicester went into freefall. Akinbiyi had been the replacement for Emile Heskey and life in the Premiership, against top-quality defenders, was far harder than anything he had experienced. Today he suggests that whilst Wolves played to his strengths, Leicester City did not. Eventually Taylor was sacked.

All these things conspired to make him look like a fish out of water in many games, and it was at Leicester that a long spell when he was unable to find the net earned him some cruel comments and national notoriety when at last the drought was broken and the match was featured on *Match of the Day*. But in truth, Ade Akinbiyi was never as bad as his time at Leicester might suggest. His goal record there was not that much inferior to the low-scoring Emile Heskey. Emile Heskey too went through periods when his detractors were numerous.

Crystal Palace rescued Akinbiyi from his misery but his stay there was short-lived as Tony Pulis, now at Stoke City, took him on loan and then made the signing permanent. At Stoke it was 19 goals in 63 games. Not prolific you might say but certainly not disastrous.

Steve Cotterill took Akinbiyi to Burnley and it was an inspired purchase. He was 30 and it could be said hit peak form in his first spell at Turf Moor. 16 goals in 39 games was excellent and some of them were stunning. His infectious enthusiasm, huge smile, willingness to run and pressure the opposition; his workrate, all endeared him to Burnley fans. The latter can spot a phoney a mile away and they recognised in Akinbiyi a genuine player. His own explanation for his popularity is simple. "I think if you work hard the fans will give you praise and if you aren't working hard they'll give you stick so that's part and parcel of it all. I want to go out there and, even if I'm not scoring, I want to work hard and give 100%. There are going to be days when I don't play well, because as good as you get, you can also be bad too but I want to work hard every week and keep going."

His departure from Burnley was for the same old reason, his club needed the money. But having said that, even if cash-strapped Burnley had been better off, it was still an offer that was too good to turn down – £1.75million for a 30 year old. Neil Warnock wanted an in-form striker for his Premiership team but his appearances there were just three.

It was not a happy stay and there were stories of a major training ground confrontation involving himself and Claude Davis. Allegedly the incident happened after insulting text messages were sent to Akinbiyi by Davis. These followed Akinbiyi's jokes about Davis' poor performance in a game at Everton when United lost 2 – 0. The face to face row broke out when Davis reportedly made remarks about one of Akinbiyi's parents and the pair decided to resolve their differences at the training ground. Sources claimed that punches were thrown and it was also alleged that Davis pulled out a razor, although Akinbiyi would never confirm this.

Akinbiyi was, in fact, quite angry that this story ever became public. "There was a row lasting about two minutes," he said. "But where do you get all this stuff from?" he asked reporters.

His return to Burnley after the brief unsuccessful sojourn at Sheffield United prompted Rod Liddle in the *Sunday Times* to write a delightful, tongue-in-cheek piece about him. He asked the question – just what was it that managers did in January, when the play-offs were still a distant target; the place needed a lift, the fans needed cheering up, the season needed saving or disaster needed avoiding. Bizarrely, he wrote, the answer is that they inevitably turned to Ade Akinbiyi as the solution to their problems.

'Every January, long before the hounds of spring are on winter's traces, the ground is hard with frost and the play-offs still beckon, tantalisingly in the middle distance, football managers sit themselves down, wracked in deep thought. What, they ask themselves, will save this season from being a complete and utter disaster? Is there a panacea immediately at hand, which will rescue my team and thus my job? Is there something, short of divine intervention, which when visited upon my squad of petulant and underachieving monkeys will enable them to soar?

And, bizarrely, the answer they frequently, repeatedly, arrive at is this: Ade Akinbiyi ...

... The wheeling and dealing of January rarely has a real impact upon the comparative fortunes of the teams in question, much as we supporters might lick our lips in anticipation. Poor players go to poor clubs; average players go to average clubs. The best players end up at Manchester United, Chelsea, Arsenal and Liverpool. And somebody, somewhere, gets Ade Akinbiyi.'

Such articles, (though I stress again, it is a piece and written with humour and affection), do not upset Ade Akinbiyi; nor did the catcalls at Leicester City.

"I don't care if I am playing in front of 100,000 people all giving me stick. I will never hide because I love football. People watch me and say this boy's a hard-working boy, he's not hiding. I can miss as many chances as I want but I won't care, I will carry on playing. I would die for football. Football's a short career; you have to earn as much as you can and enjoy yourself. Ten years ago, a lot of professionals enjoyed football. Now it's totally different, football is more of a job for players. It's more about politics and money. It's a 50 – 50 split between those players who enjoy football and those for whom it's a job. Me? I enjoy every minute. The more that fans and media try to hammer me, the more I enjoy football. Criticism just gees me up more. Even though I don't read the papers, my friends do, and the criticism gets back to me. I don't have to prove them wrong. I just have to prove to myself right that I can rise above this."

Ian Wright said something to him in his teens when he was briefly at Arsenal. "Wrighty made one statement which I have never forgotten: 'I never care whether I am playing in the reserves or the first-team, as long as I am playing.'"

Overall, his goal-scoring record is just about a goal every three games. It is no Jimmy Greaves (but then Greaves was a one-off), but it is very acceptable and only his short time at Leicester City was a disaster.

Three of those goals came in one memorable game. It was November 5th, 2005, bonfire night, and oh how the fireworks went off after the astonishing result at Kenilworth Road. Steve Cotterill was Burnley manager and he had placed his faith in Akinbiyi when he bought him. Burnley had only won six games up to this point, but the Luton result came in a spell of four consecutive wins which gave grounds for optimism and the club moved up the table. That promise never materialised. There were a number of reasons and Cotterill, in a later season, would eventually take the club to a record sequence of 20 games without a win. On November 5th, however, the trials and tribulations that would beset team and manager were yet to come and the supporters who had made the trip to Luton went home with their disbelieving heads in the clouds after a quite remarkable game, an extraordinary team performance, and a quite superlative individual display from Akinbiyi.

Barry Heagin also wrote a report on the Luton 2 Burnley 3 game in *Something to Write Home About*:

I guess when Stan Ternent let Marlene Beresford go some years ago after a particularly disastrous season as regards the goals against column, he could not have envisaged said keeper performing successfully at Championship level in season 2005/06. After 300+ games for the Clarets in three separate spells starting in the early Jurassic period, I have to acknowledge a modicum of pleasure in seeing the old girl again, albeit on the opposition side. Only David Eyres, that well known footballing pensioner, challenges Marlene on that score. Anyway, I digress, as the story I am about to reveal dear readers, is one of heroism shown by the greater Claret empire against great odds. It involves three keepers, one of the 'parks' variety, and provides a denouement that Hitchcock would have been proud of. In years to come, more people will have claimed presence at this game than at the infamous Plymouth play-off away game back in the last century. Sit down and enjoy.

Once upon a time there was a football ground, Kenilworth Road by name, with a very silly entrance to the away supporters' cage. The turnstiles, as some will know, are situated where the front room of some long deceased Lutonian's terraced house had been, before the bulldozer moved in. To the left of the entrance was the kitchen, now masquerading as a gents' toilet, and in front are the steps leading up to the back of the away cage entrance over some poor soul's bijou back yard. How they must hate match days. One then pays the 20 quid-plus entrance fee for the privilege of joining 800 or so Clarets for an almost unimpeded view, whilst sitting on seats bolted to the terraces. Well that's entertainment! My particular favourites here, however, are the 'boxes' to the left of the away end, down the whole of a long side.

Little beauties these are, about the size of my shed, with netting over the top to stop the loss of expensive footballs in the adjoining back yards. It is also incredibly odd that alcoholic refreshment is available throughout the ground except for the away end. Why is this?

Apparently Luton FC were looking to move out of Luton to a new site near the airport. Not a bad move, you would have thought, given the lack of attraction in this sixties, slightly Watfordish place. It's one of those places where you would be tempted to call in a napalm strike if you just happened to be George W Bush for the day. It looks even worse on the sort of overcast, drizzly afternoon that was the setting for this fixture. The football club board allegedly made a complete arse of the exercise and have lost the opportunity, which has caused their manager Mike Newell to be a trifle upset. Apparently he was the last person to be told, sometime after the world at large.

The game started slowly for us, as Luton tested the young debutante full-back, Duane Courtney, with Feeney's movement and Howard's height. The latter had strength in the air and on the ball, but the full turning circle of the QE2. Jensen had hardly broken sweat, however, before we took the lead on 15 minutes. Ade and Spencer combined well from a quick throw-in before the latter released the former on goal. Ade outstripped Perret with ease before a snap shot left Marlene well beaten and we were on our way. Goal one for Ade, if only he knew what was to come. It was to be his afternoon.

A good Jensen save from a Howard free kick shortly thereafter neatly led to a doubling of the lead with a tremendous goal on the half hour. Spicer, having robbed Foley, again released Akinbiyi behind the Luton defence with a superb chip. This left THE man still with something to do as Marlene steadied himself for the shot. But the ex-Claret man needn't have bothered, as a tremendous half volley from the edge of the box arrowed its way to the top right hand corner of the net. It was a simply stunning goal, as good a goal as Akinbiyi has ever scored, as good a goal as you will see anywhere.

But then, in the 38th minute, a key moment when a long hopeful ball made its way towards Jensen with the Luton forwards some distance away. Not for the first time Jensen had options and couldn't make up his mind. Kick the ball into the stands, or wait for the ball to reach him in the safety of his own box. Nothing here to disturb the decision-

making capability of the average twelve year old, you might think, but not our Brian. With time to spare he runs out of the penalty area and catches the ball. Cast iron, red card and the team then made their way to the bench to waste a good deal of time until we were ready to start again. The only problem was that not only did we not have a keeper on the bench, but also our 'potentials' Duff and Branch were absent. Enter the frame, a very slight 22 year-old in a rather large keeper's jersey/tent. Master Spicer of all people had decided to resurrect his goalkeeping interest from his parks football days.

Inevitably Luton put the pressure on with a series of corners, from which Howard pulled a goal back with a firm header on 43 minutes with Spicer crunched between two defenders on the line.

Down to ten men, a rookie goalkeeper normally a deft, subtle, polite, gentle midfielder, the pressure on, Luton trailing by just one goal; but enter the man of the game again – one Ade Akinbiyi who has spent the game terrorising Luton with his every touch.

Luton tried the up and under game, meat and drink to the aged ones at the heart of the defence – not really very bright and known as doing a 'Prescott' in the manner of one of the more celebrated icons of the political establishment. For their dimness they were duly punished.

Micah Hyde an old head on young shoulders plays a long ball down the wing for Ade to chase. Ade in full flight is an awesome sight even on one of his bad days – but this day is one of his good ones, nay brilliant ones. The Luton defender is left for dead but for his impudence Ade is dumped in the penalty area for a blatant penalty.

Ade takes the ball; he has never taken a penalty in his life before, except in the school playground. Marlene at Burnley had a great reputation as a penalty saver but this one he does not save. Akinbiyi sends him the wrong way and claims his hat-trick wheeling away with extravagant exultation and wild, unrestrained joy.

A hat-trick is an achievement on any day, but in the context of this particular game was astonishing. Luton stepped up a gear, more pressure, more shots, but saved by rookie Spicer. Eventually though Feeney scored the Luton second. The support from the away end reached fever pitch, the minutes ticked by. When a last gasp Luton free kick sailed over the bar we knew Burnley had done it. The Clarets engaged in a post-match huddle and at last Ade emerged from the pack to retrieve the match-ball from the officials.

Exhausted and hoarse, Clarets spilled out from the ground into the night to ruminate upon the afternoon's entertainment. This is what real, live football is all about. If you weren't there for some reason, shed a tear.

***

The record books show just a 3 – 2 win. What they do not explain is that two men were heroes. Of those two however, one was a giant on the day and virtually unplayable. Time flies. Only one of the team, Jensen, remains at Burnley in 2009. Nobody who was there that day will forget his gigantic performance. It was one of those matches of a lifetime and a game to remember for a long, long time.

ADE IS NEW BIONIC MAN wrote reporter Chris Boden in the local *Burnley Express*:

'And Ade Akinbiyi will go down in Burnley history as their own bionic man after this superhuman effort. Akinbiyi performed incredible feats of strength and speed to fire the Clarets into a 2 – 0 lead, and, as part of a monumental team effort put in a selfless shift of great discipline down the left after the break as ten-man Burnley reshuffled following the dismissal of Brian Jensen, winning and scoring what proved to be the match-winning penalty. He was simply unstoppable, occupying and terrifying Luton's back four with devastating pace and power. Now, only Lee Trundle and Frank Lampard have scored more goals this season in the entire country.

And all that in boots he only picked up at 2:50 p.m. He had split his normal pair in training on Friday and, after a frantic dash, he got a new pair just in time. They may now be hung up after one incredible 90 minutes.

It was six years virtually to the day since his last treble, scored for Wolves against Grimsby. They were part of a tally of 18 that earned him a big move to the Premiership with Leicester, but they could scarcely have been more impressive than Saturday's haul. He looks an absolute steal by Steve Cotterill at £600,000.'

"This was the best victory of my career," said manager Steve Cotterill. A major factor was the performance of Ade Akinbiyi. I think a few people raised their eyebrows when we signed Ade, but they probably have their eyes shut now. Everyone has been signing the match ball. I love him, the players love him and a few girls in the office love him. I thought the first two goals came out of absolutely nothing and he showed his power and pace. I told him at half time to make sure he collected the match ball. His hunger and desire to do that was fantastic and he tucked the penalty away nicely."

One Burnley fan who was there, Matt Trickett, will never forget the day. "Ade ripped Luton apart single-handedly, grabbing a stunning hat-trick. It's fair to say his resurrection as a footballer began at Stoke – but during his short time at Burnley, it was complete. I'm confident Burnley could add an extra digit to the fee paid for his services earlier this year. This was one of those games where you willed the ball to be sucked towards him at every opportunity; such was his presence and superiority over the Luton defence. He appeared to have gained an extra five yards of pace and was simply unstoppable running at them."

Matt Trickett was particularly impressed by the second goal. "Outpacing the defence Ade slammed a stunning half volley into the roof of the net and went on a victory run around the pitch that silenced three sides of the ground and had the away end going wild. It's a long time since I've seen such a display of pace and power from a Claret forward.

"We'd seen something special," said Trickett. It was the game of a lifetime and a match to remember for all who were there.

* * *

Ade's career at Burnley ended when he moved to Houston Dynamo towards the end of 2008/09 with manager Coyle looking to reduce the age of the strike force and the wage bill. There was conjecture at the time that Burnley were leaving themselves a little thin on the ground up front but with the emergence of Jay Rodriguez the cover was there. "You never know what's round the corner," said Akinbiyi as he jetted off to Major League Soccer with everyone's best wishes. He missed out on the great day at Wembley as it took place between away games at San Jose Earthquakes and Toronto FC. Given the chance he would have flown back to be there. His sojourn in the USA was not to last long though. He had been rushed out there, he wasn't fully match fit, Houston were winning and it was hard for him to get into a starting eleven. He was coming on as a sub for 15 or 20 minute spells, but never really got used to the jet lag and constant flying between games. In hindsight he feels that he should have gone out there just to look at first and he is now back in the UK following his release by Houston. The Houston interlude did not go to plan at all but he has no regrets and thinks he may well return there one day to do some coaching.

He had two surprises on his return. Firstly there was a letter and a medal waiting for him sent by Owen Coyle. "I'd just got home from America and there was a parcel with a medal and a letter in it from Owen Coyle," he said. "I'm going to frame it along with the letter." Although he only started one game in that magical season he had made 15 appearances. His medal was therefore justly deserved. He had thought about ending his career at Burnley but it was Coyle who persuaded him to carry on for as long as he could.

If the medal and letter was a surprise, perhaps an approach to sign for Notts County in September 2009 was an even bigger one bearing in mind that the top man there was none other than Sven Eriksson and County were aiming high with big financial backing. At the League Two club he was also united with former Burnley assistant manager Dave Kevan who had been at Burnley with Steve Cotterill. (More than just a few of us raised our eyebrows when Kevan left Burnley for the then backwaters of Notts County, wondering exactly what was going on behind the scenes at Turf Moor.)

Kevan, assistant at County, retained the role even though Eriksson eventually brought his own man in as manager to replace Kevan's friend Ian McParland.

"Dave knew I was finishing in America and asked if I wanted to go there," explained Akinbiyi.

So there he now is, with a lot of media attention on the club, and huge ambitions to work their way up the Leagues.

Perhaps we all thought we had heard the last of him as his career wound down. Maybe, though, one swansong season would remind everyone that Ade was back again.

7

The Magic of McIlroy

From *Jimmy Mac: Prince of Inside Forwards* by Dave Thomas (Hudson and Pearson)

Somewhere in the film *Shakespeare in Love* written by Tom Stoppard, there's a memorable scene.

"How does a play come together?" says the stage manager, played by Geoffrey Rush.

"I don't know, it's magic," is the reply.

You could ask the same about Jimmy McIlroy, and ask how a 'footballer' comes together.

Jimmy himself might well say that it is not magic, but that it is skill, and that the skills he possessed were learned in boyhood with the hours and hours he spent with his tennis ball. But then, I ask myself, why is it that all the rest of us, who played with a tennis ball in our backyards, or in the school playground, didn't go on to become another Jimmy McIlroy.

There is a magic, and it is a magic that cannot be taught. It is something indefinable, something inherent, something natural and instinctive. It is why great painters can paint, and great actors can act. It was in Tom Finney, Stanley Matthews, it was in Jimmy Greaves, it was in George Best. They and Jimmy Mac never really needed coaching. It was why Brian Glanville called his *World Soccer* piece 'The Magic of McIlroy'.

Reporter Don Smith wrote about the same magic of McIlroy shortly after a Burnley win over Tottenham in 1959. He described the same goal that Glanville had seen at White Hart Lane.

'When asked about my outstanding memory, I had no hesitation in recalling an April evening in 1959. Over 32,000 had roared Spurs into a 2 – 1 lead after Albert Cheesebrough had given the Clarets a 1 – 0 early advantage. Time was running out with Burnley facing apparent defeat after a run of eight matches without a loss. Spurs mounted another attack to seal the result but the move broke down on the 18-yard line.

'Here Jimmy McIlroy gained possession in the inside left position, slightly left of centre. Mac had been the mainspring of Burnley's raiding power, prompting and inspiring and generally playing too well for the comfort of the home team whose skipper Danny Blanchflower decided to give his personal attention throughout the second half. Consequently when Mac controlled the ball at this particular moment in the fading minutes, Danny snapped into the tackle. McIlroy's flickering footwork outwitted him. Spurs fell back to close ranks.

'Instead of releasing the expected forward pass Mac moved forward with deceptive variations in pace, with swerve and sway, the feint to pass and the sudden dart ahead, he weaved a mazy way through a baffled defence in an astonishing solo dribble – a slightly diagonal run into the penalty area where he was at inside right with only goalkeeper Hollowbread to beat.

'There was a roar as the keeper came out. Mac realised that Cheesebrough had come up in support and that there was a desperately racing defender rushing back to cover the goal line. Mac coolly slipped a square pass as if to say, "Albert, finish it off." Albert obliged.

'The crowd erupted. Probably that last unselfish touch added the final touch of lustre to the incredible run. The whole stand rose, arms waved, they applauded … a Tottenham crowd mark you. They were clapping at the restart as their tribute to a moment of sheer artistry.

'It was the finest goal Mac never scored. Yes, one of the three longest dribbles I have ever seen under pressure; a rare and golden cameo of football history.'

Granville Shackleton remembered one piece of sorcery in a piece he wrote called 'The Magic of Mac'. (The word 'magic' seems to be a popular word in any discussion of him).

'He tantalised and baffled experienced opponents to the point of despair and if I had to pick out just one moment of McIlroy magic, this would be it. Burnley were playing Birmingham City at St Andrew's and needing just another goal to really sink the home team's challenge.

'He picked up the ball in their half, suddenly swept forward chased by two opponents and ran diagonally to the corner flag on the far side of the field.

'I saw him backheel the ball during one of those delicate skips and moments of acceleration and so did about 25,000 other people in the main stand and behind the goal Birmingham were defending.

'But his two markers didn't and carried on until Jimmy stopped by the flag, still with his back to them, and started his swaying.

'In the meantime Burnley had picked up the ball Jimmy had left behind and with the rest of the defence cursing their two lost colleagues Ray Pointer rammed it into the net.

'Then, Mac stopped his doodling and pointed out where the ball now was, to the two defenders.'

Towards the end of March, 1999, Jimmy was surprised and delighted to learn of his inclusion in the Football League's Centenary list. The official invitation, issued by the Football League's then Chief Executive, Richard Scudamore, explained what the occasion was all about.

'At the start of this season, the 100th League Championship, you were recognised as one of the 100 best players ever to have graced professional football in this country. The 100 League Legends were honoured for their individual contribution to the game and to mark this achievement the Centenary Season culminates in a celebration "Evening of Legends" (London Hilton, evening of 13th May 1999). This will be a unique gathering, never again will so many of football's greatest ever players join together to honour our national game.'

No greater tribute could have been paid to Jimmy McIlroy.

In the writing of this book I have read dozens of written references about Jimmy McIlroy and spoken to no end of people about him, either face to face, or on the end of a telephone many miles away.

Typical was Les Gold who lives near the Spurs White Hart Lane ground in North London, and whose support for them goes back to the fifties. "Jimmy McIlroy," he exclaimed in his broad Londoner voice, "it's a pleasure to talk about him. I saw him play so many times. I know so many players from that era and he was the best. He's the greatest player Burnley have ever had. I'm just so glad you're writing a book about him."

Author Ivan Ponting, who has written no end of football books, expressed the same sentiments. "Wonderful, it's time someone did a book about him." If Jimmy was worried that no-one would be interested, two publishers expressed immediate interest.

Pete Ellis is typical of the supporters from the sixties who saw Jimmy Mac play, and yet, Pete is from Fareham in the south of England. So many people, years ago, who lived far from Lancashire chose Burnley as their team. Why? They read and heard about Adamson, Connelly, Pointer and the rest, but above all McIlroy. They came to love and admire the skill of their football. In the seventies it was Adamson's team that played with poetry in their feet. Pete wrote to me to say that he had been born in 1947 and later noticed that this coincided with Burnley's Cup Final appearance. At boarding school in Winchester he and a friend played football with a tennis ball (Jimmy Mac would be proud to hear that) allowing themselves only to head it. It was the start of Pete's love affair with football. Like so many young lads he picked a team to follow and fancied a team that played in claret. One of his pals told him: "Well there's Aston Villa and West Ham but there's also this up and coming little side from Burnley who are turning a few heads."

But it was Pete's story of the radio in the English classroom that was most intriguing. "Another thrilling time I had was in the 1961/62 season when the Clarets were in a class of their own. Well I didn't have a radio of my own back then but in our English room we did, but it was totally out of bounds. But Burnley were on a fantastic ride with a possible double looming and most of the media were following them. Anyway nothing was keeping me away from those matches and by hook or by crook I was determined to put up with any punishment if I was caught with the radio in the English room. So I used to sneak in on Cup match days and listen on the school radio. The school was so strict I dread to think what might have happened. Now, today, I can look back and am so pleased I did. I've got all those vivid memories as though it were yesterday."

"I don't know Jimmy personally," wrote Pete, "but the pleasure he gave me in the sixties, and the memories, will live with me to my dying day. I didn't actually get to meet the great man at a book launch at the club last November but would love to have had a chat. But you know what it's like, he never had five minutes to himself, he was continually signing autographs. What a player, God bless."

Somewhere way back in these pages I think I wrote about how we as supporters grow up with our team; how they are part of our boyhood, and we can remember the milestones in our own lives through the events at our football club. Pete wrote to say something similar. "Growing up in my youth, they were my life. I've had some pretty tough experiences and they took away a great deal of pain."

Norman Giller, author of 80 books, one of them being *Fifties Football* and co-author of books with Jimmy Greaves, had this to say: "If Jimmy McIlroy was at his peak today the bidding would probably start at £30million … and Bob Lord would probably want a few pounds of sausages thrown in. When Danny Blanchflower was about to place the ball for his penalty against Burnley in the 1962 Cup Final, Jimmy Mac said to his good friend and countryman: 'Bet you miss it'. Danny, one of the most accurate penalty specialists, duly steered the ball past Adam Blacklaw and as he ran back past Jimmy said: 'Bet I don't'. Give my regards to Jimmy Mac and tell him that I considered Danny and he poetry in motion."

Cliff Jones of Tottenham remembered McIlroy well, having played against Burnley several times and also against Jimmy at International level. Jones was without doubt one of the finest wingers of the time, and always considered Spurs to have been very lucky to have beaten Burnley in the 1961 FA Cup semi-final. Jimmy Greaves said he was so fast that not even wearing an over-coat would have slowed him down.

"Ah Jimmy McIlroy, the 'Prince of Inside Forwards', he was known as," said the former Spurs winger and Welsh international. "He was a lovely player. We had such rivalry between the two clubs. We used to pinch a lot of their free kicks. I played against him so many times and remember the games against him and Burnley well."

"He was a great player," said Burnley's John Connelly who went on to mention that among his cherished memories of Jimmy are the times he had the ball in the corner not letting anyone take it off him.

"There was one game at Everton one Christmas, it was a record crowd something like 78,000, and we were as good as down to ten men but winning 3 – 0. They had this giant clock at one end and I remember watching that clock in the last minutes with Jimmy in the same corner underneath it with the ball by the flag. And they just couldn't get it off him.

"It was against Wolves where I think he did that for the last time. Ron Flowers told me this story about how they knew Jimmy Mac would hold the ball by the corner flag so they told Eddie Clamp to do something about it. So Jimmy had the ball in the corner, and Eddie Clamp set off towards him from something like 25 yards away. Then with two yards to go he just launched himself at Jimmy and took him, ball, flag and everything six feet over the touchline. They'd figured out how to stop his tricks and in those days you never got sent off for anything like that. I'd guess that was the last time Jimmy ever tried that."

Writer Brian Glanville was delighted to hear the name Jimmy McIlroy after so many years of not knowing how he was or what he was doing. "What a lovely man," was his immediate reaction to my first telephone call. As he went away to fetch pen and paper I could hear him talking. "Chap on the phone writing a book about Jimmy McIlroy, how wonderful." He came back to the 'phone. "Whenever Burnley were in London the two Jimmy's, McIlroy and Adamson, would come to my house for coffee. Then I'd have lunch with the team at Bailey's and go on the coach to the ground with them."

Stanley Matthews felt that Jimmy Mac was the last piece of the Tony Waddington promotion jigsaw at Stoke City and spoke glowingly of him in his autobiography *The Way It Was.*

"Jimmy was a marvellous inside forward. In fact, I am given to say, he was the complete inside-forward. As a person Jimmy was genial. As an inside-forward he was a genius. When play was congested in the middle of the field, up out of the trapdoor would spring Jimmy. A will-o' the-wisp player, he glided rather than ran about the pitch with the ball seemingly hypnotised on the toe of his left boot. A sudden drop of a shoulder and a flick with the outside of his boot, the ball would leave his foot at some acute angle and another rearguard was breached. On releasing the ball, it was as if Jimmy disappeared into the ether. He would re-emerge inside the opponent's penalty area, take the return pass and pass again into the net. I would say Jimmy passed the ball into the net because more often than not that is what he did. His cool, calculating brain enabled him to size up the situation and choose his spot. Not for him the robust shot into the roof of the net; Jimmy simply guided it between the outstretched hands of the goalkeeper and the post. He succeeded in doing so 150 times during his career. In my time in football, I'd come across players, who, it was said, could make the ball talk. Jimmy could make it sing like an aria and along with Dennis viollet, he made my life easy at Stoke City."

Geoff Crambie is a Burnley supporter of nearly 60 years. He went to his first game in 1950 and saw the young 19-year old McIlroy in what might well have been his first game. He is unashamedly a McIlroy admirer and in 2000 wrote this in his local newspaper column after he had taken his grandson Nathan to Turf Moor for his first game. He had heard the news that Jimmy Mac would be opening a new stand which was to be named 'The Jimmy McIlroy Stand'.

'This was an occasion not to be missed and also, more important, this was the ideal match to take grandson Nathan, age seven, to his very first football league game. As we arrived at Turf Moor, both excited, me for the ghosts of the past, Nathan for the things to come, suddenly there was a most tremendous cheer as the dignified figure of Jimmy McIlroy walked across the ground he graced for 13 years.

'It was still the same warm Irish smile, although the once coal-black hair had now turned to snow. The crowd of more than 14,000 stood to give a mighty ovation to the great man. Then as I pointed out to Nathan my all-time football hero, who I first saw on this very ground when I was his very age, more heroes of the past strolled onto the pitch. "Look there's Pilky, Robbo, big Brian Miller, the wizard winger John Connelly and stalwart Tommy Cummings.

'As the crowd's cheers rang out, Jimmy, surrounded by his team-mates of 40 years ago, cut the tape and the newly named stand was enshrined in glory. As thousands of balloons were released into the December sky, anything that followed had to be an anti-climax. But no, this day had more surprises for us …

'As the minutes tick by Glen Little and John Mullin team up to play superb football and then, in the very last minute, Andy Payton completes his hat-trick and Burnley have won a marvellous victory by 3 – 2. What a day to remember!'

Harry Brooks in his efforts to have Jimmy made a Freeman of the Borough, wrote this to the Council: 'It is often claimed that Burnley Football Club is the heartbeat of the town and it is indisputable that the club has been a central and significant force in Burnley, through good times and bad, over the past 100 years.

'There would be reason enough, then, for the Council to accept my proposal if it were simply to celebrate the contribution of a man widely regarded as the club's finest player. Jimmy McIlroy gave the essence of his footballing life to the town he arrived at in 1950 at the age of 18, fully justifying the intense public outrage in 1963 when he was, in an act of supreme folly, forced out of the club before his playing days were at an end.

'How can one encapsulate his unique world-class quality as a player? Grace, style and exceptional skill were allied to pace, strength and unselfish effort in the cause of his team. It is difficult to convey his distinctiveness to anyone who did not see him play. There is no one quite like him in the game today – individual genius of that kind can never be replicated precisely – but those who saw the brilliant young Russian playmaker Arshavin run the European quarter-final against Holland, will have had a flavour of a McIlroy command performance.

'But it is not for football alone that the town should honour him. For nearly sixty years in Burnley he has been a fine example of citizenship, lending his name, his presence, his interest and his time, in response to constant requests to support local good causes and worthwhile public events.

'Modest almost to a fault, fame never rested more lightly on any man's shoulders.'

Bob Lord paid Jimmy a fine tribute, except this was not *the* Bob Lord but a chap Jimmy used to meet in Scott Park when he took his granddaughter for a stroll in the evenings. This particular Bob Lord was a 94-year old musician who had once played in the dance and music halls in Burnley. They would often chat and this was a fellow who harked back to the days of Halley, Boyle and Watson. He had seen them all, including the wonderful Bob Kelly. Jimmy remembered this particular Bob Lord fondly: 'Darling,' Bob once said to Tara. 'I hope your granddad doesn't reach 94, there's not much fun.'

And then one evening he told Jimmy: 'Ah McIlroy, you weren't a bad player but Bob Kelly was that much better.' And as he said it he held up his thumb and first finger just three inches apart. Jimmy still smiles at the recollection of being told he wasn't quite Burnley's best ever player, and says it was this that always kept his feet on the ground.

In 2002, when a Burnley FC shirt that once belonged to Jimmy Mac came up for auction at Bonhams (the shirt worn in the European Cup-tie against Reims when Burnley won 2 – 0), it was bought for nearly £4,000. Jimmy had swapped it after the game with French player Raymond Kopa, and it was Kopa who put the shirt and other items up for sale. The successful bidder was Peter Hodson from Cambridgeshire. One of the unlucky bidders, Mervyn Hadfield, another Burnley fan, desperately wanted to buy the shirt for his grandson. Though he did not take the shirt home, he did have his bidding card framed. He penned his thoughts afterwards and called it *Jimmy Mac's Shirt.*

'And there it is, lot '389, in the Bonham auction sale,
Last time I saw it, Jimmy wore it: To me it tells a tale.
Of football played with passion, and verve not oft repeated,
Till Reims, champions of France, trooped off Turf Moor defeated.

Eleven heroes played that night, for Burnley were a team,
As modest Mac has always said, when the Clarets were supreme.
I keep on looking at the shirt as other lots go down,
And I think back to Jimmy Mac and the pride he gave our town.

In the fifties and the sixties with super soccer skill,
Today in his adopted home, there's great affection still.
And now the time has come to bid, I'm full of apprehension,
The auctioneer has made it clear, this lot has claimed attention.

And so it proves, my humble bid, is soon left far behind,
As hundreds turn to thousands, perhaps I shouldn't mind.
At least I tried for Jimmy's shirt, and can't help feeling proud,
It reached the highest price today, and truly stirred the crowd.

As Jimmy Mac so often did, but now before I leave,
I stand before my hero's shirt, and touch the light blue sleeve.
I gaze at it with reverence, the famous number eight.
Over fifty years have passed; it's been a long, long wait.

One lingering look; one final touch, and now I turn to go,
I hear a French voice say to me, "This man, a great one, no?"
I face the Gallic football fan, the question to address,
"The one who wore this Claret shirt, he is a great man yes."

And suddenly I've no regrets, for here, I'm glad to be.
Though it was priced beyond my scope, the shirt reminded me,
Of what I have that can't be sold, or even put on show.
My priceless memories of that night, Mac wore it long ago.
(Mervyn Hadfield 2002)

Even though it had been nearly 40 years since they had last met, Ken Bates referred to Jimmy in his Leeds United programme notes in November, 2008. Bates still remembered what a model player he had been. In his notes he was critical of the modern international world that awards over 100 caps to someone like David Beckham, when the caps have been devalued so much, and have been awarded for appearances in the most meaningless friendly games and for appearing for just minutes as a substitute. He described Jimmy Mac as the Gianfranco Zola of his day and playing in an age when a cap meant something and every one was thoroughly earned.

Burnley FC author David Wiseman devoted several pages to Jimmy in his *'Vintage Claret'* book and saw him play throughout the fifties. He makes an observation that makes you wonder. At the end of season 1961/62 Mac was injured with ten games to play. It was those ten games that cost the club dear. He missed five of them and was not fully fit in the ones in which he did play. Burnley did not win one of the five games he missed. If only … just two more wins would have won the title again. If Jimmy was placed on the transfer list because he had allegedly "stopped trying" or, "not giving wholehearted effort," then David Wiseman points to a newspaper report that undermines that allegation. It was a game at the end of 1962 against Sheffield Wednesday and Burnley won 4 – 0.

"Despite the ice-rink surface this was a vintage McIlroy who gave a performance his fans won't forget in a hurry … who said McIlroy is finished."

Wiseman went to Stoke to see him play after his transfer, but says it just wasn't the same.

On Tuesday, December 9th, 2008, Mac became a Freeman of the Borough of Burnley. The websites and the match programme, the local paper, were all filled with fans' tributes. Typical was this from Brian Sellers:

'I was fortunate enough to see you in action during the late 50s and until your departure to Stoke in '63. It is hard to put into words what you and the team meant to the supporters of Burnley Football Club during those vintage years of League Champions, FA Cup finalists and the wonderful European evenings on the Turf. Probably the best example I can give relates to my father who was a lifelong Burnley fan. When he heard the news of your departure he was so incensed, upset and shocked, he vowed never to pass through a Turf Moor turnstile again and, despite my best efforts during the Adamson era, he kept his word.

Jimmy you leave many lasting memories of how the 'wonderful game' should be played. I can still vividly recall you with the ball at your feet by the opposition corner flag surrounded by 2, 3, or even 4 defenders. Moments later, following a shimmy or two and magic footwork you would be bearing down on goal, leaving the defenders in your wake. Then there was the penalty taking where you almost seemed to mesmerise the opposition goalkeeper, like a rabbit trapped in car headlights. Three or four steps up to the ball, a sway of the hips to leave the keeper rooted to the spot and you would stroke the ball into the bottom corner of the net.'

But Mac had worried about the occasion; he had worried about what he would say up on the platform in his response. But his heartfelt speech was a gem, acknowledging both his roots and the place of Burnley in his heart. His words were typical of his modesty.

Jimmy and I had been meeting and talking for much of the year and when Jimmy asked me to be one of his guests at the Town Hall ceremony and at the football club afterwards, I have to say I was quite speechless. It says much about Jimmy that he will never understand why he induces these moments of unashamed admiration in the people who saw him play so many years ago, and even in people who never saw him play when they are in his charismatic company. He has continually questioned the 'need' for a biography about himself as a result of his quite humble modesty. And this, from a man of whom Stan Matthews once said, "Had he been born an Englishman his name would have been one of the biggest in world football."

As I sat and listened to his acceptance speech, and accompanied him to the meal afterwards with his other guests, my mind went back to when he was a player and I was a wide-eyed, young supporter convinced on every Saturday that Jimmy Mac would win us the game, and who every Friday night said a silent little prayer in bed that Jimmy would have a blinder. All these years later I know exactly how I ended my prayer: "And please dear Lord let Jimmy Mac win us the game."

Whilst Jimmy's father, who wanted so much for his son to become a footballer, might never have imagined the fame and glory that would come his way; neither would my father have ever imagined that I, the once hero-worshipping, day-dreaming schoolboy, would one day write the biography of this 'Prince of Inside Forwards'. Life works in mysterious ways.

Today, when Jimmy Mac reads and receives tributes such as these, of course he enjoys them, but at the same time is embarrassed and will be the first to say that he was part of a team; and that he had great players playing alongside him. He remembers the occasion when he and most of the players of that great Championship, and Cup Final team, assembled on Turf Moor for the naming of the Jimmy McIlroy Stand some years ago. He made a short speech in which he said he thought it should be named the Champions Stand. What he omitted to say to the fans that day, and wishes today that he had, is simply this, and perhaps he can say it now:

"What a treat you missed; not having seen these fellows play."

Some of us did and can still see their magic when we close our eyes; Blacklaw, Angus, Elder, Cummings, Miller, Adamson, Connelly, Robson, Pointer, Pilkington, Bobby Seith, Trevor Meredith, and not forgetting McIlroy himself; golden names from a golden era.

How lucky we were.

* * *

2008 The One and Only Jimmy Mac

This article would have been part of the Paul Fletcher book Magical *that we wrote together. But, as we went seriously overboard with the word count, we were asked by the publisher to lose several thousand words from the draft that was sent. The Jimmy Mac chapter was one of the sections taken out, the other one being a chapter about the formation of the University College of Football Business that was set up within the Turf Moor stadium.*

The book, Magical *published in October 2012, covers all of Paul's varied years in football up until his resignation as CEO at Turf Moor. Those years include his 10 playing years at Burnley, his move into life-after-football, his time at Colne Dynamos and then Huddersfield. It was at Huddersfield that the job of CEO morphed into that of the new stadium builder and organiser. From that, there were spells at The Reebok, The Ricoh and Wembley until he returned to Burnley as CEO during the period of promotion to the Premiership and then the year in the Premier League. His after-dinner speaking career started quite soon after he stopped playing and continues to this day and he continues to work for the UCFB with its campus at The Etihad.*

In 2018 he had his novel published, Saturday Bloody Saturday, *written in collaboration with Alastair Campbell; a novel based on 70s football, politics and the IRA problems of the time. DT*

* * *

In my four more years at the club, few events gave me more pleasure than overseeing the club's involvement with Jimmy McIlroy. Our paths had crossed at Bolton when I was a young player there and he was part of the management. I remember he once drove me somewhere – it might even have been to Burnley to see Jimmy Adamson and sign for the club. I remember asking him football questions and one sticks in my mind. I think it was to do with how I could become a better player. "Play with better players," he said. When I signed for Burnley I certainly did that and everything I did at Bolton, I did better at Burnley. In the 70s when I was a player there, his name would crop up in training sessions at Gawthorpe. I sometimes saw his columns in the local paper when he worked as a journalist – and a damned good one too. His football writing was filled with sense and perception.

One of the nicest things that happened in November of 2008 was the presentation of Jimmy McIlroy to the crowd at the home game against Cardiff City. Just a few hours earlier he had been given the Freedom of the Borough of Burnley by the town council. One of the driving forces behind the award was Harry Brooks, a long-time Burnley supporter and shareholder, former councillor and a huge admirer of the great man. The club was delighted to cooperate and support the award. Chairman Barry Kilby and the Lady Mayoress of Burnley were present on the pitch alongside Jimmy to display the large framed document with him.

How do you cap that? You present him with his MBE on the pitch, two years later.

The award of the MBE was long overdue. But, being the quiet, unassuming man he is these days, as ever Jimmy found the award embarrassing. He is always quick to say that whatever awards he received he was only part of a team; the team that won the title in 1959/60, played in the Cup Final of 1962, and played in the European Cup of 1960/61. What he has done for years though is unfailingly accept any invitation to help with any local charity or fundraising.

The North Stand was named in his honour several years ago, The Jimmy McIlroy Stand. He is on record as saying that it should have been called The Champions Stand in honour of all his colleagues with whom he brought honour to Burnley. He has been an ambassador for town and club since the day he arrived in 1951. He wondered then what kind of a place he had arrived in when he surveyed the cobbled streets, the smoke-filled air, factory chimneys belching black clouds skywards, and the rows and rows of terraced houses. The place he came from was rural and green with just a handful of dwellings. When he looked out of his bedroom window in Burnley on the first morning and saw the market area filled with rubbish and the remains of the previous day, he wondered should he go straight back to Ballyskeagh.

The naming of the Stand took place on Tuesday, December 28, 1999. It was a significant date for it also marked the end of the 20th Century, and over 100 years of Burnley Football Club. Jimmy's team-mates were there with him as part of a parade of the legends before the game. At half-time it was the turn of the 1968 victorious FA Youth Cup team that walked round the pitch. It was a moving occasion. From the special programme that day there was a feature on Jimmy. Another one appeared in the January 1st programme, 2007. The two together make a fitting tribute to a great and gracious man.

Jimmy McIlroy was idolised by Burnley fans in a glittering 13-year career with the club. In his pomp, the incomparable Irishmen was rated the finest inside-forward in the British Isles by Stanley Matthews and his boyhood idol Peter Doherty and is the only Burnley player to be listed as one of the '100 Football League Legends'.

He made 51 of his 55 international appearances while at Turf Moor, represented the Football League twice in 1960, played for Great Britain in 1955 and was a key performer when Northern Ireland reached the quarter-finals of the 1958 World Cup in Sweden. He went on to make 497 League and Cup appearances and scored 131 goals for the Clarets.

He made his home debut four days before his 19th birthday in a First Division game at Sunderland and embarked on a memorable career which saw him compared favourably with the greatest scheming inside-forwards of all time. In the great sides of the 1950s and early '60s – League Champions, European Cup ambassadors – McIlroy was the most dazzling star in Burnley's team of all talents. The pinnacle of his career came when the Clarets were crowned Football League Champions by winning the 1959/60 First Division title – in the last match of the season.

Wolves were going for a title treble but goals by Brian Pilkington and Trevor Meredith gave Burnley a 2 – 1 victory over Manchester City at Maine Road in front of 65,981 and brought the coveted Championship trophy back to Turf Moor for the first time in 39 years. The match was played on a Monday night. Some fans even walked to Manchester. Amazingly it was the only time all season that Burnley had topped the table.

"That was some night I can tell you. I had a thigh strain, but the trainer, Billy Dougal, strapped me up and told me I was playing, irrespective of what I thought. That in a way was a compliment and when we were crowned League Champions it fulfilled a lot of ambitions. We had a good team and I was fortunate to have so many good players

around me. Looking back we certainly played some flowing football that season and must have thrilled the fans. At our peak, which was about half a dozen times a season, we would have beaten any team anywhere. The manager, Harry Potts, was one of the nicest fellows in the game – in fact too nice."

The title success brought European Cup football to Turf Moor in the 1960/61 season. It was anything but a typical November evening in East Lancashire when goals from Jimmy Robson and McIlroy gave Burnley a 2 – 0 victory over the French champions Reims in front of 36,742 fans at Turf Moor. John Connelly and Robson were on target as the Clarets lost 3 – 2 in the return but moved into the quarter-finals 4 – 3 on aggregate.

Burnley were paired against the German champions Hamburg in the last eight, and Brian Pilkington (2) and Robson scored as the Clarets won the first leg 3 – 1 in front of 47,000 ecstatic supporters. Although Gordon Harris netted in Hamburg, the Germans scored 4 times at the Volksparkstadion and won 5 – 4 on aggregate, McIlroy side-footing against an upright from close-range in the closing stages.

McIlroy said, "We were a wee bit naïve when it came to playing against good European sides. Leading 3 – 1, we should have adopted a more defensive attitude for the return leg. But we went out to score more goals, were exposed, and lost 4 – 1. We were carrying the hopes of every football fan in the country and it was all new to us. But the atmosphere for those matches was absolutely electric." Had McIlroy scored late on, rather than hit the post, the tie would have gone to a replay at Real Madrid's Bernabau Stadium.

Although this chance was missed, his goal-scoring ratio, better than one every four games was excellent for a scheming inside-forward. His primary function was to create chances for others.

"It surprised me that I scored so many goals because I was not a natural. I panicked in front of goal, yet on my own six-yard line I could collect the ball, knock it through an opponent's legs and play my way out of trouble. It didn't help me being the worst header of the ball in the Football League."

The matches he looked forward to most were those against the mighty Tottenham Hotspurs. "Every Tottenham match was a classic even before my great pal Danny Blanchflower joined them. But, when we played them in the FA Cup Final it was a real anti-climax. When we were walking on the pitch Danny said, 'I suppose you are wondering what all so-and-so the fuss is about'.

"Two thirds of the crowd were made up of neutrals and it was more of a social occasion. Danny scored their third goal from the spot and as he prepared to take it I indicated to Adam Blacklaw where I thought Danny would put the ball. Quick as a flash Danny asked me if I wanted to take it."

Another Burnley-Tottenham classic took place at White Hart Lane in the 1960/61 season. Burnley were 4 – 0 down but staged one of the greatest fight-backs in football history to draw 4 – 4.

Jimmy played in some of the biggest matches in Burnley's proud history and, while many were often high profile and memorable, for the legend from Ballyskeagh, the 'Game of his Life' was just an ordinary league game in the First Division against Bolton late in the 1957/58 season. It was a Wanderers side that had just reached the FA Cup where they would face mighty Manchester United in one of Wembley's memorable finals.

Of all the games in which Jimmy wore the famous Claret and Blue, this game stood out above all others, as almost his ultimate performance. Jimmy recalled, "They were always good, fierce matches against Bolton in what we really termed as a derby game. It was one of those days when running was effortless and I felt I could have run for hours. I genuinely could have played another game at the end of 90 minutes even though I had covered such an awful lot of ground. I felt so fit and strong, and as performances go it was as near to perfection as I ever played."

Jimmy, now 75, added, "All through my career, in bed at night, you would analyse your performance and particularly the mistakes you made. That night I slept so soundly there was not one mistake to go over in my head. The Bolton game was just special for my own personal performance that stood out. But I played in many games when as a team we just clicked and were breath-taking on certain days. Sometimes I even recall wishing I was standing on the terraces watching us when that happened. We were so good on days like that."

Jimmy had played against Bolton and their legendary centre forward Nat Lofthouse on many occasions in what he described as *'derby matches'. Indeed he claims he still bears the bruises of crashing into the man known as the 'Lion of Vienna', during this game.*

"It was like running into a stone wall, he was so solid. Nat was a superb header of the ball given he wasn't the biggest of centre forwards."

Unfortunately Nat was not the only immovable object in the Trotters' side and right back Roy Hartle was one of the game's genuine hard men. Jimmy recalled, "Off the field Roy was one of the nicest blokes you could wish to meet. But on the field he was a real tough nut. I remember in one game I could see this shadow getting near to me out of the corner of my eye and then I heard Roy say, 'Just hold it Jimmy'. I soon passed the ball.

Jimmy's stark memories of a game nearly half a century ago are naturally fading with time. He does remember taking a corner and spotting Bobby Seith in some space. "I put the ball right on his head for him to score," he insisted.

However, on checking the archives later, I found that Jimmy had actually scored twice in the game that Burnley won 3 – 1. How typical of the great man that he didn't mention being the match-winner. But then Jimmy McIlroy never was the kind of player to blow his own trumpet. World Class, certainly, a legend, he definitely was. (Two articles reproduced by kind permission of Burnley Football Club.)

* * *

How ironic that Jimmy should pick this game against Bolton. This was the season I started to go and watch with my granddad. This was the Cup Final I went to with my father. This was the Nat Lofthouse who taught me all he knew about heading a ball.

Today, Jimmy is 80 years old and how good it was to wish him many happy returns at the club on his special day. He still has a table on matchdays for himself and family. They dined well that day. Yes his memories are fading of all those games so many years ago, but he certainly doesn't look 80 years old and jokes that he would love to meet a rich widow. In fact he has a delightful and wry sense of humour. Co-writer Dave Thomas remembers the time that he met Jimmy to talk about the old days and whilst Dave was leafing through some of Jimmy's old photographs, Jimmy was reading the local paper and seemingly ignoring Dave.

"Dave, I'm so sorry," he said. "This must seem so rude. But I always look in the obituary page to see if I'm in there."

The two Dave Thomas books about him are superb. The biography *Jimmy Mac: Prince of Inside Forwards* is a wonderful large-format book packed with pictures of a golden age. Then there is another coffee table format book, *Jimmy McIlroy the Scrapbook*. This is a book the like of which no other exists, telling the story with hundreds of pictures, right up until the Freeman of the Borough ceremony in December 2008. The club once again produced a commemorative programme including this tribute:

For someone who regularly had crowds on their feet in his heyday, it comes as something of a surprise to learn that Jimmy McIlroy is nervous about his biggest ovation yet. At half-time tonight under the floodlights, the man universally known as the club's greatest player will take to 'his' stage and accept the Freedom of the Borough of Burnley in front of Turf Moor's adoring fans.

Those old enough and lucky enough to remember Jimmy in his prime will have memories jogged, while younger fans wisely acknowledge the part he played in arguably the Claret's greatest ever side in those halcyon days of the 1950s and 1960s. Young and old will therefore rise as one to acclaim the legendary inside-forward, one of only a handful of players to score a century of goals for the club and, nearly 50 years on, has still played more league games than any other outfield player in the club's history. However, modest as always, Jimmy insists he will be glad when he steps back into the shadows.

"In 50 years of facing audiences I still haven't got used to it. I still suffer agonies in the days leading up to making speeches and I have to write everything down. I have reached an age where I couldn't risk remembering where I am. Some mornings when I get up, I look at the newspaper to see what day it is."

Take no notice! The great man is in fine fettle, save for a dodgy knee that is currently curtailing his favoured passion, the freedom of the golf course. The honour of being awarded the Freedom of the Borough is a well-earned recognition for a genuine ambassador, not only for Burnley Football Club but his adopted town as well. The honour was scheduled to be bestowed on Jimmy earlier today by the Mayor of Burnley, Councillor Ida Carmichael, at a special ceremony at Burnley Town hall.

When news of the award first broke following a successful fans' campaign led by the Burnley Express newspaper, the Clarets legend admits to being "embarrassed" at the whole affair. Jimmy who was born in Ballyskeagh, near Belfast near 77 years ago insisted, "I couldn't believe it."

"First of all I didn't know quite what the Freedom of the Borough meant and then I thought it was all a joke. When the Council people explained it to me, I was amazed. I was even more amazed when the Burnley Express told me that supporters have been backing up the proposal. This is the biggest honour a town or borough can give to anyone and I think you have to do heroic things to earn something as special as this. All I have ever done is kick a ball around and enjoy it."

Modesty again from a man who claims to be "as conceited as anyone", adding that despite his reputation for humility, his late wife Barbara used to mutter, "They don't really know you."

Yet the joy Jimmy gave to thousands of people remains his biggest unwitting attribute.

"It is a tremendous honour. I know I am embarrassed but at the same time I am so proud that so many people have paid me so many compliments. Over the past few years I have been amazed at the number of people who stop me and thank me for the pleasure I gave them. I almost feel I am a better player now than I was then. In fact I'm certain I am. I remember once walking through Belfast Airport with one of the English journalists on the way to cover a Northern Ireland match for a local newspaper. The England team were walking right behind us, but people kept calling my name. The journalist said he wondered how many of those players would get that recognition over 40 years on. It's just a tremendous feeling to know that people still remember you. Even at the golf range the other day, two old boys were talking when I walked in and one of them said how much he had enjoyed watching me play. I just feel that would apply to so many of our players because seriously, I am embarrassed to be picked out above all the other lads I played with. At that time I think we had nine internationals, and these guys were the top players in the UK. I think of players like Ray Pointer,

John Connelly and Colin McDonald, who suffered a horrendous injury at the peak of his game. We had some of the best players around and it was easy to play with them. There's nobody in football I feel sadder for. He was a goalkeeper who made everything look so easy and was in the England team at the time."

It's the magnitude of the First Division title victory achieved on the final day of the 1959/60 season that Jimmy still sees as the pinnacle of his playing days. "It's something that will probably never happen again for a town this size to produce a team that finished Champions of England. It really was something special and it's a medal I am so proud of. I can't believe it will be the 50th anniversary next season and how amazing that 50 years on, that team and those players are still remembered. I can't think of a better celebration than seeing the current team back in the top flight and you know what … for the first time in years I actually believe we can do that." (Reproduced by kind permission of Burnley Football Club)

***

Was Jimmy psychic? That piece, written in season 2008/09 foretold in the last paragraph the wonderful triumph of reaching the Premiership so that the year in the top-flight did indeed coincide with the 50th anniversary of Jimmy's title win.

What exactly is the Freedom of the Borough? It is the highest honour a Council can award and is restricted to residents who have made a significant contribution to the borough over a period of 15 years or more. In the distant past 'free men' enjoyed special status and enjoyed various privileges. Today it carries no special privilege and simply reflects the standing of the person upon whom it is bestowed. It is never given lightly and in Jimmy's case was thoroughly earned.

And then there was the MBE. Jimmy chose to have this presented at Turf Moor instead of Buckingham Palace. I was absolutely delighted to be involved in the organisation. The Lord Lieutenant of Lancashire, Lord Shuttleworth, acting on behalf of the Queen, was dressed in all his ceremonial pomp and finery to read the citation on the pitch before the game. Alongside Jimmy were his daughter Anne and son Paul, Barry Kilby and the Deputy Lieutenant, Peter Robinson.

Jimmy himself claimed it was all because of an old school friend that he was receiving the award. "He's called Alf McCabe and I've known him for a long time since I was at school. He probably worked harder getting me this award than I ever did on the field. Sometimes I think I can't be worth all this. It came completely out of the blue. I was supposed to go to London to collect it but there were so many people who wanted to come that they would have filled a bus. I was bound to upset many of them because you can only take so many guests. I just thought, let's have it at Turf Moor so that everyone can see. I wanted the fans to feel it was for them as well. I've three grand-daughters, a son and a daughter, and then of course there's Alfie, nephews and nieces and I knew a lot of them would be upset if they weren't included on the Buckingham list. It's the medal that is important and it doesn't matter where you get it or how. It's perfect that it was at Turf Moor. Honours are for sharing and this is what I'm doing. I am so pleased to be called Burnley's 'adopted son.' How lucky I was to come here and I've never wanted to leave. I'm treated now as if I was still a player. But nobody should ever think that Burnley was a one-man team. Far from it, and it makes me continue to ask, 'why me?' In fact that was the title I nearly chose for the book that Dave Thomas wrote. The one thing I am sorry about is that my friend Alf wasn't at Turf Moor to see the occasion."

It was a masterstroke to choose Turf Moor as the location for the award and the applause was rapturous. The club weren't quite finished with him. He was made Club President in 2011, a thoroughly popular decision and he celebrated his 80th birthday at the club. A wonderful man and I'm proud to have known him for so long.

Paul Fletcher

8

Clarke Carlisle, the Wembley Play-Off Final

His Game to Remember, from *Something to Write Home About*, the magazine of the London Clarets. Article by Dave Thomas

It isn't too often that *The Spectator* waxes lyrical about Burnley Football Club or one of its players but in May 2009 there was an exception to this rule: *'Thank heaven for Burnley who played their hearts out to win the Premier play-offs. Afterwards their heroic defender Clarke Carlisle picked up the MOTM award and in a short and graceful interview he gave every sign of being one of the most impressive human beings on earth. Moved to tears, he spoke with wisdom, articulacy and passion about the game, players, supporters and his own personal journey through a host of injuries as well as alcoholism. If anyone should carry a torch for all that is great and good in the beautiful game – it is Clarke Carlisle'.*

Nor is it very often that *The Guardian* picks out Burnley as being one of the shining lights of football. But it did on May 30th, 2009, when David Lacey bracketed Burnley's football ethos with that of Barcelona: *'In football it has been a good week for fundamentalists, those who believe that amid the hustle and haste of the modern game the basics of good passing and movement plus the ability to make space and not give the ball away are too often taken for granted. To which might be added the willingness of players to run with the ball when the opportunity is there, a habit in danger of being coached out of teams fearful of losing possession and being caught on the break.*

'On Monday Burnley displayed many of these qualities in beating one United, Sheffield, to win promotion to the Premier League. On Wednesday Barcelona did as much, and a bit more besides, when they outplayed another United, Manchester, to win the Champions League Final in Rome. In each case the match was run and won by medium-sized men with the brains and technique to outwit the athletes whose power and pace are beginning to dominate football at the expense of the subtler arts …

'Forty-nine years ago Burnley set standards which were embodied in the Tottenham double side the following season. So it is good to see Turf Moor back in the big time and the Lancashire heartland is promised a rare pantomime now that Burnley's Cinderellas have joined the Ugly Sisters – Sam Allardyce's Blackburn and Gary Megson's Bolton – with Wigan playing Buttons …'

There are those who would say that the game against the powerful athletes of Sheffield United was no classic. But try telling that to the 36,000 Burnley supporters who were there. It was the match of their lives.

Lacey was right in his assessment. No-one could call Burnley's Wembley team that day a team reliant on nothing but muscular, powerful, physical athletes, good at running and pressing, but lacking in flair and deftness. This was a team, and it was a team in the proper sense of the word, where the sum of the parts is greater than the individuals. In this respect it continued in the tradition of the McIlroy/Adamson Championship team of 1959/60 and then Adamson's golden team that flowered so briefly from 1973 to 1975. What the team of 2008/09 had was a blend of strength at the back, creativity in midfield and pace and skill up front. Above all there was flair and as Lacey says it was the small men who ran the show: Wade Elliott, Robbie Blake, Graham Alexander, Joey Gudjonsson and Martin Paterson, not one of them a giant. Burnley played well and their goal came from a mazy run from deep by a player with the skill, confidence and bravery to take the ball forward almost to the edge of the box from inside his own half. He passed, it came back to him, and from 25 yards the ball was stroked home with a level of skill that would have made that great legend Jimmy McIlroy proud. In their victory Burnley demonstrated to the nation that passing skills and ball control can prevail and succeed over might and muscle.

Ironically the only physical giant in the Burnley outfield was Carlisle, at 6' 3" a powerful colossus who, on the day, was unbeatable in the air and impassable on the ground.

In an interview after another game, ironically against Sheffield United again in a League game only a few weeks earlier, Carlisle described the experience as like playing in the Land of the Giants. Again it had been a game where Burnley's smaller men had won although Carlisle was honest enough to describe some of his defending as "industrial," a case of needs must. This is an articulate man indeed, and in that single word, he conjured up the image of his approach and method. He is not a man to weave his way out of defence with elegance and sophistication. He is not a man to make pinpoint 40 and 50 yard passes to the feet of a colleague on the other side of the pitch. He is direct, simple and uncomplicated. He wins it, he makes the simple pass. His job is simple – to defend. "It is up to the likes of Chris McCann, Robbie Blake, and Martin Paterson to produce the pretty, eye-catching stuff, but the defensive unit to keep clean sheets." At corners in the opposition half it is his job to move up into the penalty area, steam in, and attack the ball. Burnley's progress to Wembley in the final weeks was marked by a string of games in which there were clean sheets and he received the MOTM award.

Club programme notes outlined the key role he played in 2008/09. They referred to his never-say-die attitude, the way he was able to dip into his own well of strength after a dip in form briefly cost him his place. "I have got to a stage in my career where I can't be dipping below a seven out of ten. I've played 300-plus games and I am approaching 40 games this season and I haven't done that for a while. I should be experienced enough to know what is expected of me and produce it every week. It's about having a mindset and knowing that when you cross the line you are not going to take any chances or risks and just focus on your job. I get paid to defend and sometimes it may not be as aesthetically pleasing as some might want and it might be quite industrious at times, but as long as the ball is not in the back of our net my job is done. I am feeling great, probably the fittest I have ever felt at this stage of the season, having played more games than in the last six or seven years."

Wembley on May 25th, 2009 was certainly the match of a lifetime for this dignified centre-back in which yet again he received the best player award. It was clear from the on-pitch interview that this was a day he will never forget. The story of his journey to get there is that of a fall from grace and then a lesson in self-appraisal, determination to recover, rehabilitation, and then ultimate triumph. This is a man who faced his demons and found his renaissance.

Born in Preston in October 1979, his first club was Blackpool. There he made 100 appearances between 1997 and 2000. His form was such that QPR paid £250,000 for him in the summer of 2000. He made appearances for England at U21 level and really was seen as an emerging star. However, the injuries began and a cruciate ligament tear kept him out of the game for a year. Doctors thought he was finished. In his first game back, a reserve fixture at Bristol City, there were fears he had repeated the injury when he was forced to limp off. Fortunately it was not as bad as feared, and he was back within a month.

Carlisle spent four years with QPR, helping them win promotion to the Championship and in January 2002 he won the title of Britain's Brainiest Footballer in a TV Quiz. In a close final he beat Alan Brazil 6 – 5. It was QPR's first major trophy since 1967, one newspaper pointed out not without humour.

But, by the 2003/04 season there were problems and he was admitted to the Sporting Chance Clinic for treatment for alcohol problems. The trigger came when he was axed from manager Ian Holloway's squad after going AWOL on the eve of a game.

"With the knowledge I have now, I realise it had been affecting my performance for a long time. I had been playing at nowhere near 100%. At one stage I found I wasn't actually that bothered. Then, suddenly, I had a moment of clarity and thought: Clarke what the hell are you doing? It was when clarity set in I felt at my lowest. To be honest I was scared."

Tony Adams' Sporting Chance Clinic nestles in the tranquil Hampshire countryside. There are several football stars who have attended the centre but wish to remain anonymous. Clarke Carlisle has never wished to do that. There is no pampering to ego or salary, the kitchen is a place where beans on toast are on offer. There are facilities for retaining fitness but definitely no facials. Instead of pampering there is a regime of individual and group counselling sessions. TV is allowed only in the evenings. It was at QPR that he turned to drink.

"After training I'd go to my local and have a few pints and then when I was bloated I'd shift onto cocktails or shooters and then when my friends had finished work we'd crack on into town."

His turning point was when he arrived for a match looking the worse for wear and was sent home. He was days away from getting the sack. It was then that the realisation hit him that his career was going rapidly downhill. Once there he found it mentally and physically draining going through all the emotions that came to the surface. "There are reasons for behaviour and getting to the roots of the problems was liberating."

He acknowledges now that what the clinic and its staff did for him was lifesaving. He acknowledged them again in his interview on the pitch immediately after the Burnley Wembley Final.

The effect they had on him was not only to combat the drinking but also to help him realise that it was his reaction to certain situations that triggered the drinking. "It was an intense and emotional 28 days."

"Clarke's shown bravery and was man enough to face up to his problems," said manager Holloway. "I can only applaud him for what he has done. Nobody has seen the best of him yet and my message is to watch out for him. He can go on to play in the top flight with the new tools he's been given to deal with the rest of his life."

Carlisle's prophetic comment was: "I do believe I can do a lot more than almost anything I've shown in football so far."

His contract at QPR ended in 2004 after 212 appearances and 6 goals. Kevin Blackwell took him to Leeds United on a free transfer. There he spent just one year, playing 38 games and scoring 4 goals. Here too there were injury problems; torn ankle ligaments during a game at gloomy Rotherham, when there was a 0 – 1 defeat, keeping him out for six weeks.

Leeds accepted £100,000 for him from Watford (Stoke City too would have signed him) and he signed a three-year deal. His potential remained clear and manager Aidy Boothroyd tipped him to become one of the best defenders in the Championship. It would be five years later that Boothroyd's prediction was proved correct. Boothroyd identified that he had enormous strengths and was certain that he would become an even better player. Watford finished third in the table in 2004/05 and gained promotion to the Premiership. But by the time of the play-offs Carlisle had been injured again, this time a thigh injury, and he took no part in the final games or the Final. Nor did he take much part in the Premiership season. He missed eight months of the season finding it hard to cope with and by the time he was able to play again Watford had been relegated. He regarded the small number of games he played when he returned as a taster of Premier football. He could not have known that in 2009 he would be instrumental in another club's promotion to the Promised Land.

In the summer of 2007 Burnley manager Steve Cotterill was the next man to recognise his abilities, signing him for a reported £200,000. He replaced Wayne Thomas who was sold to Southampton for over £1m. These two moves were amongst the smartest of Cotterill's deals and once he arrived at Burnley Carlisle was an almost ever-present.

The move back north was not in Carlisle's script. He had just forced his way back into the Watford side after injury and presumed he would figure in Aidy Boothroyd's plans for the season. Cotterill's phone call changed all that.

"I was all set for Watford's season and this phone call came out of the blue – apparently not so for the gaffer – he said he'd been after me for a few months, but I was completely unaware of it," said Carlisle. "It all just fell into place. It was excellent. I don't just want to tag along in the background, I don't believe that's a stage of my career I'm at. I believe I'm definitely a first-choice centre half and that's what I'm here to prove."

If constant injuries had been a problem for him until joining Burnley, he avoided them at Turf Moor. But tragedy might have struck if he had not had a miraculous escape from a car crash on October of 2007 when his car spun into a ditch on the way to training ahead of a game against Crystal Palace. The car was a write-off yet he emerged unscathed. In fact his wife collected him and they continued the journey to training. The following weekend he played against Crystal Palace.

"Anybody else doing another job might have had a week off work in a neck brace and a doctor's note signing him off," commented manager Cotterill. "Clarke did remarkably well even to play on Saturday."

It could certainly be argued that the arrival of Owen Coyle as manager at Burnley took Carlisle's game to another higher level. As Steve Cotterill's term reached its end, this was a disenchanted group of players, several of whom he had alienated and had lost confidence in him. Nine of the Burnley Wembley team, including Carlisle, had played under Cotterill. These same nine players had established a club record run of 20 winless games. With Owen Coyle they achieved promotion to the Premiership.

"The manager, Owen Coyle," said Carlisle, "tells us week in, week out, it doesn't matter what other teams are going to do or who they've got in their side. It's all about what we do and how we can perform, because he believes – and it'd filtered all through the club and the squad – that if we play to the best of our ability we're more than a match for anyone … There's a lot of pressure … but when we cross that white line, a freedom to go and express ourselves and play the game in the right manner has been instilled into us, with a knowledge that the manager supports you in that – and that if we, as a team, play to our strengths and abilities, we can win the game."

On Monday May 25th, 2009, that philosophy took Burnley to an improbable triumph. "Little old Burnley," is how Peter Beagrie, a smile etched on his face, referred to them with clear affection at the end of the day. This was the club with one of the smallest budgets and one of the smallest squads in the Championship. The season had begun badly with two defeats and two draws. Slowly but surely things were turned round. Then over the Christmas period there was a run of five consecutive defeats. Again things were turned round so that by the final game of the season if Burnley won the last home game they would progress to the play-offs. This they did with a thumping 4 – 0 win over Bristol City, not a bad side themselves.

Behind the scenes, however, the club was in financial turmoil. In April administration was imminent. The club could not meet the wages bill. The payment instalments for the purchase of Chris Eagles had already been re-negotiated. Four directors: Barry Kilby, John Sullivan, Ray Griffiths and Mike Garlick saved the day with more loans totalling nearly £1m. All this was a well-kept secret. Without those loans, the push for the play-offs and the Premiership could have taken a far different turn. It made the Wembley play-off even more of a match to remember. In the great scale of things it was up there with the Orient

Game of 1987 when basic survival was at stake and Burnley might just have folded.

The two semi-final games against Reading were won, 1 – 0 at Burnley and 2 – 0 at Reading. Yet again Clarke Carlisle was immense in both games. To reach Wembley within the context of all the background problems, limitations and pressures was a miraculous achievement. To have actually won it was quite simply an astonishing fairy-tale and with a £60m jackpot at the end of it, how those directors celebrated, although one of them, Ray Griffiths, lay in a hospital bed unable to attend this most marvellous of days. It is not unreasonable to say that the win over Sheffield United saved Burnley Football Club from eventual financial meltdown.

BURNLEY ARE BACK said the *Burnley Express* report in the May, 26th edition: *The day was all the sweeter for those who have traipsed around, with all due respect, places like Aldershot, Maidstone, Halifax, Rochdale, and those who witnessed Hereford win 6 – 0 at Turf Moor, an FA Cup embarrassment at Telford, a defeat to nine-man Rochdale, and those who refused to let their club die on that fateful day in 1987.*

The teams came out to Ian Brown's FEAR, which starts, "For each a road …" and it certainly has been a long old road since 1976. The Burnley supporters wondered which path this wonderful team would take on a day of destiny. But any early nerves were settled in sensational fashion.

If the goals in the semi-final second leg were special, Wade Elliott's 12th minute strike was every bit as good – and it will now acquire legendary status – the goal which took Burnley up.

It started with a driving run, typical of the former Bournemouth man, whose piercing movement when played through the centre has been instrumental in Burnley's success over the second half of the season.

The Blades backed off, and after he laid the ball off for Chris McCann to try his luck, when his effort broke, Elliott effortlessly whipped the ball inside the top left-hand corner to spark mass celebrations in the stand, but not on the pitch where Elliott remained calm.

He knew, as has been the mantra throughout the season, nothing was won yet.

The game took a lot of winning. As is often the case, the Clarets did things the hard way. They created a raft of chances, Martin Paterson curling an effort inches wide, Steve Thompson nodding just past the post. Joey Gudjonsson had an effort scuffed off the line after the break, and then Kyle Walker somehow got back to deny Robbie Blake from Thompson's pass.

You wondered if the missed chances would come back to haunt them, but with Brian Jensen untroubled all afternoon, all fears were unfounded.

We dared to dream, we believed in this team, and my, how they have delivered.

BURNLEY ARE BACK.

They came from all over the world, from Bermuda, Philadelphia, Sydney, Adelaide, Melbourne, Wellington, Mexico, Bulgaria, California, Vancouver, Seattle, Yemen, Kazakhstan, Florida, Belgium, Malta, Norway, France and Cyprus. They came from all points of the UK compass, Ireland, Dublin, Belfast, from the tips of Scotland to the ends of Cornwall. There is a family of Burnley expatriates for whom the umbilical cord will never be stronger. And Burnley itself was half empty.

How many miles did people travel during the season to watch them, how many thousands and thousands of pounds did they spend? Which of them during the opening month of the season did not think that disaster lay ahead? Which of them did not live on their nerves towards the season's end when the prospect of success was close? Who did not feel despair when we could only draw at Southampton, or Derby scored their last minute equaliser with just a handful of games remaining? When were the first thoughts that something special might happen?

"Little Burnley," we kept saying and little Burnley became the 'peoples' club' as the feeling grew in the outside world that here was a hard-up, modest club from a small town battling against the odds. The pundits and the great and good wanted us to succeed. They remembered as we did that horrible night against Tottenham in the Carling Cup when Burnley were just two minutes away from the Final.

None of us dared contemplate with certainty a win over Sheffield when the actual day came. To be there was a bonus we consoled ourselves but for Graham Alexander it was his seventh experience of play-offs, the previous six all failed. Surely this time he will be lucky we implored the football gods.

I know that I spent the Sunday wondering if just one moment would settle it. Would it hinge on a referee's decision or would one man seize the moment and strike home a winning goal? As it turned out, the football gods were indeed on Burnley's side. Every Burnley player played his part, none more so than Carlisle who gave a masterclass in the art of defending. But they were all on top form. Blake twisted and turned until he sent us all dizzy. Caldwell was not far behind Carlisle. Paterson ran and ran and did the work of two players, in attack one minute, defending the next. Elliott was all guile and darting runs, Duff and Kalvenes solid at the back. Thompson up front was more than a match for the physical Morgan. And the Beast, the player of the season, had a quiet day, rarely troubled by Sheffield, but was there on the rare occasions he was needed.

The spectacle at the end was stunning. Mike Dean blew his whistle and the claret and blue end erupted. The tears flowed. Exultation, exhilaration, exhaustion, joy and more joy, cascaded down from the terraces and engulfed this band of brothers who had defied the odds and achieved this miracle. The noise was deafening as we danced and hugged with strangers and pinched ourselves and asked was this really happening. The Sheffield end had emptied by the time skipper Caldwell lifted high the trophy. Another roar filled the stadium and more tears flowed.

This was little Burnley, a founder member of the Football League and no-one could say that they had not earned their place in the Premiership. On that warm sunny afternoon the members of that team had they lost would have been heroes still. But in winning they, and Clarke Carlisle, became legends forever.

Carlisle afterwards described his feelings on the day.

"Words will not describe how it felt at the final whistle to stand in that centre circle. I didn't know what to do, whether to laugh or cry. It was unbelievable – such a magnificent achievement.

"It was awesome. I cried like a little girl on the pitch. It was an unbelievable time and a moment to savour. What an achievement, 61 games, 23 players. It was such a compressed workload but we did it.

"Every single one of us, from the gaffer and Sandy Stewart and Steve Davis and Phil Hughes all the way through the playing staff, what I'm so proud of is from a town of 80,000 there were 36,000 out there, more wanted to come, and we performed and we gave them something to sing about. We respect their support and we're Premier League now. It's awesome.

"I'm just trying to say to the lads who have always been on the fringes of success, and young lads like Alex Macdonald, Adam Kay, Jay Rodriguez, savour the moment. Moments like this don't happen ten a penny in your life. Just enjoy it and make sure you experience the 36,000 out there and all the trappings that come with it. It's an awesome day.

"It had to be a normal 90 minutes, and that's why we stayed at the Bull where we stayed before the Cup games against Chelsea and Arsenal, and we made it as normal and down to earth as possible because when you step into the arena, the last thing you want is to have been daunted already.

"The lads went out, did what they had to, and I was just blessed and privileged to have been a member of this."

There is no doubt that the media and the experts widely welcomed Burnley's return to the big-time, and just about everyone who saw Carlisle's after match interview could not fail to have been deeply moved.

Neutrals sighed with relief at not seeing Sheffield United playing Stoke in the Premier League next season ... instead Burnley will grace the top division, 33 years after they left it and 22 after they nearly slipped into the Conference. It gladdens the heart and makes you feel good about the old game ... **Daily Express**

It was settled by a goal that deserved to win any game. If Burnley's tale, on a club level, is a romantic one for having been away from the top division for so long, then the goalscorer encapsulated the fairy-tale nature of their ascent. Wade Elliot, 30, who settled the outcome after only 13 minutes, was a free transfer from Bournemouth having previously played in non-league football at Bashley ... **The Independent**

Grown men cried, strangers embraced, and under a shower of ticker tape Wembley saw an emotional outpouring that brought an end to 33 years of hurt ... it was hard to avoid being consumed by the euphoria that greeted the minor miracle overseen by Owen Coyle ... among the Claret and Blue hordes few ever imagined they would see this day come to pass ... nobody can say they do not deserve it ... **The Times**

For all ages of Burnley fans, yesterday was special ... for the older supporters it was all about the restoration of the natural order, a return to the time when Burnley were an established force in the land ... **The Telegraph**

All over the pitch there were Burnley heroes ... Carlisle didn't put a foot wrong. Then there was Elliott who can dine out for life on his winner ... make no mistake the better side won ... **The Telegraph**

Burnley are back in the big-time and ready to bring a touch of much-needed romance to the billionaire world of top-flight football. They are the smallest town ever to boast a Premier League club and their entire population could fit inside Old Trafford. What Owen Coyle and his players have achieved this season is little short of a miracle ... and no-one could begrudge brilliant Burnley their long-awaited return to the big-time ... **The Sun**

It will be 50 years next season since Burnley won the title and the anniversary will be celebrated among the elite. A Lancashire town has burst into the limelight, their elevation back among the elite constituting a staggering achievement by one of the Championship's thinnest squads ... **The Guardian**

The enormous significance of this match was that a town was united both during the game and afterwards. Supporter Mark Griffiths was both at the game and the celebrations and parade afterwards. "I can't get over what I witnessed. There's real poverty in Burnley – there were young women with teeth missing holding their grubby babies up like it was some kind of papal blessing. There were whole Asian families waving and shouting at the roundabout by Centenary Way. It was magnificent.

"Our little town turned itself inside out to applaud – nay worship our team. They were stood on walls and rooftops and leaning perilously out of office windows and hanging banners from the bridges over Yorkshire Street and Finsley Gate. It was still magnificent.

"Leaving the Town Hall the chill descended and the crowds thinned out a little, but the busses were pursued by young girls and middle aged men waving homemade flags and tattooed adolescents who'd ripped their shirts off. When we approached the Turf again the crowds were still there, deeper and even more urgent, with some having sprinted across the town to get there. When we crossed some of the junctions you could see people running along the parallel streets. In a 'zombie' flick it would have seemed threatening, but instead, here, it was utterly heart-warming to see that people cared so much.

"Burnley has had its well-documented problems in the past, both social and political. But this was a match and victory that brought a town together. It was a glorious triumph."

In the Premiership, Carlisle appeared in the fabulous wins but was as stunned as anyone when Owen Coyle left Burnley and just as surprised when Brian Laws was appointed. It was then the next manager, Eddie Howe, who saw that he was a player that Burnley could now release.

At the beginning of the 2011/12 season he signed a season long loan at Preston North End. Howe had informed him that he was not in his plans, something that Carlisle wrote about in his book *A Footballer's Life:*

'He said he was looking to build a squad of players who were mostly in their mid-twenties and he explained that he would not be renewing my contract at the end of the year either. I was almost in tears on the other side of the desk. A couple of months earlier, after Burnley had just missed out on a play-off place the season after being relegated from the Premier League, we had discussed the possibility of a new contract and I had been under the impression that I was definitely part of Eddie's plans. The apparent U-turn was so painful that I didn't have the wherewithal to react. I calmly wished Eddie the best of luck for the new season, jumped in my car and drifted home in a haze of uncertainty.

'Burnley was without doubt the most successful, the most enjoyable and closest-knit club that I have ever been at. As players we had risen from Championship relegation favourites to the heights of the Premier League, all via a League Cup semi-final against Tottenham Hotspur and the most monumental day at Wembley. Our wives had formed a friendship that I haven't seen at any other club before or since, and we all felt comfortable in each other's company. I didn't want to hear this news.

'What made it worse was that Eddie didn't even want me to come back for pre-season. He said that I could if I wanted, but I would no longer be required to attend. What had I done that meant I wasn't even wanted around the place? I don't think I'm a bad egg. I am not unprofessional around the club, and I don't bad-mouth people or sit on the bitter bus. So I didn't understand why I was being kept at arm's length. I tried to be a good example to the younger pros at the club and, if anything I did was unbecoming of a professional, I made sure to let them know. I spent so much time with lads such as Adam Kay, Alex MacDonald and Jay Rodriguez, all of whom I have a great fondness for and huge admiration for their ability. The club knew that they could trust me and that I would bring anything to the table and do all I could to help and guide the younger ones. I felt that surely my input in that regard was worth keeping me round a football club. It really was the worst way to leave a football club: unwanted.'

Many months later: *'Gem and I met up with some of our Burnley friends for a spot of Christmas dinner in Manchester. We ate with Graham Alexander, now the manager of Fleetwood Town, and his wife Karen; Steven Jordan now at Dunfermline Athletic in Scotland and his wife Katy; and Michael Duff still at Burnley and his wife Jess. We had a great time and a good catch-up, but afterwards both Gem and I had pangs of longing to be back at Burnley.*

'This is very abnormal for me. Gem calls me "The Littlest Hobo" because I wander from club to club, making new friends and dropping old ones off with very little emotion; it's just the way of life that football is. This is the only time that leaving a club has had a lasting impact on me. We loved it there. I would happily have stayed there for the rest of my career; so much so that I tried to have discussions with Eddie Howe and Paul Fletcher about having a dual role at the club, as Burnley is the site of the campus for the University College of Football Business.

'This is an interesting initiative where they roll out courses on the specifics of running a football club, an industry that is completely different to any other. They had been asking me to get more involved with it and I went in as a visiting lecturer one day to share my experiences of the football world. I really enjoyed it and thought that I might be able to tie in some kind of role with them alongside being a member of the squad.

'Alas it wasn't to be. All good things must come to an end but at least the friendships that we made don't have to and I can see this group gathering in 30 years' time and still reminiscing about our heyday at Turf Moor.'

If Burnley fans wanted to see Carlisle's book reveal some of the events behind the scenes at Turf Moor, with particular reference to two managers, Owen Coyle and the manner of his departure; and then Brian Laws and the relegation he oversaw, they were very disappointed. He tactfully described them as two polar opposites in the context of impact as each arrived. Fans were rather more frank, seeing the impact of the former as quite astonishing; and the impact of the latter as an unmitigated disaster.

'When Owen Coyle took over from Steve Cotterill, there was a palpable shift in the atmosphere around the club. Cotts had been at Burnley for many years and I think he had taken the squad as far as he could. His forthright and often tough manner had instilled a level of fear around the place. Owen came in and completely shifted the dynamic. His focus was on total enjoyment. It was fun at training, something that a lot of the squad hadn't encountered for a few years. This change led to a happy workforce and a happy workforce is a productive one as any business person worth their salt will tell you. This joy-infused team that was high on confidence went on to be incredibly successful considering the players it contained. We were definitely a classic example of a team whose total was greater than the sum of its parts.

'When Owen left the club we experienced the other end of the spectrum. We were in a run of bad form in the Premier League but still in 13th place. The new boss needed to be dynamic, charismatic and someone who could make an immediate impact. After a couple of weeks it was plain to see that Brian Laws didn't have those traits. The lads asked a few questions among ourselves when he was appointed because he had recently left Sheffield Wednesday after taking them to the bottom of the Championship. We believed the club was in a position to attract one of the bigger names in management, but obviously not. Had we done so, we might have drawn confidence from that, rather than wondering if he was the right man. I genuinely believe we would have remained in the Premier League had Owen stayed, but we'll never know.'

Carlisle did describe one incident from which we can deduce there was a damaging lack of respect shown by the players towards Brian Laws.

'We were on our way down to Cardiff for a Championship fixture in early December and had made our plans to stay over afterwards and spend two nights in the Welsh capital. We were travelling down on the team bus the day before and the snow was falling with intent. Just as we passed Junction 16 of the M6 the manager Brian Laws received the phone call that we had all been hoping for: the game was off. Anyone would have thought we'd won the league. The two-day party had become a three-day event and there was no hiding everyone's excitement at the prospect. The coach pulled over on the A500 as we held an emergency meeting at the back. We didn't want to carry on to Cardiff and the roads were murder and that would cost us several hours valuable drinking time. After a couple of phone calls and a round or two of voting, it was decided. We could take the bus to Nottingham and spend the weekend there. We could be in the pub in less than two hours and begin the mother of all Christmas parties. But there was just one problem: the manager and his staff were still with us on the bus.'

Carlisle described the brief conversation between the players and Laws regarding what might be done with him and the staff. It was agreed the coach would take them back to the last service station from where they could get a taxi home. The next paragraph sums up the situation that existed at the club and is a sad indictment of a failed appointment.

'I don't think that any other manager I've worked under would have allowed that to happen. But there was far more power in the dressing room than in Brian Laws' hands.'

Carlisle went to York City and then soldiered on at Northampton, re-united with Aidy Boothroyd, and appeared in the Wembley play-off final of 2013 having clocked up over 70 games after he left Burnley. Alas he was on the losing side but it was a fitting place to play his final game. He announced his retirement on Thursday 23 May and thus enabled himself to concentrate on new career roles; the chairmanship of the PFA being a role he would now have to relinquish. In a radio interview on his retirement he described himself as a player of moderate ability, but always giving 100% had made full use of it, and he'd had some phenomenal moments, the greatest being Wembley, 2009. He was a bargain buy by Steve Cotterill and a giant in the promotion season especially in the final stages. He becomes another player who will always be welcome back at Turf Moor.

It was in December, 2014, that we all heard the sad news that he had been involved in a dreadful incident whilst walking on the A64 near his home on the outskirts of York when he was involved in a collision with a lorry. Details were scarce other than he was air-lifted to a Leeds hospital, and that just a few days earlier he had been apprehended for drink-driving; that he was walking by the road around 7.30 in the morning, and the A64 is the fast ring-road around York that sees most traffic moving at between 50 and 60 mph. It is not a road where you go for an early morning stroll.

It was easy to speculate that the incident might well have been promoted by the recurrence of depression. Even in mid-January no details had emerged, save for the fact that his recovery would be long and slow, but that he was now awake. We could only wish him well and that by some magic or medical process, his demons could be permanently banished.

9

2010 Robbie Blake, the Little Magician

From *Something to Write Home About,* the magazine of the London Clarets. Article by Dave Thomas

So to our great disappointment Robbie Blake left Burnley FC, unable to accept the terms offered to him by Brian Laws at the end of season 2009/10 – one year with the option of a second had he appeared in a certain number of games. By and large there was general agreement that what he was offered was appropriate for a player of his age. But, Robbie felt that he deserved a straight two years deal. His name was linked with Hearts and places like Huddersfield where his experience and class might have been well received. Staggeringly he left for Bolton Wanderers and Owen Coyle, tempted by the lure of another year in the Premiership, serving as an impact player coming off the bench.

He left with our heartfelt thanks for what he had done for Burnley Football Club and the entertainment that he had provided. But that gratitude was tinged with some regret that he had gone to re-join the man destined to be derided in and around Burnley for years to come.

Probably, it will be season 2008/09 that we will most readily associate with Robbie Blake. It was a wonderful time to be around Turf Moor. Not since the days of Jimmy McIlroy in the 50s and 60s at Burnley Football Club, have supporters been able to use the word 'magician' in their tributes to any Turf Moor footballer. But that is how Robbie Blake was described more than once during season 2008/09, one of the greatest seasons in the club's history. Demoted to the bench early in the season, with more than a few people wondering if his legs had gone, he came back to enjoy a simply sparkling season, rolling back the years, and demonstrating his full range of talent and skills. The media and the TV pundits drooled over his performances particularly in the Carling Cup games and the Wembley play-off final against Sheffield United. And yet this was a player, by now 33, with self-confessed weight problems, and who had been around the block not once, but several times. With just a little more pace Robbie Blake might well have been an England player. But his lack of pace was more than compensated for by his touch, awareness, intelligence, anticipation and passing skills, and all that is before we even mention his shooting and free-kick, dead-ball skills.

He had a number of outstanding games during 2008/09, was MOTM on seven occasions, scored some superb goals, and at the end of the season shared the player of the year awards with Brian Jensen. The main Clarets website *Claretsmad* voted him player of the season over the year. His superlative goal against Reading early on in the Championship decided the game.

One game in particular though provided a platform for the nation to watch his sublime talents and this was in the semi-final Carling Cup game against Tottenham at Turf Moor. The first leg had been lost 1 – 4 but on a wild, wet night, in front of a packed Turf Moor, Burnley clawed their way back to parity with a 3 – 0 score by the end of the 90 minutes. Blake had a foot in each of the goals. He scored the first with a wonderful long-range free-kick, made the second with a darting, weaving run that left Spurs defenders on their backsides in the penalty area, and assisted the third with a floated free-kick into the six-yard box. That Burnley lost in extra time was a travesty and was the result of the rule that away goals did not count double in the event of a draw. Spurs scored with Burnley just two minutes away from the Wembley Final. Blake, amongst others, was heartbroken and the tears flowed in the dressing room afterwards. But the fact that they had come so close to Wembley on that night arguably whetted their appetite, and increased their desire to make it there in the Championship. This they duly did and in May at the season's end the tears were those of joy not despair.

Sometimes referred to as the Band of Brothers, this tiny squad funded by one of the division's smallest budgets, in front of an average crowd of just 13,000, triumphed in the Wembley Play-off Final in what was the season's outstanding football fairy tale.

* * *

Born in Middlesbrough, Blake began his career with Darlington in the 1994/95 season. Bradford City snapped him up on the strength of his games at Darlington where he scored 21 goals in 68 games. The Bradford offer of £300,000 was accepted by Darlington and Blake played first under manager Chris Kamara and then Paul Jewell scoring eight goals in his first full season.

With Lee Mills he formed an excellent partnership and the 40 goals they scored between them earned Bradford City promotion to the Premiership. Blake scored 16 of those goals and his winner against Wolves in the final game of 1998/99 saw the side finish as runners-up. Bradford City was hardly the most glamorous club in the division and it was a marvellous season for both him and club.

In the Premiership though, he failed to make an impact, starting just 15 games and with another 12 as substitute; so he was loaned out to Nottingham Forest for three months. "He will bring to the team something we haven't got at the moment," said manager Platt, "the ability to score a goal out of nothing. We drew up a short list of players during the summer and he was on that. Robbie has shown in the past he can score goals in this division." Having been frozen out at Bradford he had done himself no favours when he criticised their chairman, Geoffrey Richards, in the Forest programme.

On his return, to a new manager Jim Jefferies, he insisted he would have no problems fighting for his place. He started 14 games and scored four goals but Bradford were relegated at the end of their second season in the top division.

Nottingham Forest and their manager David Platt would have taken him back permanently but their final bid was rejected.

A few months later in 2001/02 the club received a £1m bid from Burnley and, because Bradford were in severe financial trouble, they accepted the bid and Blake moved to Turf Moor and new manager Stan Ternent.

He signed a three year contract and at this point Burnley were ambitious and the ITV Digital money deal was enabling them to compete with the top clubs and aim high. But he had a poor start and initially the fans wondered just what was going on with the signing. He featured little in the first few months owing to a hernia injury and the sense of his arrival was questioned. In one game he played, Stan Ternent famously likened his performance to someone wearing divers' boots.

But Blake came good and in season 2003/04 he was the club's leading scorer with 22 goals in all competitions. It was a tough season though, by then the ITV Digital deal had ended acrimoniously; Burnley were as good as penniless, and though Ternent worked miracles keeping the club in the Championship, albeit only just, he was replaced in the summer by new man Steve Cotterill.

Blake continued to shine, scoring another 13 goals by January, but was unsettled by bids that came from Wigan Athletic and Paul Jewell. Wigan's final bid was £700,000 but was rejected despite Burnley's precarious financial state. The whole tone of the dealings left a lot to be desired and accusations flew back and forth that the player had been 'tapped' and deliberately unsettled.

Out of the blue, however, came a bid from Steve Bruce and Birmingham City. Burnley accepted the reported bid of £1.25m. To a degree the whole affair left fans with the feeling that they had been deserted and that with the financial limitations at Turf Moor and the best player sold, that the future held little promise.

He made his debut for Birmingham in the FA Cup against Leeds United and was confident he could succeed back in the Premiership.

"Clinton Morrison and Emile Heskey have done fantastically well, but hopefully I can push them for a place. I can play in a few positions, behind the strikers or dropping deep, and that gives the gaffer some selection to think about. I thought if anything a bottom four team in the Premiership would come in for me. But Birmingham, with the quality of players they have, was an even bigger bonus."

His time at Birmingham was unsuccessful and he played just 11 games and before the year was out he had signed for Leeds United and manager Kevin Blackwell for £800,000. The financial problems that Leeds United had been through are well documented but they remained ambitious and determined to get back into the Premiership and Blackwell saw the signing as an indication that things were on the up at Elland Road. He signed a three year deal.

"It's a step back in terms of divisions but hopefully I can get back into the Premier League with Leeds. With the quality of players we have got, I'm sure there will be no end of goals going in."

To a degree he was right and there was a Wembley play-off final against Watford. But it was Watford who won and from that point on Leeds' financial problems increased. The problem he faced was that he was one of six strikers at Leeds and he failed to become a first-team regular until Blackwell left and new manager Dennis Wise arrived. He managed eight goals in 2006/07 but Leeds were relegated to League One, money problems became even worse, the club filed for administration and there was a ten points deduction. Players had to go and Blake was one of them.

It was Burnley who re-signed him for a bargain fee of just £250,000, Leeds being eager to get him off the wage bill. Steve Cotterill, who admired him enormously, announced that Blake, by now 31, had "unfinished business" at Turf Moor. The club ran a season ticket promotion campaign on the back of the signing. "Don't miss the chance for a reunion with Robbie Blake; it's not too late to secure your season ticket." Burnley still had little money to play around with but the arrival of a new director, Brendan Flood, had resulted in a small increase in available funds. Flood revealed that they had been working on the deal for a few weeks and doing their best to keep it quiet.

"With strikers, once it gets mooted that they may be on the move, it invites others to join in the hunt. Being able to keep it under wraps is therefore vital; otherwise you get competitive bids coming and the price spirals. Robbie is a proven entertainer and one of the top strikers in the Championship and we know he is always going to score goals. But the really important factor is that he is happy and keen to play for Burnley."

The truth, as well we know, is that footballers in this day and age follow the money as a general rule, but that said, there is an element of truth in the observation that Turf Moor may well have been his 'spiritual home' as pundit Peter Beagrie described it. After his return in July 2007, notwithstanding the occasional dip in form, he blossomed so that in 2008/09 he was certainly one of that small band of brothers who flourished, entertained and provided an outstanding season beyond the wildest dreams of any Burnley supporter.

His return in 2007 was a popular one; the Turf Moor fans are loyal to their favourites and his return debut in August saw a 2 – 1 win over West Bromwich Albion. Steve Cotterill had faith in him but eventually he too was replaced as manager as wins and entertainment dried up.

In came Owen Coyle from Scotland. Encouraged by Coyle's brand of football philosophy and style; the same players who under Cotterill had set a club record of 19 games without a win, then proceeded to play, to entertain, to attack, and to blossom. Nine of them, including Robbie Blake, formed the team that started the game at Wembley in May 2009 and won promotion to the Premiership.

This is not to say that all was sweetness and light between the manager and Blake early in that season when Blake was demoted to the bench. "I had a little sulk," said Blake albeit with a cheeky grin on his face. Nevertheless he appeared in every one of Burnley's 61 games, a tremendous achievement and only one of two players at the club to do so. If anyone had said to him at the beginning of the season that he would play 61 games he would have shook his head no doubt in disbelief. Only Manchester United played more games than Burnley with a squad of players twice as big. The scale of Burnley's and Blake's achievement was truly monumental for although they had a squad of 23, small enough in itself, an even smaller number of just 18 players, week in week out, played the vast majority of the games.

It was at the time he signed for Birmingham City, when he was 28, that Blake made a prophetic statement. "I feel I'm the type of player who will improve with age so you never give up hope of getting back into the Premiership." To say he improved with age was indeed an understatement.

A list of his magic moments during the promotion season would begin with his home goal against Reading when he received a pass on the edge of the box and with pure guile threaded a low shot into the corner of the goal. A perfect, long-distance free-kick strike away at Preston was a trademark goal. A goal at Coventry during the win was class but his celebration has entered folklore at the club.

Apparently well known for his failure to win at poker on the team coach, even when possessing a winning hand, a 'bad-beat-bob' hand, he was presented by Clarke Carlisle before the Coventry game with a commemorative pair of red underpants inscribed with 'bad beat bob' on the rear. After his Coventry strike in his glee he lowered his shorts and revealed the briefs to the delight of the Burnley crowd. The club shop cashed in of course and sold hundreds. Director Brendan Flood in his elation after the win at Chelsea wore a pair over his trousers into the Chelsea directors' room. He was asked to remove them. The briefs took a bow again at Wembley when after an on-pitch interview he skipped over to the Burnley fans, and revealed them to the utter delight of the crowd as he danced across the turf. The studio pundits were in hysterics.

Perhaps it was the game at Plymouth when the belief really took hold that the play-offs were achievable. Again it was a superb Blake strike that decided the game when he half-volleyed the ball as it came to him 18 yards out and lashed it home. Another superb strike came at QPR just a few days after Chelsea had been disposed of.

But if there is one truly memorable free kick that still lives in the memory it is a goal that he scored against Preston North End at Turf Moor from 30 yards out and wide of the penalty area. With minimal back-lift he struck a shot of such power and accuracy that it arrowed into the top right corner of the net before anyone could blink. The ground was stunned and for a brief moment there was a sort of speechless silence until the sheer magnificence of this goal registered.

If one game defined Robbie Blake's career at Burnley it was the Carling Cup game against Tottenham Hotspur at Turf Moor in season 2008/09.

Over the years, Burnley versus Spurs games had always been special. There were the games of the early sixties when McIlroy and Adamson pitted their skills against those of Blanchflower, Mackay and Greaves et al. In 1984 Second Division Burnley went to White Hart Lane and won 4 – 1 in the Milk Cup as it was then known, to provide a massive upset. And then during Stan Ternent's tenancy Burnley, then a Championship side, had beaten Spurs 2 – 1 at Turf Moor in the Carling Cup to provide another upset, reminding the fans of what life was once like at Turf Moor in the glory days.

Spurs arrived at Burnley for this 2009 semi-final game in no great shape. Harry Redknapp had done a reasonable job in bringing some semblance of stability and recovery to a side that had done really badly until his arrival. The first part of their season had been dreadful. The possibility of relegation was quite clearly there the way things were going. Somehow they had won the first leg of the tie 4 – 1 and the Burnley team and supporters who were there still wonder how. The first 45 minutes of that game had been a showcase for all that was good about Burnley with one-touch passing, slick moves, speed and acceleration and they certainly deserved to go in at half-time at least 2 – 0 up. Robbie Blake sent a glancing header half an inch wide. Had that gone in to make the score 2 – 0 it was reasonable to assume Burnley would have gone on to win the game. As it was, the one goal they scored was buried beneath the four goals that Tottenham scored in a 20 minute second-half spell.

When they arrived in Burnley for the second game the pundits agreed that they had the game in the bag with their healthy three-goal cushion. It seemed hardly possible that a small Championship side could overturn such a lead against a side containing the multi-million pound stars that Tottenham had assembled. But in atrocious conditions with cold, swirling rain that battered the ground, in front of almost 20,000 soaked people and millions more on TV that is exactly what happened on a night of drama, excitement, passion, pride and then ultimate heartbreaking disappointment.

In a game like this, three goals down, the classic game plan is usually to bag an early goal, get one more to set up a charge for the finishing line, and then a late winner to give the opposition no time to come back. Burnley did this by the book, and did exactly that to level the overall score.

Harry Redknapp handed the Clarets some hope by including a rookie goalkeeper and the young lad, who had already tipped away a goal-bound back-pass, had not one clue about Blake's free-kick taking ability. In the 34th minute he curled a wonderful dead-ball kick from 30 yards, wide of the defensive wall, and into the net at the near post. The Spurs defence and the Burnley players mostly at the far post presumed that was where a hopeful cross would go. Not so: the magnificent free-kick with a low trajectory curled its way in and the jubilation was simply immense. Game on.

At half-time the topic of conversation was simple: could Burnley get a second whilst at the same time keeping out the talents of Defoe, Modric and Pavlyuchenko? Hybrid side this might have been, but it still contained some impressive players. In truth other than an occasional attempt on goal they hardly seemed interested and Burnley ran the game. The second goal was no surprise.

Blake again: another moment of brilliance. He received the ball someway out on the left-wing. He weaved his way this way and that, twisting, turning, changing direction, cutting in, cutting out, leaving Gunter flat on his backside, leaving Bentley flat on his backside before firing across a fast, low ball that McCann pounced on at the far post to fire home. The creation of this goal alone was worth the entrance money. This was skill, flair, dazzling footwork, a man on top of his game, and it left all of us open-mouthed. In a word it was exquisite.

2 – 0: Was it really possible that Burnley could do the impossible? Burnley pressed even harder and with nine minutes to go Coyle brought on the young fresh-legged Rodriguez. Now it was all out attack. Nerves were close to breaking point when suddenly Pavlyuchenko was clear but missed the target. Four minutes to go, death or glory, you just sensed that something was going to happen. It was one of those nights.

And then: a free kick way out on the left. Of course it was Blake who took it and the kick, the flight, the trajectory was perfect. The young goalkeeper dropped the ball and it was Rodriguez who immediately lobbed the ball into the net. The tumult that followed was like nothing ever witnessed before at Turf Moor and that includes European nights in the sixties against Reims and Hamburg. Some people really thought that Burnley had won the tie but alas when the euphoria died down there was the realisation that there was now 30 minutes of extra time.

"Keep playing the way you are and you're there," Alex Ferguson texted Alastair Campbell.

Those minutes were agony for all Burnley fans. They ticked down slowly, agonisingly. The wet, heavy, boggy pitch now counted against Burnley who had run themselves into a state of exhaustion. Paterson was dead on his feet and was replaced by Akinbiyi, Eagles could hardly move. But Blake was still working like a Trojan to defend deep in his own half. Spurs who had done so little and hardly broken sweat all night did even less in the first period of extra time.

But, in the second period, the fatigue that the Burnley players felt was like a deep pit and with the fans whistling and screaming for the final whistle, believing that Wembley was within touching distance, Spurs made a foray into the Burnley half. The ball was squared across the penalty area and suddenly Pavlyuchenko had the ball in the net with just two minutes to go. The curtain of silence that fell from three sides of the ground was instant, one of stunned shock and heartbroken disbelief. Jensen had in fact got a touch to the Russian's perfectly placed shot. Then on the stroke of full time insult was added to injury when the invisible Defoe who had been appalling all night, advanced on goal and finished clinically.

The ovation that rained down from the stands on Blake and the Burnley players was no consolation to them. They had been heroes and had deserved to win, but for some there was the clear feeling that this game was the last chance they would have of playing at the new Wembley in a Cup Final. Sometimes the football gods decree that heroics will count for nothing. Heads drooped, shoulders slumped, some sat down in disbelief, and some were clearly in tears. No one deserved to win more than Blake but life and football is cruel. If only we could have said to them, "Don't worry you will win the Championship play-off at Wembley in May."

After the game Blake was inconsolable.

"I don't think you can think of being proud at the moment, it's just sheer devastation. We've come so close to the final of a major competition. The lads have turned in an outstanding performance and I can't put it into words, we're just devastated. It was an unbelievable performance, you couldn't have written it to be honest. Everybody made a contribution to the game and we deserved to go through, but that's the way it goes and we'll just have to take it on the chin. You look at the run we've had and we haven't been lucky, it's all deserved and if anything, we were unlucky down at their place. We didn't deserve to be 4 – 1 down. Yes we can be proud, but at the moment it's devastating.

"They have fantastic players and it was a great finish from Pavlyuchenko. Brian was unlucky he didn't manage to keep that one out, he can't keep them all out. He got a good hand to it but it was just a sickener. To get done in that way at the end, it's cruel. We've beaten them 3 – 0 over 90 minutes but with the rules, not having away goals counting after 90 minutes, it's just so frustrating. To come so far and get so close, to get the three goals and then concede with 27 minutes gone in extra-time, it was a sucker-punch. To beat them 3 – 0 in 90 minutes took a lot out of us, and we tried to play it out and keep the ball in their half, but they punished us at the end.

"It was a great feeling, my goal. Grezza said, 'The keeper's well over there; have a go'. I gave him the eyes, he stepped a yard and there was enough power on it to make sure it went in. It was a great feeling but I'm devastated now. I'm not thinking 'what a goal'; I'm just gutted about the result.

"The fans were amazing; they really were our twelfth man. I'm sure the players are proud of the fans and the fans are proud of the players and the way they performed. It's just so disappointing, so many Burnley fans in the wet and the wind. It's just one of those things."

Owen Coyle tried to put the emotions we all felt into words:

"The lads have shown tonight that when they get to the levels we've set, we're a good side. So there's a lot to take from that. There's disappointment but I've been there as a player and a manager and you go again. They must have the mental strength to go along with their ability to bounce back. We have that disappointment but they can go out with their heads held high because some of the play was magnificent. There's no doubt it was very cruel on us but that's why we all love football. Hopefully further down the line it will work for us. But I couldn't have asked any more of these players. We're a Championship club so to recover that deficit and look the team in charge, I think it has in essence, been a wonderful night for Burnley Football Club. The fans have turned out and shown what the club is all about. The atmosphere was unbelievable tonight, that's what I want as a manager and it's what I want on a game to game basis. It's not always going to be possible but the fans played their part. They were magnificent and roared us on from the start.

"When you analyse both legs, I think we were the better side. But you don't always get what you deserve in football and that's what happened tonight. We were two minutes away from going to that Final but they were terrific finishes from their two lads at the end. I think at that point our lads were out on their legs, if you think about the amount of games they've played and what they gave tonight. I really couldn't be any more proud of the lads and what they offered. I couldn't have asked any more of them individually and collectively. I asked them to go out and reach a standard tonight and not to have any regrets. The only regret is that we've not reached the Final. It's important that we pick ourselves up and dust ourselves down now. We've got a massive game on Saturday against West Brom, because we'd love to have an FA Cup run now like we've had in the Carling Cup.

"They're such a grounded group of players who want to do their best for the club and they'll be hurting, but we'll look to use it as a motivation to drive us on.

"It would have been nice to have had that gala day at Wembley and I really believe we could have made a game of it, but it's not to be."

"We need to climb Everest," Coyle had said before the game. They so very nearly did. The Press unanimously praised Burnley to the skies and there wasn't one reporter that didn't say Tottenham should be thoroughly embarrassed by their win.

Henry Winter in *The Telegraph* wrote some memorable lines. His final one: "The tears began to flow for Burnley but really their eyes should glisten with pride."

Alan Pattullo in *The Scotsman* wrote that Owen Coyle must have felt that his heart had been ripped from his chest when Pavlyuchenko scored.

"Robbie Blake was the star of the night, the best player on the park," said *The Daily Mirror*.

Afterwards Harry Redknapp, totally discomfited, said this had been the most uncomfortable night of his football life and that after the third goal went in he thought they were dead and buried.

"It would have been a nightmare if we'd lost," said Jermain Defoe, "and it would have been difficult to recover."

Radio phone-ins after the game were filled with Spurs supporters wondering how on earth they had won, and saying that their overpaid, spoilt, pampered superstars had deserve to lose. Turf Moor on the night of the game opened its doors as the Theatre of Dreams. It closed them as the Theatre of Broken Hearts.

There was only one season in the Premiership with Burnley but two goals will be imprinted in Burnley minds for years to come. Blake's goal that beat Manchester United was utterly sublime; a volley of such accuracy and power that it almost broke the net. That it was captured by Sky cameras during the live transmission of the game made it all the better. This was a goal and result of such significance that they flashed round the world. If just one goal put Burnley on the international map from New York to the Far East, then this was it.

The goal against Blackburn Rovers at Ewood Park put Burnley into a 1 – 0 lead. Taking the ball from just inside the Blackburn half he made ground and then let fly from distance with a shot that had the Burnley crowd roaring with joy and elation. It was a goal good enough to win any game but alas Blackburn went on to win 3 – 2.

All good things must come to an end and it is one of the great sadnesses of football that truly accomplished players grow older. Time takes its toll and they are caught in possession more and more often. Though the head may be willing, the legs simply will not function quite as fast. For some, the waist becomes a little thicker; it becomes harder to stay fit.

Thus, they have to depart – either to retirement or another club. That moment came for the wonderful Robbie Blake in the summer of 2010. Some players are forever welcomed back at Turf Moor. If they step onto the pitch in the colours of a new club they are applauded with affection and appreciation. Robbie never did make it back as a player for someone else. His contributions to Bolton Wanderers were limited and when he then moved to Doncaster Rovers he was eventually released having made few appearances there.

Making a total of nearly 250 appearances for Burnley, Robbie Blake goes down in Burnley history as a player who made a real and lasting contribution to the club. At his best there were certain moments when he really was the nearest thing to Jimmy McIlroy that some supporters might have seen. He was, in fact, one of the few modern players that Jimmy actually enjoyed watching.

Some years later in 2015 in a poignant interview with Suzanne Geldard, Blake revealed his sense of regret at leaving Burnley in the way he did, particularly the second time when he felt unable to continue at the club as long as Brian Laws was there. He confessed to meeting director Brendan Flood and telling him that as long as Laws was at the club, then he couldn't be. There were arguments he said and even astonishment when the assistant manager asked him what it was like in the Premier League.

"Laws didn't want to play me," he told Geldard. "He told people I was injured when I was fit. It was a personality thing; it was everything, on the field and off the field. I told Brendan but the hard thing was not being able to say anything in the press."

At the time this is what we suspected but it all remained under the carpet, such a sad way for a man and supreme entertainer to end his time at Turf Moor.

Dave Thomas.

10

2017 Little Old Burnley

As the days became shorter and the nights progressively darkened, Simon Hughes commenced a journey through the country's most successful football region during the winter of the 2016/17 season. From the Premier League to grassroots, Hughes met the individuals shaping the game; those able to explain how and why trends and moods are shifting.

Hughes' book On The Brink *features interviews with Jurgen Klopp, Sean Dyche, Gary Neville and many other managers, players, owners, chairmen, directors and politicians. The book studies the modern state of the North West's professional clubs, also slipping into the semi-professional ranks and amateur levels.*

Hughes began in Carlisle and went south, through Barrow, through Morecambe and towards the Fylde coast. He trekked inland to Preston, to Burnley, to Accrington. From Southport he moved into deepest Merseyside and then to Chester, Greater Manchester and inner-city Manchester itself. Part social examination, part travelogue, Hughes re-discovers and laces together some of the personalities and moments that have helped define football history.

Simon Hughes is a journalist, author and editor. He covers Merseyside football in The Independent *and travels elsewhere for* The Sunday Telegraph. *He has written several football books about Liverpool FC. DT*

***

On The Brink: A Journey Through English Football's North West by Simon Hughes (De Coubertin Books) From Chapter 7: Little Old Burnley

At first and second glance Sean Dyche does not appear to be the most sympathetic of characters. He is judged to be the toughest looking manager in the Premier League. He is six-foot tall with shaven ginger hair, a ginger goatee beard and ginger sideburns that are sharpened at the ends. He is the manager with the voice that sounds like it has passed through a cheese grater, a voice that nevertheless commands authority. He is the manager with the presence of a warden at a maximum security prison who possesses the sort of tough humour that can deal with dangerous inmates. He is the manager of a football club from a struggling Lancashire town where there are blizzards in late April.

Dyche could be the Lord of Winterfell. With his arms folded and his sensors activated, he is looking out of the sliding windows in his office and scanning the treacherous terrain of Burnley's Barnfield Training Centre, as youth team players try to control passes in the wind. The snow has turned into bullets of hail and this has been the pattern for a few days. It explains why, on Dyche's desk, there are tissues and a bottle of cough medicine. In Burnley the frosts are longer than they are elsewhere in the north-west due to its meteorological position high beside the Pennines. You have to be prepared to play for Burnley; to play, indeed, for Dyche. This cold is not defeating him however. He is wearing his Burnley training kit: short sleeved shirt and shorts short enough to reveal the enormous thighs of a central defender, the sort forwards would bounce off during an eighteen-year career in the Football League. Beneath his flip flops there are mud stains on his socks. The marks point to the probability that training sessions earlier in the day had taken place with the help of Benylin.

Dyche is the longest serving manager at a Premier League club in the north-west. That three of his five seasons were spent in the Championship is a testament to both the vision and understanding of

Mike Garlick, the chairman who appointed him, and his own resilience; to rise, to fall, and to be able to rise again. Burnley were promoted into the Premier League, relegated and then promoted, this time returning as champions. When I meet him, he is on course to becoming the first Burnley manager to survive relegation from the top flight since 1975. In terms of what clubs spend in relation to their league position, Burnley were the third highest achieving team in the 2016/17 Premier League season. Despite breaking their own transfer records the summer before, Burnley had still spent the lowest amount on players in the division by some distance. Their fourteenth position in the table represented a gap of six above expectations.

Despite his achievements, Dyche had become a categorised manager at Burnley, a manager who favours 4-4-2, a manager who favours hard-working, direct and physical football over technique and flair, a manager who prefers British players over foreign. Whilst his supporters admire him for speaking in plain facts and commend his ability to cut through all the surrounding hyperbole, critics say that simply answering questions about why British managers get overlooked for top jobs, makes Dyche a Little Englander; that considering Burnley voted overwhelmingly to leave the EU, Dyche is in the ideal place, where people will truly believe him, working for a club that might as well rename itself Little Old Burnley, because he mentions it so often when discussing the challenges that face him.

I wanted to know from Dyche what it was like being the Premier League manager with the lowest budget while working in an industry where everyone thinks you have everything. I wanted to know to what extent Burnley geography has dictated the club's fortune. I wanted to know as well what he was really like, whether preconceptions about who he is and what he thinks were true and how he manages them; and can he shift them?

There was a simple question to start with and it related to endurance; how he'd remained as Burnley's manager for nearly five years when so many of his contemporaries had been sacked, especially those that faced relegation or been sucked down the Championship plughole.

Dyche jumps straight in, quoting Howard Wilkinson, Leeds United's old manager, not known for his charisma. '"Win, survive, succeed," Howard used to say. Football is very different to other industries, though it is often compared regardless. If I was planning a financial strategy for, say, HSBC, you wouldn't plan for success in three weeks. You'd look ahead to six months, lay a mark in the sand, and then have a recap on progress. Six months later you'd have another recap. After 18 months you'd be able to assess whether a plan was working, or a year maybe. In football, after three weeks, people are already making decisions about you. You are thrown into a pot and you have to swim immediately. You feel like you are floating on a melting icecap. He's right, Howard: "Win, survive, succeed." Win meaning literally: can you win your next game? Survive meaning: can you win enough games for people to trust you. That then gives you the chance at succeeding, whatever that might constitute.

'My definition of success isn't just about results, it's the general state you leave a club in compared to when you join it,' he continues. 'I don't like the term project because it sounds so transient, like you flip from one project to the next, and some managers do, by the way. It's not just about the eleven on the pitch. Are you affecting the welfare of a club positively? It's dangerous term to use, caretaker, but that's what I am, a caretaker. The keys are with me for a while. It's my duty to take care of the place.

'Now, recruitment is very, very important when you talk about first-team football and winning. Whether you get it right or wrong it can have a massive effect because of the short-termism that I've just been talking about. Whereas if you are in charge of the academy and you are recruiting sixteen-year-olds; you've got a two-year window to try and make that sixteen-year-old become a player. As a first-team manager, there's no way you're going to get two years to see if that teenager can become a player. He needs to be ready and settled within six months max.'

The themes of man-management, coaching techniques and recruitment appear regularly throughout this book. I ask Dyche what he thinks are the most important.

'I must say, man-management is not a new thing. It's been around a long time. It started, I think, with Brian Clough, or Bill Shankly before him. I was at Forest as a player when Clough was there. It's more vital now because of the higher standards players set in terms of the way they live their lives and what they have experienced having come through the academy system. Players are more educated in the mechanics of football than they were; they have certain expectations from managers in terms of the information they receive and the quality of that information.

'I think analysis of off the pitch wellbeing is the future of football personally, that's where the breakthroughs will be because the demands are getting so, so high. The information circulated by your camp (the media) can be so brutal and social media can be so acidic. I think the players need help to deal with the intrusion and be in a prime state to perform at the highest level. As players get older they get an understanding of modern life but they still need aid, no matter what they earn, because dealing with the fact that everyone has an opinion on you is not a thing the overwhelming majority of teenagers and young adults have to deal with.

'Coaching is still important,' he says. 'We've been through an era where coaches have become the managers but I think it will return to the way it was before where the managers manage and the coaches coach because at the top level the demands are so high; that includes the Championship where the pressure on managers is becoming similar to the Premier League in terms of lifespans because owners are so determined to earn promotion.

'There is a difference between stretching and panicking. Stretching is good, testing yourself, the players, the staff, seeing whether you can deal with a target that usually would not be a target. But when you are stretched to the point where there is so much going on, how are you meant to see the wood for the trees?

'Years ago I did a football course with the LMA. A fella whose name I can't remember came in and did a presentation. It was about politics in football, about managing upwards. It was also about leadership. He spoke about definitions of leadership, about knowing what to do when you don't know what the answer is. That for me sums up the pressure of football management because everyone is looking for you to lead. You know what you are doing but do not always have the answer immediately because there is so much going on. You're often thinking, there's that much to do here, where do you want me to start?

'I remember speaking to managers in the past who were devastated when they lost their job. I mean really devastated. They cared; they had big plans and all that. Now they are almost like, "Oh well." The change has happened because they were being measured on such an unrealistic landscape; there's not that kind of broken biscuit thing, "Oh well, that happens."

'The cult of the manager thing; it's gone too far in my opinion,' he concludes. 'I'm amazed at the media attention that's on managers. It used to be about the players and the teams. Games used to be about Keane versus Vieira. Now it's Wenger against Mourinho. Now they mention the teams and automatically it becomes a war between the managers. Pep coming to the Premier League and managing City at the same time Mourinho's in charge at United has taken it all even further.

'I appreciate this is because managers are the first point of contact for the media now, before and after matches. We act as spokesmen for the clubs we represent because we are accessible through contractual obligations and the players aren't quite as much. That means that what we say becomes newsworthy and because the cycle of news relies on the most up-to-date thing that has happened and because press conferences follow matches, hey presto.

'In press conferences I go to facts. Where does it leave us immediately? How was the performance? Did they do what I wanted them to do? Did I make good decisions? I try not to get too carried away with the highs or too low with the lows. I always try and find positive realities, appreciating the reality of where we are but reflecting on the positive side of the situation. That's my internal measure.

'I like having conversations like these because you can see authentically how I'm conducting myself. But after a game, there is little room for context in reporting about clubs the size of Burnley. Nigel Pearson came for me after we played Leicester out of the blue a few seasons ago for no reason at all. I told the media that my only concern was Burnley and what we did. The reaction was headlines: "DYCHE GOES ON MORAL HIGHGROUND." You can't win. I meant it genuinely. This job is fraught with pressures, stress, emotion, outside influences and inside influences so that I understand why Nigel may have said what he said. But I also appreciate that by fanning the flames you usually bring more focus on yourself.'

Two days before meeting Dyche, Burnley had lost 2-0 at home to Manchester United. They were not safe from relegation but Dyche was satisfied with the performance, insisting, 'You can't always get above where you are.' Burnley's season had been reported as a season of two halves; the first good and the second, not so good at best, largely due to a run of away matches against the best sides where they had lost each time. Burnley had not won an away game in the league all season and their survival was hinging on home form. Dyche says that management becomes more difficult when perception gets in the way of facts. In fact, in Burnley's first seventeen games, they had earned seventeen points. In the second seventeen, they had earned nineteen points.

'I don't read the papers, not because I don't value the art of the industry, but because I don't need the extra noise; there's enough already,' he says. 'I don't want distractions. When we became a Premier League club in 2014, one of the pundits on Sky said, "The only way Burnley will win a game is when they go back down to the Championship." I was told about this. Saw him later in the season didn't I. We were third bottom but making a fair fist of it. I went over all smiles, shaking his hand, getting him sucked in. "How are you doing, family well?" all that kind of thing. And then I said, "It was interesting what you said early in the season. That's funny, isn't it, now we've got something like seven wins." He denied that he'd said it and started flapping. "This is what I was told; maybe they'd misheard your name and the name of the TV show." If you're going to say something acidic, I think as managers we should be allowed to challenge it. I didn't abuse him, by the way. I was just playing with him. Part of my job is to try and bring balance to a discussion and say, "Hang on a minute …"'

'At the start of this season every single pundit, columnist, and newspaper, every single one, tipped us to go down. We would go down! You start well and they are saying, "Here we go, a wobbly run-in." In an odd way I'm quite proud they're speaking of us wobbling because it means we've changed perceptions about our abilities. If it's a shock that Burnley are on a tough run in the Premier League, each person at the club can be very pleased with the work they've done.

'I go into businesses and talk to workers,' he adds. 'At the beginning I'd ask them why they wanted me to do it. "Because you're constantly in a form of crisis management; the next thing is always the biggest thing." In the business world a crisis might come around every blue moon. Football management is not a crisis in the truest sense. If I said that in the media for example it would be dressed up as "DYCHE IN CRISIS." But you are constantly able to see the edge of the cliff. You're not there but you know it's there. You are constantly looking over and behind you, checking: am I tied to the tree? On the horizon you can see the knives being sharpened. You know, Wile E. Coyote was always trying to catch the Road Runner, trimming the fibres of the warm tarmac below. It feels a bit like that.'

* * *

In his book *The Football Man*, Arthur Hopcraft described Bob Lord, the chairman of Burnley Football Club, as 'The Khrushchev of Burnley.' Presiding over his football affairs and butchery business from the office at his Lowerhouse meat factory, he coordinated feuds with governing bodies, newspapers, supporters clubs, television companies, other teams and even Burnley's greatest player, Jimmy McIlroy, sold to Stoke City because Lord found out he was friends with Reg Cooke, who was the club's former vice-president and someone Lord had previously warred with.

Lord ran Burnley in such a belligerent manner that he became the first football club owner to have a national profile. Having had his attempts to take control of Burnley denied by other directors for the best part of nine years, Lord became chairman in 1955. In the following seasons, Burnley were competitive in the First Division and were crowned champions of England in 1960 before becoming runners-up in both league and FA Cup two years later. It was not sporting achievements that brought him into the wider public's consciousness, however.

His first controversial move came when he suppressed Burnley fans in their attempts to form an official supporters' club. 'We're not having an official supporters' club at Burnley,' he decreed. 'They cause a lot of problems because the people that run them eventually want the football club power.'

Between 1964 and 1969, Lord banned television cameras from covering matches at Turf Moor, citing they would 'damage and undermine attendances.' When he ruled that the BBC would not be allowed into a home game, there came a warning. 'If the BBC don't shift their cameras from Turf Moor, I'll be down there myself and will personally burn them. They are on our ground without consent and I don't care if even Harold Wilson has given them permission.'

Lord tried to justify his concerns by saying at a Variety Club function in 1974, 'We have tried to stand up against a move to get soccer on the cheap by the Jews who run television.' He then took great offence at the reaction of Manny Cussins, the Jewish chairman of Leeds United, who said he would leave the Elland Road boardroom if Lord attended a match there. Lord was furious that Cussins had been critical of him and ordered his own board to stay away from the game; with that, the offender turned into the offended because, somehow, he got away with it.

If Lord thought his boycott of television access would be followed by other club chairmen he was wrong, however. While Burnley decided to forego the television exposure and the money on offer, other clubs cashed in during a period where football was adjusting to a new world which did not include a maximum wage cap, as it had done before Jimmy Hill's campaign to have it lifted in 1961. It meant richer clubs could now outmanoeuvre Burnley financially.

Brian Miller had been a wing-half in Burnley's 1960 league championship winning side, having signed his first contract as a fifteen-year old when his responsibilities included the sweeping of the famous Longside terrace at Turf Moor. By 1987, he was Burnley's manager and the club was the bottom-placed team in the Football League, a 2-1 win against play-off chasing Leyton Orient on the final day keeping them up. Fifteen thousand supporters were inside Turf Moor that day, five times the average home gate. During the 1960s when Blackburn Rovers, Blackpool or Preston North End travelled over the hills on Bank Holiday, Turf Moor's attendances could be as high as 54,000. For a club that had been champions of England just 27 years earlier, it had taken only nine seasons to slip from the First Division to the Fourth.

Burnley's existence was being threatened by a new order in east Lancashire. In the late 1980s, Colne Dynamoes, bankrolled by millionaire chairman-manager Graham White, who had business interests in property and the timber industry, charged through the non-league pyramid on a budget to make even Burnley jealous. In the summer of 1989, White took the club full-time, even though the Fourth Division was still two promotions away. As White's team raced towards the Northern Premier League title in the season that followed, their Holt House ground was graded unfit for the Conference, prompting White to offer a reported £500,000 over two years to share Turf Moor with Burnley, the club he had previously tried to buy. Burnley's board were panicking about Colne's rising popularity but remained firm enough in their decision making to reject both of White's offers. When Colne were denied promotion to the Conference because of their ground, White walked away from football and the club folded overnight.

The Premier League era and SKY were a few years away and this was still a time when football clubs were the fiefdoms of the local mercantile class made good. You cannot mention Burnley without mentioning Blackburn, who, like Burnley, were champions of England having won the Premier League in 1995 after huge investment by Jack Walker, an industrialist from the town, only to slip into the third tier 22 years later. Under Indian ownership group Venky's, Blackburn were £100million in debt and paying wages they could not afford when relegation to a level they had not played at in 37 years was sealed. A month before, the Blackburn Rovers Supporters Trust met Sports Minister Tracey Crouch to discuss ownership reform and push the Supporters Direct idea of club licences to protect professional clubs from incompetent owners.

'The whole thing is a shambles,' said Trust chairman John Murray. 'We all wanted Blackburn Rovers to survive but even if they did stay up, this miserable existence would have continued.'

It might be suggested that this area has a history of boom and bust, that Blackburn will have the opportunity to rise again, just like Burnley did, but it is difficult to see who might have the means and motive to save this deeply indebted club from an economically challenged former mill town struggling to attract gates of 10,000 in League One.

Burnley might have followed the same path as Blackburn before promotion to the Premier League was earned on three separate occasions. Mike Garlick the current chairman, someone who made his relative wealth through IT consultancy and was born 200 metres from Turf Moor, had joined the board as a director in 2007 in the aftermath of the ITV Digital collapse, which forced Football League clubs into dramatic decisions. Burnley sold Turf Moor and its Gawthorpe Hall training facility and Garlick was dispatched to Rome to discuss a deal that would have seen Burnley link up with an unnamed Serie A giant, resulting in a string of young Italian players heading to east Lancashire for loan spells. Thus Burnley might have become a foreign club's junior side rather than a local priority.

Considering one of the biggest critics of televised football had been Bob Lord, there is an irony, indeed, that Sky's television money has changed Burnley's financial landscape. Although Burnley is the smallest town to host Premier League football, although Turf Moor's main stand (a stand that still carries Bob Lord's name) is one of the smallest structures in the Premier League with 4,000 wooden seats, although the club has the lowest wage bill and although it has the lowest gate receipts, Sky's money accounted for 90 percent of Burnley's revenue during the 2016/17 season.

Sean Dyche was keen to stress that Burnley had used Sky's money sensibly. It had not only cleared all of Burnley's debts but ensured too that Turf Moor and Gawthorpe Hall were assets again. Burnley had since spent nearly £11 million transforming their training ground, which under Bob Lord's instructions had become the first purpose-built training facility in England after he stressed the economic importance of Burnley producing its own players. Gawthorpe had since fallen into disrepair and the new Barnfield Training Centre became one of Dyche's pet projects, the manager joking that his rugged appearance made him look like one of the builders rather than a Premier League manager. With so much money washing about in the Premier League era, Dyche says the biggest challenge is managing perceptions, 'the realities and the non-realities,' as he calls them.

'When I came here, the club was completely out of sync, and it will go there again, just by the nature of football and human beings,' he believes. 'The club had forgotten what it really is. It had been in the Premier League two years earlier. Why are we languishing in the bottom half of the Championship when we should be in the Premier League? I got here and we quickly rose from sixteenth-ish to seventh and everybody thought, "Right here we go." But the team was nowhere near good enough. We were lucky to get seventh. The reality was out the window by then and so we had to remodel the thinking and, of course, people don't like to be told they need to think differently. Slowly but surely you have to nibble away at it.

'Results didn't go so well, which they didn't for me, but there was a lot of good work going on behind the results, things that I was aligning differently to make sure the club was stronger. The majority of people can't see those things and you are only measured on the pitch. Finding an owner or a chairman that can see the bigger picture, one who doesn't panic when the pressure comes, is getting harder. The misalignment of where clubs are is rife and it never used to be.

'When I was at Nottingham Forest from 1987 to 1990 it was a given that young players would play. The crowd knew it, the board knew it, the manager knew it, and the team knew it. All stakeholders were in the loop. So if a young player played and the result didn't go your way the crowd weren't necessarily lenient but they'd understand it. They realised that it was improbable that you'd get instant success with young players. Therefore, it was accepted as part of the club's identity at that time. All of that now is out of the window. People want bang, win, win and win. There's no reality of thinking behind it.

'"Why aren't they winning?" Some say, "Give young lads a chance." Then when they don't win the same people say, "The young lads aren't good enough." There is only a small amount of players in this world that can enter a first team and be good enough straight away; that has always been the case with football. The overwhelming majority need a bit of time. But they don't get the time because everybody wants to win the league.

'To get balance here, I'm not crying this in, I'm stating facts. If this was a post-match press conference the reaction would be "DYCHE LAMENTS FOOTBALL." My words would be spun all over the place. I'm not moaning about it at all. I'm just saying this is how the game has changed and if I fail to appreciate the environment I'm working in, I'm one step behind already. I buy into the working environment. That's why you don't see me upset. These are the realities. I love the challenge.'

In the summer after Dyche arrived at Turf Moor, having been sacked by Watford after the Pozzo family from Italy bought the club, expectation levelled out because he had to sell leading scorer Charlie Austin to QPR. Dyche replaced him with three free transfers and overnight it 'was back to us being little old Burnley.' The bonus of this was, there arrived a reality. 'If you have a common reality you've got a chance.' Then, in the summer of 2016, Dyche spent £30million for the first time in Burnley's history. Although it was nowhere near what other clubs with relegation concerns were spending, the unprecedented transfer deals at Turf Moor inevitably raised expectations at a local level.

'Relegation should be an invaluable experience for a club the size of Burnley and should not mean the end of the world, because survival in the Premier League is already a massive challenge,' Dyche says. 'No benefactors, no one who is going to write massive cheques; the club has to be run properly by absorbing the money and redistributing it appropriately. The club has to survive over the next five years, not just in year one, covering all the contracts. At the end of that we still need to be in a healthy shape. Relegation doesn't necessarily mean you are moving backwards providing you learn from your mistakes and stick together. The problems come at clubs who bet the ranch and, oh-oh, it doesn't work. Then you have heaven and hell, a club in bits. I witnessed this at Watford. I left the club as a player the season they got promoted into the Premier League. Then Aidy Boothroyd brought me back as youth coach three years later. By the end of that season we were nearly out of business, twenty four hours away from the administrators moving in. If mismanaged, relegation can mean real chaos for a club, and I don't mean football managed. That helps of course, I mean as a club, reality, the perception of reality, facts within the perception; remodelling it again. It becomes hard because there are a lot of business people now involved in football and they are not used to so many voices in their world saying, "Why are you not doing that?" '

'I'm 46 so I've seen the change in front of my own eyes, in my lifetime. There is a demand for everything now, the throwaway lifestyle, throwaway fashion, and throwaway goods. Growing up I remember watching my dad trying to fix the washing machine when it was broken. He was a consultant for British Steel but he'd try his hand at fixing anything off his own back. When that didn't work he'd ring the geezer that knew how to fix washing machines. Only then, if all else had failed, he'd decide to buy a new one. Now, people are on the Internet straight away buying the cheapest washing machine they can get. They don't worry about paying the bloke that can fix it.

'This attitude has fed into football. A few bad results; sack the manager. "He ain't good enough". Bad season, sell all the players. Soon enough the new generation of fan will only know Twitter, Instagram and Facebook. I never cry it in, as I say. But this is how it has factually changed. If we live in a throwaway society, why should football be any different? Opinions are made instantly. There is less of a desire to look at the situation and try and fix things. Instead it's bang, change now. The downside or the upside, whichever way you want to look at it is, the managers get thicker skin. They think, look, I'm going to work really hard, give everything I can to be successful. If it doesn't work out, then c'est la vie. They walk off into the distance, not broken like I used to see managers. You'd see them and say, "Sorry it didn't work out," and months later you'd see them and they'd still have a face on them. Not now, I don't think I'll be like that (not caring as much), though that isn't me saying I'm better or stronger than other managers.

'You have to wear a coat of armour. When I signed for Bristol City as a player a lot was expected of me and it didn't work out. There were lots of cliques in the dressing room and I didn't fit in. I'd had great times at Chesterfield before and this disappointment taught me that you have to maintain your independence. The fans might think you've been a waste of money but they don't always know the off-the-pitch circumstances.'

On perfect spring days at Turf Moor, from the top of the main stand the sunlight shimmers off slate roofs. Beyond the old mills, the terraced houses and chimney smoke, the Pennines when smeared with frost, make it one of football's most picturesque settings. The football under Dyche, though practical, has seldom threatened to match the beauty of the backdrop. A lot is made about Dyche's preference for a certain type of player, specifically British workhorses over foreign flair. The perception about what Burnley are doing is reinforced by Dyche's willingness to talk about the lack of opportunities for British managers in the Premier League.

'Think about it, what business would you be in if you didn't want good people working around you, to at least work hard and care about what they do?' he says of the players. 'I don't think I'm the only manager who thinks along those lines. Surely if I'm the only one that does, then the world is in trouble. It's basic values in life, work hard and I'll do everything I can to help the individual succeed within a collective. I'll help try and rub off any edges; I'll try and guide you towards being the best you can be, and at the very least, give us a bit of respect and honesty.

'We signed Steven Defour from Anderlecht. He's played for Porto and he's played in the Champions' League. A lot was made of it because he was a big-money signing and because he wasn't British. We've made other non-British signings and they haven't really got a mention in the press. Freddie Ulvestad was one and Rouwen Hennings another. Then there was Johann Berg Gudmundsson who came from Charlton. We signed Defour and everyone was like, "Oooh Burnley have signed a foreign player for once". We've had foreign players here before. I've said this many times but I couldn't care less whether players are green, blue, or brown. They can come from anywhere on the planet as long as they can play football. You have to think logically when signing someone though – the business thinking.

'Do you know anything about them? Do you know the agent? Does the agent want to play ball? Does the player want to play ball? Do they fit your finance? Do they fit the club? Are they willing to move to the north-west of England where, as you've seen today, it can be minus-six at the end of April and we've just been hit by a hailstorm during a training session? Do they want the challenge of being at the smallest club in the Premier League? Well if they tick all those boxes why wouldn't you sign them? People speak about recruitment as if everyone is equal, not appreciating that this club is in its infancy with regards to recruitment. We're still hand to mouth. Which division are we going to be in? How much money do we have?

'Admittedly, the geography has changed. A lot of players now live in south-west Manchester, no matter which club in the north-west they play for. It could be Liverpool, Everton, Man City, Man United or Burnley. Players travel from that area to Stoke. When you sign a player he is more likely than ever to know another player from one of those clubs who will say, "South-west Manchester is lovely." I don't think geography is the major issue it once might have been before for Burnley. The major issues concern whether we will be in the Premier League because there are no guarantees; certainly at the beginning of the season when most analysts were saying, "You've got no chance." Can we pay as well as other teams, no. Can we advance your careers? Yes I believe we can, our record suggests that we can help move careers forward; that is a big one for us. Will the player be in a good working environment? Certainly, as you can see the training ground has changed significantly over the last two years compared to what we have been used to before. It's the balance of yin and yang: the good things balanced against the not-so-good things and then the buy-in from all parties. Does the player really want the challenge – because we don't sugar-coat it? Does the agent want the challenge – and they are ever more important? It's not just one element. It used to be way easier when I was playing. You either wanted to play for the team or you didn't.'

Dyche says his proudest moment as a manager was sealing promotion to the Premier League for the first time in 2014 when Wigan Athletic were beaten at Turf Moor, 'because the team performed exactly how you'd want your team to perform on a big day after a year's work.' Up, down and up again Burnley went, though Dyche insists he has never asked to be interviewed for jobs at clubs where the ambitions exceeded Burnley's.

'Ownership has changed massively in my lifetime,' he reasons. 'You'll have to check the stats but I think fifteen out of the twenty Premier League clubs are foreign-owned. In the Championship, there are thirteen from twenty-four. That's a start point. So if you've got foreign owners there's an increased chance you'll get foreign managers. Within that, I think 60 percent of first-team Premier League squads are made up of foreign players. To manage those players it might be an easier option to appoint a foreign manager. These are considerations before you analyse what has been successful and which clubs want to achieve that level of success. If you are Chelsea, Arsenal, Tottenham, Man City, Man United, Liverpool and to a degree Everton, who are climbing now because of their new backer, do they want a young British up and comer or do they want someone who has probably been successful in their own right already? Chances are they are going to go for the second option.

'The demands of being successful are huge. If you look at the careers of those managers, Klopp has been very successful in Germany; Pep's record speaks for itself, Conte and Wenger the same, and then Pochettino who is one of the newcomers. He did a great job in difficult circumstances abroad with Espanyol then established himself here with Southampton. He's since built it steadily at Tottenham and he's my favourite, if you like. There's more to come from him, I think. But the point is, these guys are not novice hurdlers. I've done a bit but not in relation to their achievements. We need someone to break the mould. I'm a big backer of Eddie Howe because if it goes right for him it goes well for me and all the other British coaches. The media might misconstrue that as some sort of patriotism when the reality is, it would be good for the health of our national system, for the good of coaches that would filter through the system and down into the grass roots.'

Dyche has sacrificed family time to become Burnley's manager. He travels back to his home in Kettering usually on a Tuesday or a Wednesday to see his wife and children. As this has been his life for the last four years, I wonder how long he can go on for, or whether he'd jump at the chance if an opportunity came to manage a club closer to home. He compares his job to 'working away' like a businessman from Kettering going to London, or a builder to Birmingham.

'Football management is a wonderful industry but the challenge to succeed is enormous because there are so few jobs and so many people wanting to do it,' he says. 'I tell loads of young coaches they should be prepared for what is to come if they really want to succeed. "Make sure you are ready to deal with the knockers," I say. If you can handle that, compartmentalise criticism and put it in a box while still moving forward, then that's no problem. If that's not your bag then don't do it because the job is fraught with people picking on what you do constantly. There will be a thousand managers who have done it better than you and they'll still be deemed to have done it wrong. Look at Arsene Wenger.

'You wouldn't want a stadium full of people sitting on their hands though, because it would be boring,' he concludes. 'Football is driven by passion and opinions and people should always feel free to express them. But there's got to be a moment where you can reason with people who disagree with you and you part by shaking hands. Social media means everyone is so desperate to have their voice heard and to be proven right. Sometimes the line is overstepped and it's becoming more of a regular thing.

'When we got promoted the first time, which was an amazing

achievement considering the budget; I don't think any team assembled for such a small sum will ever reach the Premier League again, there was still a fan who came up to me at the players' awards. "What an amazing season," he said. "But I still think you should have played this guy more than that guy."

'What did I say back? I said, "OK, nice to meet you sir …"'

About the Author

Dave Thomas, born in 1944, is the author of innumerable Burnley books, the first of which appeared in 2003. Since then he has written a book a year and there are more in the pipeline. His first full season at Turf Moor as a supporter was in season 1959/60 when the Clarets landed the First Division title. He has been hooked ever since although there have been intervals when attendance has been interrupted by family matters.

He has written biographies of Harry Potts, Jimmy Adamson and Jimmy McIlroy. A Bob Lord book written with Mike Smith is scheduled for 2019, this completing the quartet of books about the four great characters of Burnley's golden years in the late '50s and the early '60s. The story of Burnley's time in the Premier League with Sean Dyche has been chronicled in five books so far.

With Vertical Editions he ghosted the Paul Fletcher and Roger Eli autobiographies, and wrote the story of Steve Cotterill and Owen Coyle at Turf Moor. Vertical also published the two Best of Burnley volumes.

He was a headteacher for 15 years in South Leeds until 1996 and then did supply work in several Leeds schools. Neither pupils nor staff could ever understand him being a Burnley supporter. Retiring fully in 2002 gave him the chance to turn to full-time writing which he always thought far better than painting the garden furniture or creosoting the shed. Whilst a teacher he always dreamed of writing bestsellers that would make him a fortune. He is now living proof that there is little money to be made writing football books.